# Down From Heaven:

The 11th Airborne Division in World War II
Volume 1: Camp Toccoa to Leyte Campaign

Copyright: Jeremy C. Holm
1st Published: September 1, 2022

The right of Jeremy C. Holm to be identified as author of this Work has been asserted by him in accordance with sections 77 and 78 of the Copyright, Designs and Patents Act 1988.

All rights reserved. No part of this publication may be reproduced, stored in retrieval system, copied in any form or by any means, electronic, mechanical, photocopying, recording or otherwise transmitted without written permission from the publisher. You must not circulate this book in any format.

This book is licensed for your personal enjoyment only. This book may not be resold or given away to other people. If you would like to share this book with another person, please purchase an additional copy for each recipient. If you're reading this book and did not purchase it, or it was not purchased for your use only, then please return to Amazon.com and purchase your own copy. Thank you for respecting the hard work of this author.

Find out more about the author and upcoming books online at www.jeremycholm.com and www.511pir.com.

# Table of Contents

Prologue .................................................................................. i
1: Airborne All the Way ............................................................ 1
2: Glider Wars ........................................................................ 26
3: Haugen's Heroes ................................................................ 32
4: Forming the 11th Airborne ................................................. 59
5: Jump School & Camp Mackall ........................................... 85
6: Knollwood Maneuvers ...................................................... 105
7: Les Bon Temps ................................................................. 118
8: Heading West ................................................................... 132
9: So, This is New Guinea ..................................................... 144
10: King II Operation ............................................................ 169
11: Leyte Mountains ............................................................. 181
12: Operation Wa ................................................................. 209
13: Pushing West .................................................................. 225
14: Breaking Out .................................................................. 253
15: Down From Heaven & Healing Waters .......................... 277
16: On to Tokyo, Via Luzon .................................................. 290
Postscript ............................................................................. 297

> "The harder the conflict,
> the more glorious the triumph."
>
> -Thomas Paine, 1776

# Prologue

January 12, 1946
New York City, New York

The sun shone brightly over the streets of New York City. The day's radiance was matched only by the smiles of an estimated 3,500,000 of New Yorkers who braved the crisp air that morning to witness such a historic event.

World War II had been officially over for four months and with the war's end had come four months of victory celebrations the likes of which the world has rarely seen since.

And yet, New York City's victory parade promised to be one of the biggest yet, one that wasn't just for some general or world leader. No, this parade was for the average G.I., the boys from Brooklyn and Atlanta and San Diego, "all the guys who walked through the mud-- the sloggin G.I." who won the war for their Uncle Sam, for their ma's and pa's and for the girls back home.

Cameras rolled as Major General James M. Gavin, just 38 years of age, led 8,000 men of the 82nd Airborne Division, the All-Americans, at the front of the 13,000-man march through the Washington Square Arch and down Fifth Avenue to the thunderous roars and cheers. The crowds packed the city's sidewalks, balconies and rooftops. It was a spectacular afair with a ticker-tape blizzard pouring down on the four mile-long procession that thrilled a nation still laboring to heal from the wounds of a war. 400,000 young American lives had been lost in the war and those now marching past the Flatiron Building and Madison Square Park did so to honor all those who did not come back.

General Gavin's 82nd Airborne was proud to lead the way and as one headline declared, "Millions Acclaim Airborne Troops," including New York's governor Thomas E. Dewey, NYC's Mayor, William O'Dwyer, and the city's former mayor Fiorello LaGuardia.

Appropriately, the review stand was on 82nd street and was also "manned" by former WWI-82nd Divisioners General Jonathan Wainwright and Sergeant (now Major) Alvin York.

This was the second such event for the the 82nd Airborne which had participated in the Berlin Victory Parade on September 7, 1945. And just as in Berlin, each of the 13,000 marching men wore battle dress with uniforms adorned by appropriate decorations.

45 C-47s from the 316th Troop Carrier Group soon roared over the city, each towing a WACO glider surrounded by 100 P-47 Thunderbolts of the 1st Air Force. It was an impressive display of America's air and airborne power and one of the division's chaplains proudly proclaimed, "No other outfit pulled together like the 82nd!"

A few days later, and 7,000 miles away, in Sendai, Honshu, Japan, one of the United State's most experienced airborne commanders disagreed.

Major General Joseph May Swing, commander of the historic 11th Airborne Division, sat in a darkened room at Camp Schimmelpfennig as a recording of the 82nd's Fifth Avenue march played through a projector.

His headquarters staff sat quietly as "Jumping Joe" watched General Gavin's men march smartly through the ticker tape storm as tens of thousands of cheering New Yorkers waved American flags.

Hailing from Jersey City, New Jersey, Swing was prematurely grey, Hollywood-handsome and was recognized throughout the service as a pioneer in airborne concepts and tactics. Swing had graduated from the United States Military Academy in the famous Class of 1915, the Class the Stars Fell On since of the 164 graduates, 59 (36%) attained the rank of general, more than any other class in the history of the Academy. Swing excelled at West Point alongside his roommate and football teammate Dwight Eisenhower (Omar Bradley also played with them under head coach Charles Dudley Daly).

In 1916 Swing served as a young 2$^{nd}$ Lieutenant under General "Black Jack" Pershing in Mexico during the "Punitive Expedition" against Pancho Villa in the 4$^{th}$ Field Artillery. When America entered World War I, he served in France between 1917-1918 with the 8$^{th}$ Field

Artillery under Chief of Staff General Payton C. March, earning France's Legion of Honor and a position as March's aide de camp.

Swing returned stateside to marry March's daughter Josephine on July 8, 1918 then graduated with honors from Fort Hood's field artillery school in 1926. Swing taught at Hood until 1931 when he entered Washington's Army War College until 1935 then bounced between units from 1935-1942.

As the film of the 82nd Airborne Division's 1946 New York victory march continued, Swing must have thought back to 1942 when he was assigned command of the 82$^{nd}$ Infantry Division's (later Airborne) artillery where he helped his old teammate Brigadier General Omar Bradley organize the division's units.

Had he stayed with the 82nd, perhaps Swing would have marched alongside (or in place of) General Gavin down Fifth Avenue. But given his penchant for daring leadership, Swing was instead given command of America's third airborne division, the 11$^{th}$ Airborne, at Camp Mackall in November of 1942 and promoted to Major General.

General Swing had led the 11th Airborne on its own extraordinary march through the history books as "saviors of the airborne" during the Knollwood Maneuvers of 1943 then on to literally helping to save the Philppines from the cruel domination of Imperial Japan in 1944-1945. 2,431 of Swing's men had become casualties in the liberation of Leyte and Luzon and over six hundred had made the ultimate sacrifice for the cause of freedom.

Swing and his men had successfully liberated over 2,100 men, women and children from behind enemy lines at Los Baños, had helped destroy the last remnant's of the enemy's forces on Luzon, had been hand-picked by General Douglas MacArthur to be the first foreign unit to land on Japan in that country's long history and form MacArthur's Honor Guard for his historic landings at Atsugi on August 30, 1945. When the well-tanned GEN Swing dropped his six-foot frame onto the Atsugi tarmac at 0600 on August 30 (Z-Day), he was the highest-ranking Allied officer in Japan.

MacArthur himself would land several hours later, and while England's Prime Minister Winston Churchill noted, "Of all the amazing deeds in the war, I regard General MacArthur's personal landing at Atsugi as the bravest of the lot," the fact that General Swing landed at Atsugi with only his 8,000 Angels around him speaks volumes of "Jumping Joe's" courage and daring nature.

As one of those Angels, HQ3-511's PFC George Doherty noted, "It was.... the most courageous and daring maneuver by a conquering general and his army of occupation in the history of the world."

A few days later, Swing's Boys had then guarded the departure docks for the Surrender Ceremony onboard the USS Missouri on September 2 and then admirably performed Occupation Duty as "ambassadors of democracy" until 1949.

Indeed, as Secretary of War Robert Patterson once noted, "They are the best representatives the nation could have…an army of which the American nation can be proud."

General Swing and his staff noticed that while all the soldiers in the recording of the New York City parade wore the 82nd's "AA" on their left shoulder, nearly 5,000 wore the patches of the 101st Airborne's Screaming Eagle, the 17th Airborne's Golden Talon or the younger 13th Airborne's Golden Unicorn on their right.

Swing was painfully aware that the patches represented four of America's five airborne division, including the 13th which had not even seen combat in the war. Only his beloved 11th Airborne Division had been left out of the day's celebrations.

The recording ended and a few staff officers quietly smoked cigarettes. The lights stayed off, as if to match the darkened feelings of the room. No one felt anything close to resembling the celebratory atmosphere of the New York Victory Parade. Instead, the mighty Angels, even their recent transfers, felt… overlooked.

After minutes of painful silence ticked by, General Joe expressed everyone's sentiments when he whispered to no one in particular, "That should have been us. That should have been us."

After asking the film to be played again, Swing got up halfway through and walked out with tears in his eyes.

His greatest fears were already beginning to be realized: after achieving the impossible on Leyte, effecting the improbable on Luzon, and just plain making history in Japan, his beloved Angels of the 11th Airborne Division were being relegated to a footnote in the history of the war, one that would continually be overshadowed by the legacies (and publicity) of the 101st and 82nd Airborne Division's for decades

to come. Thousands Swing's Angels would live long, well-earned lives and then die without such fame, attention or fanfare.

None were seeking publicity. Rather, as one of those combat-hardened Angels would tell me nearly 70 years later, "I'm afraid we are being forgotten. Soon no one will know what we did over there. What I buried my friends for. Where is our movie? Our documentaries? Our newspaper articles? Does no one care? The world should know about the Angels."

It was sentiment that was shared with me time and time again I befriended and interviewed Angels for my book, WHEN ANGELS FALL: FROM TOCCOA TO TOKYO, THE 511TH PARACHUTE INFANTRY IN WORLD WAR II first published in 2019.

When that book hit the shelves, readers, World War II-enthusiasts and even some historians were incredulous. "There were airborne troops in the Pacific?!"

This book is dedicated to Major General Joseph May Swing and the thousands of Angels, including my grandfather 1LT Andrew Carrico III of D-511 PIR, who fought under his command.

May it, and we, forever honor "The Band of Brothers of the Pacific."

It is also dedicated to our modern Angels, and their families. When we first heard from USARAK that the 11th Airborne Division was going to be reactivated, there was excitement and pride.

I pray this book only serves to strengthen the resolve of the reactivated 11th Airborne Division's leadership and troopers to wear the 11th Airborne patch with honor as they serve out great country.

May they never forget those who have gone before them, whose story is told in this historical series, and who look "DOWN FROM HEAVEN" as they carry on the traditions of the Angels.

I must thank the numerous Angels, Angelettes, family members and museum staffs who helped make this volume possible, who opened their archives, treasure chests, memories and hearts. The challenge became which stories to tell and which to leave out as the story of the Angels is far too large to tell everyone's story to satisfaction. I confess to moments of worry over what to include and what to painfully cut.

This book is the first in a two-volume series that is my effort to tell the full World War II history of the 11th Airborne Division. Since the history of the 511th Parachute Infantry Regiment, the subject of my first book WHEN ANGELS FALL, is part of the division's history, readers of that book will find selected pieces and portions in this book. I hope that such repetitions can be forgiven since they deserve to be told and the full history of the 11th Airborne could not be told without them as the 511th PIR played an integral role on Leyte.

To all who read this book, and WHEN ANGELS FALL, as well as the second volume of this series, I feel the words of HQ-188's SGT Edward Hammrich said it best: "I do hope that I, in some small way, have given you an insight of the thoughts and reactions of the civilian soldier trained and led by my estimation, one of the best leaders in military history, General Joseph Swing."

Down From Heaven Comes Eleven! Airborne all the way!

**-Jeremy C. Holm**
*Salt Lake City, UT 2022*
Historian, 11th Airborne Division - 11thairborne.com
& 511th Parachute Infantry Regiment - 511pir.com

*I am a trooper in the 11<sup>th</sup> Airborne Division of the United States
Army—a protector of the greatest nation on earth.
As a soldier, I uphold the principles of freedom for which
my country stands.
As a trooper, I am a superior soldier—in physical fitness, combat
readiness, military bearing, courtesy, character and self-discipline.
My actions always reflect my pride in my country, my flag
and my uniform.
I trust in my God and in the United States of America.
I am an American soldier."*

-The 11<sup>th</sup> Airborne Soldier's Creed

While the mighty 11th Airborne Division served with distinction in World War II and Korea, the division's "theme song" did not come along until the fall of 1950 after the Angels had returned to the United States following Occupation Duty in Japan.

A contest was held throughout the Pacific Theater to encourage the composition of songs and marches that would become anthems of the 11th Airborne Division. Perhaps none of the final four entries is as well-known as the marching-ballad which was sung in bars and pubs by Angels since 1950 titled "Down From Heaven", an original song submitted by Colonel Byron Leslie Paige (SSN 376405509, USMA 1932) of Shelby, Michigan.

The music that accompanied COL Paige's lyrics was arranged by Sergeant George Whissen and you can listen to this piece by visiting www.511pir.com/march.

# Down From Heaven

By Colonel Byron L. Paige, arranged by Sergeant George Whissen

*Stand in the door!*
*Stand in the door!*

*Down from heaven comes Eleven*
*And there's hell to pay below*
*Shout Geronimo! – Geronimo!*

*Hit the silk and check your canopy*
*And take a look around*
*The air is full of troopers*
*Set for battle on the ground*

*Till we join the stick of Angels*
*Killed on Leyte and Luzon*
*Shout Geronimo! – Geronimo!*

*It's a gory road to glory*
*But we're ready – here we go*
*Shout Geronimo! – Geronimo!*

*Stand in the door!*
*Stand in the door!*

*Down from heaven comes Eleven*
*And there's hell to pay below*
*Shout Geronimo! – Geronimo!*

*Hit the silk and check your canopy*
*And take a look around*
*The air is full of troopers*
*Set for battle on the ground*

*Till we join the stick of Angels*
*Killed on Leyte and Luzon*
*Shout Geronimo! – Geronimo!*

*It's a gory road to glory*
*But we're ready – here we go*
*Shout Geronimo! – Geronimo!*

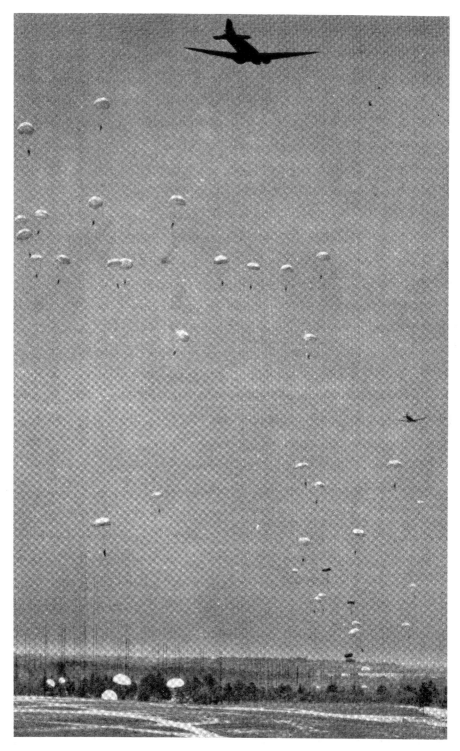

# 1: Airborne All the Way

Fort Benning, Georgia

*"I'll never forget the look on the face of the aircraft crew chief as we left the plane. His expression clearly said, 'Are these guys crazy?'*
*-2LT Stephen Cavanaugh, D-511 PIR*

When Imperial Japanese aircraft bombed, torpedoed and straffed Pearl Harbor on December 7, 1941, Japan attacked a nation that was far from prepared for war. While America had positioned itself as "The Arsenal of Democracy", she had yet to "put some skin in the game", to use the vernacular of the day.

Political leaders from all sides of the spectrum were far from in agreement on what to do. Isolationists felt that Hitler's war was Europe's responsibility while Japan's aggressions in the Pacific were, well, someone else's problem.

William Allen White, Chairman of the Committee to Defend America by Aiding the Allies, declared that, "If I were making a motto for [this] Committee, it would be 'The Yanks Are Not Coming.'"

Interventionists, on the other hand, argued that as with The Great War just two decades earlier, America had a responsibility to fight against the evils of tyranny. And with England the last major European power left to oppose Hitler's lust for conquest, how long would the Atlantic (and by default the Pacific) remain the defensive barrier that it had been for decades?

By April of 1941, several polls indicated that roughly 68% of Americans favored war against Germany and Italy if that was the only way to defeat them. The problem was that while comfortable in the former roles of isolanist and even neutrality, the United States was not ready to fight another global conflict if it came down to it.

In 1935, there were fewer than 119,000 troops in the U.S. military. That number increased slightly to 200,000 when Hitler invaded Poland on September 1, 1939, sparking the outbreak of global war.

America's president Franklin D. Roosevelt saw the writing on the wall, despite the desires of many to remain neutral. On September 5, 1940, President Roosevelt began preparing for military involvement by declaring a state of national emergency, increasing the size of the Army and National Guard, and authorizing the Selective Training and Service Act of 1940 — the first peacetime draft in US history.

As if in response to America's actions, on September 27, 1940, Japan, Germany and Italy signed the Tripartite Pact, pledging mutual support if attacked by a nation not already at war. The alliance sent a direct warning to the United States that any military intervention would lead to battles both in Europe and the Pacific.

America's future was balanced on a knife's edge and Japan's attack on Pearl Harbor pushed her over. The next day, December 8, 1941, at 12:30p.m. during a solemn joint session of Congress, President Roosevelt declared, "Yesterday, the United States of America was suddenly and deliberately attacked...No matter how long it may take us to overcome this premeditated invasion, the American people in their righteous might will win through to absolute victory..."

The President's speech, which lasted seven minutes, set the tone for the next four years. Within the hour, Congress voted to declare war on Japan as the nation's opinion shifted to mirror Greek philosopher Aristotle who said, "We make war so that we may live in peace."

Secretary of the Navy Col. Frank Knox summed up the country's sentiment's during a press conference, saying, "The Japs started this war; we are going to finish it."

To help "finish it", America's young sons rushed to defend "life, liberty and the pursuit of happiness". Contrary to the words of William Allen White, once again, the Yanks would not come back 'til it was over, over there.'

One of the new manners in which the war would be fought was being developed over 750 miles to the south at Fort Benning, Georgia.

# Vertical Envelopment

To fully tell the story of the 11th Airborne Division in World War II, we need to review how America's airborne arm laid the foundation of the division's historic creation and history.

In the pre-Pearl Harbor years, the concept of "vertical envelopment" was, like America's involvement in the war, hotly debated. Some career officers who had fought in World War I immediately recognized the advantages of providing field commanders with the option and capability to parachute men, supplies and support at almost any given point on the battlefield. These air-dropped or air-landed troops could, in theory, attack the rear and flanks of a force, in effect encircling or enveloping the enemy.

It was a concept that had first been tested limitedly in combat during World War I by Russia and Italy. Winston Churchill suggested dropping parachute troops to destroy bridges and enemy supply depots while America's Ace of Aces Eddie Rickenbacker described to GEN John J. "Blackjack" Pershing how bombers could be loaded with infantry who would parachute behind enemy lines so ground forces could attack from the front and rear.

Pershing's famous air service advisor COL William "Wild Bill" Mitchell even put together plans to experimentally drop a battalion from America's 1st Infantry Battalion, The Big Red One, behind enemy lines. The war ended before plans could be put into play, but Mitchell would go on to create a study section named the US Army Air Service to test parachuting at McCook Field near Dayton Ohio.

Of note, included in COL Mitchell's staff in France in 1918 was a young MAJ Lewis H. Brereton. On August 2, 1944, then-Lieutenant General Brereton was named Commanding General of the 1st Allied Airborne Army which oversaw all airborne operations in Europe from August of 1944 to May of 1945.

Ever the visionary, American Founding Father Benjamin Franklin understood the havoc such air-dropped troops could, and would, cause. After watching one of the first manned hot air balloon flights in France, Franklin said in 1784, "Where is the prince who can afford so to cover his country with troops for its defense, so that ten thousand men descending from the clouds might not, in many places, do an infinite deal of mischief before a force could be brought together to repel them?"

Franklin's observation displays one of the main effects of airborne-capable troop deployments. If the enemy knew that airborne troops could be dropped in his area of responsibility, he would have to be conscious of the whole field, not just a few key locations. Gone would be the typical concern for the front and the flanks; now commanders would have to watch the rear (and the sky) as well.

Thus, even enemy troops far from the traditional front had to maintain a level of vigilance for airborne attack. And even if that attack was the result of scattered troop landings, Paratroopers possess the ability to confuse the enemy into thinking he is being attacked by a larger force.

Americans would display the feasibility of such mass parachute jumps out of a transport at Chanute Field, Illinois, on April 16, 1928. To show that passengers could escape a commercial plane in flight if it was on fire, ten graduates of the Chanute Field jumping course parachuted at an altitude of 2,000 feet in 8.1 seconds. The demonstration was "jump mastered" by Harry "Tug" Wilson who would go on to help train some America's first parachutists of World War II.

Little progress was made, or attention given to, utilizing parachutes strategically in America's military until in 1940. Nazi Germany was the first to successfully employ this form of warfare on a large scale when their *Fallschirmjäger* (Paratroopers) participated in the "annexation" of Austria and the occupation of Norway and Denmark. Noticing their successes, Britain began training her own airborne units and soon thereafter America gave her own greenlight.

This, of course, created a lasting turf war between the military's various branches. The Army Air Corps felt that Paratroopers should fall under their umbrella (no pun intended) since it would be their planes that transported the parachute troops to the drop zone!

The Army felt that while planes would transport the Paratroopers to the target area, once on the ground they would become ground fighters and therefore the Army should retain control!

Given that the concept of vertical envelopment likely would consist of demolitions work to remove enemy defenses and fortifications, the Engineer Corps felt that *they* should be in charge of Paratroopers.

After listening to all the arguments, America's Chief of Staff George C. Marshall turned to GEN George A. Lynch, Chief of Infantry for the army, and said, "George, can you take this over?"

Lynch replied, "Sure, and I will pass it over to William Lee."

MAJ William C. Lee, who was also present and would become known as the "Father of the U.S. Airborne", answered, "We are late, but we have to go ahead."

# 1. Airborne All the Way

On May 1, 1939, the War Department's G-3 MG R. M. Beck sent a directive to the Chief of Infantry which in part read:

"It is requested that your office make a study for the purpose of determining the desireability of organizing, training and conducting test of a small detachment of air infantry with a view to ascertaining whether or not our Army should contain a unit or units of this nature."

Under the command and guidance of forty-three-year-old MAJ William C. Lee, on June 26, one day after France surrendered to Germany, the initial group of forty-eight parachutists were selected out of 200 volunteers from Fort Benning's 29th Infantry.

Fifteen officers had submitted their names to led the new test platoon. Twenty-seven-year-old 1LT (soon CPT) William Ryder, West Point class of 1936, had made a name for himself by studying both Russian and German parachute tactics and then writing articles on their practices in Operations *Weseruebung* and *Gelb*. When 1LT Ryder and the other officers arrived to take a test to see who would command the new test platoon, Ryder saw that many of the questions were based on articles he had previously written. He finished the two-hour exam in forty-five minutes. The job was his.

1LT Ryder was assisted in this endeavor by 2LT James A. Bassett, Warrant Officer Harry "Tug" Wilson (borrowed from the Air Corps) and two parachute riggers, Corporals James Wallace and Forrest Ketcherside (two more would follow).

Ryder's test platoon completed three weeks of physical and classroom training at Fort Benning (they did not even have parachutes to jump with yet) before moving to Hightstown, NJ for ten days of practice on the Safe Parachute Company's 150-foot parachute towers.

Physical training included a daily six-mile run before breakfast, then later they would endure countless pull-ups, chin-ups, pushups and numerous medicine ball exercises, including standing in a circle and throwing the ball at a comrade across the circle.

Test Platoon member PVT Thad P. Setman remembered, "We were tough. We thought we could whip anything with hair or a bark...and almost could. But they encouraged that in us. They wanted to build it; they wanted us to feel like we were superior individuals."

It was a level of confidence that would become synonymous with the airborne. For now, the Test Platoon completed their training in Hightstown and returned to Fort Benning for real jumps out of C-33 transports, first at 1,500 feet and then 750.

The highly-respected WO Harry Wilson explained to the platoon that there would be a demonstration parachute drop of an equipment bundle. To the horror of every man at the demonstration, the bundle was "pushed from the aircraft door, and plummeted to its destruction a mere 50 yards distance from the spectating volunteers." Its chute failed to open.

Undeterred, 1LT Ryder became the first American soldier to make an official jump on August 16, 1940, followed by the first enlisted man to make a jump, PVT William N. "Red" King. According to Ryder, when King jumped, he shouted, "Ground floor, please!" on his way out the door.

A few hours after Ryder's first jump, a friend called to breathlessly tell him congratulations. When Ryder asked why his friend was so rushed, his friend laughed and said, "Maybe I won't be able to congratulate you tomorrow. Maybe you'll get killed."

Parachute troops had doubters, both inside and out of the service, and many across America thought that parachute troops were just plain crazy. To these, as well as their supporters, Ryder would declare, "Take it from me, Uncle Sam today is breeding the toughest, guttiest jump-fighters that ever bailed out of a bomber with a grin and a wisecrack... We're the only fighters who make a cold-blooded habit of jumping day after day, week after week."

Ryder knew they were making history. He would go on to write in February of 1941, "I'd done it. Others would follow me. Dozens of them, hundreds, thousands... If these men turn out to be anything like the (test platoon) pioneers, my money is on the American parachute troops right now."

It would prove to be money well wagered.

## The Cavalry of the Air

Ryder and the test platoon made their first mass jump on August 22, 1940 (they would set a record of twelve jumpers exiting in ten seconds). Seven days later on August 29 the group made their first platoon jump involving a tactical problem. To further add to the thrilling and satisfactory nature of their work, everything went perfectly as observed by MG George A. Lynch, GEN William C. Lee, Army Chief of Staff George C. Marshall, and Secretary of War Henry L. Stimson.

Well, almost perfectly. PVT Leo Brown caught an updraft that carried him over a nearby hangar where he came down. The visiting dignitaries thought it was all part of the show and were impressed that the Paratroopers could land precisely on top of buildings (the story of a group of Latin America officers viewing a mass drop actually occured later on October 5, 1940).

The results of their successful pioneering efforts to develop parachuting practices and doctrines in the summer of 1940 convinced the Army that Paratroopers should indeed be trained in the art of vertical envelopment. On September 16, 1940, George C. Marshall directed the War Department to issue a memorandum which read in part, "The 1st Parachute Battalion is constituted and will be activated at the earliest practicable date at Fort Benning, Georgia."

This created one small problem, however, since the US Navy had already decided to create their own Marine parachute unit using the same name. So, the War department decided to name the Army's new parachute unit the 501st Parachute Infantry Battalion (the 500 numbers would be used to indicate parachute units)

Two jump towers were purchased from the Safe Parachute Company for use at Fort Benning. Another two were added later and three of these original four are still in use today, including the original elevators (a tornado destroyed the fourth tower in 1954).

With LTC William Lee too busy with his responsibilities in the Office of the Chief of Infantry, America's first parachute infantry battalion, the 501st PIB, was organized on October 7, 1940, under forty-three-year-old MAJ William M. "Bud" Miley (West Point, class of 1918).

If GEN William C. Lee was the "Father of the Airborne," then MAJ Miley was the "Father of the American Parachutist."

When asked about the training that future parachutists would endure, Miley responded, "We expect to develop men who do not know when they are whipped. That type wins battles, and our job in combat leaves much to the individual."

A former gymnast and athletic director at West Point, Miley was selected because of his effective leadership and extensive knowledge of physical training (he was also Fort Benning's athletic director where he graduated at the top of his class from the Advanced Infantry Course). With the help of several original test platoon members, Miley began training new parachute volunteers, as well as testing and improving new paratroop-specific equipment and procedures.

This included having jumpers initially pack their own T4 parachutes to increase confidence, focus on the horizon instead of looking down in the door to prevent freezing, jumping from lower altitudes to lessen vulnerable drop time, pivoting out the transport's door to allow their back to take the brunt of the propblast, modifying the standard calf-length boots with leggings to the early ski-boot type footwear, creating a sleek new multi-pocketed jump uniform (originally coveralls before the well known M1942) and much more.

Any Paratrooper who has jumped from a 34-foot cable tower during Jump School can thank (or blame) PFC John Swetish of the 501st PIB's Company B who designed it to help trainees experience the initial sensations of standing in the door then exiting with proper form. Some early jumpers even called it, "Ryder's Death Ride". Paratroopers can also thank CPT WiIlliam Ryder for the intense physical conditioning that they endure at Jump School.

Another of the airborne's most enduring legacies began with these initial pioneers. The easily recognizable silver Parachutists Badge, or Jump Wings, was the result of a desire among America's leadership to create a unique badge to distinguish Paratroopers from other infantry units. On March 1, 1941, the 501st's MAJ Miley summoned original test platoon member and hobby cartoonist CPT William P. Yarborough to his office. Miley asked Yarborough to come up with a design for the new "parachutist badge" and after producing several concepts, Yarborough decided to curl the wings upward as if they were descending with the parachute emblem in the center.

MAJ Miley enthusiastically gave his endorsement and sent the captain to Washington where he "walked the approved design from

# 1. Airborne All the Way

the Department of Heraldry in and out of every office in the War Department who had to sign off on its design."

The "Silver Badge of Courage" was officially accepted on March 10, 1941 and CPT Yarborough had The Bailey, Banks and Biddle Company of Philadelphia create 350 sterling silver jump wings which he proudly carried back to Georgia and the 501$^{st}$ PIB (Yarborough also developed the improved M1942 paratrooper uniform, jump boots and the felt unit circle that jump wings were attached to on their dress uniforms).

After inspecting Miley's new 501st PIB, BG Omar Bradley, the new commandant of the infantry school, called Paratroopers, "a breed apart-the toughest, best-trained infantry I have ever seen."

As one reporter put it, "They are the cavalry of the air."

The 501$^{st}$ Parachute Infantry Battalion became known as the Thunderbirds after their distinctive unit insignia, a shield bearing a Ojibway (Chippewa) thunderbird was approved on 29 March 1941. The 6'3" SGT Aubrey Eberhardt set the tone for the 501st with his shout of "Geronimo!" on a jump that fall (they had watched the western 'Geronimo' the night before).

Thirteen of the 501$^{st}$ PIB's original officers, including MAJ William Miley, would attain the rank of Brigadier General or higher, more than any other battalion in the history of the Army.

Volunteers for parachute duty began to pour in from units all across the country, creating a backlog of troopers waiting to be accepted. Adding fuel to the fire, in 1941, RKO Pictures made a movie titled "Parachute Battalion" staring Robert Preston and Nancy Kelly. Filmed on location at Fort Benning and Fort Bragg, the producers used the now-famous original Test Platoon as well as the entire 501st Parachute Battalion as extras. In fact, LTC William C. Lee himself doubled for actor Robert Preston during some scenes.

The fame of America's new parachute troops grew, at least limitedly in the service, after the Lousiana Maneuvers held in August of 1941 ("Parachute Battalion" was released one month later). The exercises involved nearly 400,000 troops who had several months to prepare, minus Company A of the newly formed 502nd PIB which several from the 501st were now part of.

During Phase I of the maneuvers, Company A's 127 Paratroopers dropped into the rear area of the "Red Force" on what would now be considered a suicide mission. The Paratroopers were on their own, with no plans to resupply nor reinforce them, but they successfully managed to take Second Army's HQ at Winnfield.

That cocky Paratroopers caused plenty of embarassment for Red Force commanders who argued with referees that the Blue Force's deployment of airborne troops was unfair! To be fair, Blue Force's GEN Benjamin Lear was given access to Company A during Phase II.

Though limited in size, the results were a demonstration of the lack of understanding by America's senior military leaders about how to fully utilize (or defend against) airborne troops.

As CPT William Yarborough said years later, "We had lots of enthusiasm in those early days, and some great men, but nobody really seemed to know how the thing was going to actually work when we went to war."

For most, Paratroopers were seen as a small-scale saboteur-type unit, one with limited scope. It was a perspective that would cause trouble for all of America's airborne units in the years to come, one that the 11th Airborne Division would correct with emphasis in late 1943.

## A Future With the 11th Airborne

While it can be safely stated that 1LT Ryder and the other 47 test platoon members laid the foundation for America's airborne, they and several members from the 501st PIB would soon help build on it in Major General Joseph May Swing's 11th Airborne Division almost three years later (and many who did not go on to serve with the Division helped train its troopers at Fort Benning).

While I have labored to research and compile a complete list of such men from the 501st PIB, it is an ongoing effort.

**CPT William Ryder**, for example, would interact with the 11th Airborne in various ways throughout the division's lifetime. After his participation in Sicily's Operation Husky, in which the 11th Airborne's MG Joseph Swing acted as GEN Eisenhower's unofficial airborne advisor, in February of 1944 Ryder was sent to Brisbane, Australia to advise General Douglas MacArthur on airborne operations. His service there led to numerous ties to the 11th Airborne.

America's original test platoon's platoon sergeant, **SGT Hobart B.**

**Wade**, of LaFeyette, GA, would go on to command Company E of the 511th Parachute Infantry Regiment, 11th Airborne, through the Division's brutal campaigns on Leyte and Luzon.

Another platoon member, **SGT Lemuel T. Pitts**, would join future-Captain Wade in the 511th PIR's E Company from Toccoa to Tokyo.

**CPT Glen McGowan** would serve as Regimental Executive Officer in the 511th PIR and then go on to serve as the 11th Airborne's Assistant Chief of Staff (G-1).

The 501st's CO **LTC William M. Miley** himself would take command of the 11th Airborne Division after MG Joseph Swing's departure during Occupation Duty in Japan from 1948-1949 at which time he led the Division to Camp Campbell, KY.

Miley's son, **1LT William M. Miley, Jr**, would serve in the 11th Airborne's 511th PIR, Company G, from Camp Toccoa all the way to Tokyo. After other assignments, he would serve with the Division once more at Fort Campbell, KY from 1950-1951.

**1LT Norman M. Shipley** would serve as commander of the 511th PIR's 2nd Battalion from Camp Toccoa through the Leyte campaign in late 1944 where he was wounded in action.

At least nine members of the original test platoon would serve in the **503rd Parachute Infantry Regiment** which would be attached to and eventually disolved into the 11th Airborne.

Truthfully, I have no way to fully document just how many of the 11th Airborne's Paratroopers were directly influenced by the 501st's men, although the percentage certainly is high. Countless Angels mentioned seeing Paratroopers in their sharp uniforms, garrison caps, and glassy jump boots on recruiting drives around their towns and cities. The Paratroopers' appearance, demeanor and the offer of jump pay while fighting with "the best of the best" led a great number of America's young and brightest to volunteer for the paratroops, including thousands who would serve in the 11th Airborne.

But one name from the 501st PIB stands out from all the rest when it comes to the history of the 11th Airborne: Orin D. Haugen.

## The Hardrock of Toccoa - The "First" Angel

By New Years of 1942, nine parachute regiments had been raised and on January 5, 1943 the 511th Parachute Infantry Regiment (PIR) was established at Camp Toccoa under former 501st PIB member, the thirty-six-year-old LTC Orin D. Haugen (pronounced *How-guhn*) of Wyndmere, North Dakota.

During his younger years, Orin's health was often poor which made him an easy target for school bullies who often picked on the future Angel. It was during these formative years that Orin decided he would never back down from a fight or run away in fear, attributes he would instill in the Paratroopers under his command nearly three decades later.

Orin D. "Hard Rock" Haugen

It was a mindset that Orin's future commander, the 501st PIB's MAJ William Miley, further reinforced. Gathering his small group of troopers together in 1940, Miley would tell them (and Orin), "It isn't a disgrace to get a black eye, but it is a disgrace to run away from a fight and let your buddies get beat up."

Orin was commissioned a 2nd Lieutenant at West Point in 1930 where he ranked third in his class (even though he hated The Point) and ran cross-country before being assigned to Fort Snelling, Minnesota. An incredible athlete, Orin also played polo internationally for the Army (although like many he began smoking heavily in the service).

Orin's first posting at the historic Fort Snelling at the confluence of the Mississippi and Minnesota rivers was made considerably brighter when he met Minneapolis-native Marion Sargent, the daughter of Dr. and Mrs. W. E. Sargent. After the two were married in a happy, but modest celebration on June 1, 1931, Marion dutifully accepted the life of a "soldier's wife". The young couple shared many adventures and common interests, including horse back riding which the two were quite proficient at. In fact, the Haugens appeared in several horse shows around the Twin Cities area and Marion's horse "Whiskey" has a prominent burial site at Fort Snelling.

On March 1, 1934, Orin was given leave then reported to the 21st Infantry Regiment at Schofield Barracks, Hawaii on June 2, 1934. It was here that for two years the Midwest-native got his first taste of the Pacific's mountains, jungles, heat, humidity and beaches. Orin served as Assistant Regimental Adjutant and Supply, Intelligence and Publicity Officer and was well into his education from the "Old Timers" about what it meant to be a good soldier and an officer and a gentleman. A year later Orin was promoted to 1st Lieutenant on August 1, 1935 then on April 23, 1936 he was given leave before beginning the Regular Course, Infantry School on August 31, 1936, at Fort Benning, a post that he would return to four years later.

After Orin completed the Regular Course, he and Marion headed to Fort Sam Houston, Texas to join the 23rd Infantry Division where 1LT Haugen served as a company commander and battalion executive officer. The post's heat and humidity would only further prepare him for service in the Pacific, a theater he was again sent close to in 1940 when he was sent to Fort Ord, California to join the 32nd Infantry Regiment, 7th Infantry Division. Making the move with the Haugens was their new son, William John who was born on January 5, 1938.

On June 12, 1940 Orin was promoted to Captain and while he was respected by those under his command and the other officers he served with, Fort Ord would prove a short posting. When COL William M. Miley was given command of the new 501st PIB at Fort Benning in October of 1940, the War Department sent an out official notice requesting volunteer officers for the new and admittedly hazardous Parachute Troops.

Without hesitating, Haugen leapt at the chance and boarded a train for a return to Fort Benning where he reported to MAJ Miley on the morning of November 17, 1940, and made his first jump that afternoon. Orin quickly became one of the first parachute-qualified officers in the Army, though since the 501st only had access to twelve jump transports and were living in tents around Lawson Field, he realized that the paratroops truly were a *new* endeavor.

Given his record and enthusiasm for and grasp of parachute doctrines and practices, MAJ Miley handpicked CPT Haugen to command the 501st's Able Company, so SGT Aubrey Eberhardt who famously shouted, "Geronimo!" on his first jump served under Orin.

Orin became close friends with several airborne legends within the 501st, including another company commander, CPT William P. Yarborough. Of note, Orin was one of the first officers to recieve one of the new silver parachutists badge that Yarborough brought back from Philadelphia's Bailey, Banks and Biddle jewelers.

MAJ Miley approved of Yarborough's updated boot design and encouraged his Paratroopers to wear them at all times, including in dress uniform. Wanting to show off their spit polished footwear, Miley's 501st tucked and bloused the pants of their trousers, a modification that the Army Uniform Board approved of (they argued it kept their pants from catching or snagging during jumps). Thus, the Paratroopers further distinguished themselves from other infantry units who left their pants untucked and unbloused, hence the oft-used terms used by Paratroopers to describe such soldiers as "straight-legs" or simply, "legs."

Of note, Miley also authorized the wearing of the iconic parachute patch on the left side of their overseas caps which his cocky Paratroopers took to wearing at jaunty angles.

On November 23, 1940, CPTs Haugen and Yarborough joined their colleagues and friends to celebrate their official jump status by creating a historic airborne tradition that initiates elite Paratroopers into the brotherhood of the airborne: the "right of passage" event better known as the Prop Blast Ceremony.

During this innaugrual Prop Blast ceremony, Haugen and Yarborough were joined by eleven other legendary airborne officers, including Robert F. Sink, William T. Ryder, George P. Howell, Roy Lindouist and Benjamin H. Vandervoort.

Orin's friends CPTs Yarborough and Ryder created the Prop Blast Ceremony (whether or not Orin was consulted is unknown). After Yarborough completed his required five jumps, he and Ryder got together in Yarborough's quarters at Fort Benning to discuss ideas for a new ceremony to celebrate an officers' new paratrooper status and to initiate them into the airborne fraternity.

Yarborough would later write, "We discussed and decided upon a ceremony which would focus upon the events and psychological atmosphere surrounding a trooper's first jump."

Thinking of the blast of propwash that Paratroopers feel when exiting their transports, the 501st officers also decided to create a drink that would hit like "a prop blast".

Perhaps with some humor, Yarborough noted, "We put together the Prop Blast drink by trial and error, tasting and sampling until we were satisfied that we had a good product."

That "good product" was a mixture of vodka, lemon juice and sugar. But what to drink it out of? Surely more than a common cup was needed. Yarborough directed 2LT Carl Buechner to take a 75mm shell and afix two reserve parachute rip cords to the sides as handles (they encoded the drink's recipe on the vessel using an M94 field encoding device with the keyword "Geronimo").

Dubbing the almost-sacramental cup The Miley Mug in honor of their highly-respected commander, Haugen, Yarborough and Ryder were joined by their comrades at Fort Benning's Horse Show Cabin. Given his expertise with horses, including those at Fort Benning, and his career of competing in horse shows for the Army, I have my assumptions that CPT Orin Haugen suggested the location to Yarborough and Ryder.

The names of thirteen participants were later engraved on The Miley Mug by a jeweler in Columbus, Georgia. They are:

MAJ WILLIAM E. MILEY
MAJ GEORGE P. HOWELL
CPT ROBERT F. SINK
CPT ORIN D. HAUGEN,
CPT ROY LINDOUIST
CPT WILLIAM P. YARBOROUGH
CPT JAMES W. COUTIS
CPT RICHARD CHASE
1LT BENJAMIN H. VANDERVOORT
1LT WILLIAM T. RYDER
2LT FRANK R. DUKE
2LT CARL BUECHNER
2LT JAMES A. BASSETT

While battalion commander MAJ William E. Miley had been injured earlier on a practice jump, some of his officers managed to sneak The Miley Mug and the appropriate alcholic concoction into his Fort Benning hospital room so he could be the first to "become blasted."

For the rest of those initiates, their wives (including Orin's wife Marion) watched in the Horse Show Cabin as one by one each officer stood on a chair, then lept down upon the command of "Go!" After performing a proper parachute landing (PLF), the officer would jump to his feet, grab The Miley Mug, and down its contents while his comrades shouted, "One-thousand! Two-Thousand! Three-Thousand!" with the goal of emptying the mug before a count of "Four-Thousand!"

The Standard Operating Procedure would soon come to state: "If the Blastee satisfies the senior member in his drinking, he will be considered blasted, but in case of a faulty performance in his exit, tumble, or drinking, the Blastee will have a malfunction called and go through the procedure again...."

This inaugural Prop Blast ceremony was a more formal and mild affair than many such airborne initiations that would occur in the decades to come. One of Orin Haugen's future 511th PIR Paratroopers, PFC Billy Pettit of D Company told me about the Prop Blast ceremonies he experienced in the Korean War when he was sent back to the 11th Airborne to fight again as an Angel.

"I saw guys barely able to get up *Monday* morning after their *Saturday* night Prop Blast Ceremony," he chuckled.

## Uncle Sam's Sky Army

After celebrating the holidays of 1940 and with war officially declared after Japan's attack on Pearl Harbor, the 501st's MAJ George P. Howell was given command of the new bare-bones 502nd Parachute Regiment Battalion in March of 1941. Forming his skeletal nucleus were companies skimmed from the 501st PIB and Howell asked CPT Orin Haugen to go with him. Howell, Haugen and the other cadre would soon grow the 502nd into a fully-manned battalion, a task that taught Orin, now a battalion commander, a great deal about running a parachute unit as he applied the lessons learned from their time with the legendary 501st.

The Allies as a whole would learn even more from Germany's airborne a few months later when Hitler's *Fallschirmjäger*

(Paratroopers) successfully captured the Corinth Canal Bridge in Greece on April 26, 1941. During Operation Hannibal, around 45 German engineers landed in gliders near both ends of the bridge to attack British and Australian defenders.

Simultaneously, German Paratroopers of the 2nd Fallschirmjäger Regiment dropped assaulted and took the bridge while their engineers removed the British demolitions which the engineers piled up in the center of the span. After taking the towns of Argos and Nauplia (and capturing over 2,000 prisoners), everything seemed to be going according to plan when suddenly the bridge blew up and collapsed on itself into the canal. The cause is still under debate.

What was not up for debate, however, was Germany's effective use of airborne troops, both Paratroopers and glider-borne soldiers. American airborne officers, including the 502nd's MAJ Howell and CPT Orin Haugen, studied the reports of the attack on the canal and made careful note of what the German's had done well and what could be improved upon.

Roughly one month later, Germany's *Fallschirmjäger* would give America's fledgling airborne troops even more to think about, only this time the results nearly put a halt to the progressive growth of the country's airborne efforts.

On the morning of May 20, 1941, Germany launched a bold, surprise 22,000-man attack on the isle of Crete. German High Command opposed *Unternehmen Merkur*, or "Operation Mercury", due to the upcoming invasion of the Soviet Union ("Operation Barbosa"), but after enthusiastic encouragement by Germany's legendary airborne pioneer GEN Kurt Student, Hitler overrode their resistance and declared "Crete... will be the operational base from which to carry on the air war in the Eastern Mediterranean, in co-ordination with the situation in North Africa."

While Germany would ultimately claim victory over the island's defenders, instead of the quick victory that both Student and Hitler assumed would occur, the roughly 42,000 British Commonwealth and Greek troops put up a fight. In fact, the German attackers were surprised at the number of troops and the strength of the defenses they were facing since their limited reconnaisance indicated that the island was only manned by about 15,000 troops.

Many of these unexpected British troops had been evacuated from the mainland and were in Crete waiting for transport to Egypt. One of the last to arrive was New Zealand's MG Bernard Freyberg whom Winston Churchill ordered to defend Crete to the last.

Germany's surprise attack on Crete was anything but; Freyberg knew they were coming and organized his disheveled forces into four zones which would soon be pounded by the Luftwaffe (Freyberg had sent his remaining six fighters to Egypt). However, Freyberg's lack of communication equipment would, from the onset, prove to be one of the defenders' achilles heels.

At 0800 on May 20, 1941, 600 Ju-52 "Junker" troop transports roared overhead and began disgorging Paratroopers and dropping gliders. But due to the intense concentration of the forewarned Allied firepower on Crete, hundreds of Paratroopers and dozens of gliders were shot out of the sky.

Others, caught in olive trees or struggling to unhook their cumbersome parachute harnesses, were bludgeoned to death by Crete's fierce locals who were well-accustomed to guerilla warfare.

To make matters worse, two battalions of GEN Julius Ringel's 5th Mountain Division was destroyed by the Royal Navy on their way to Crete aboard commandeered Greek fishing boats.

Victory seemed well at hand for the Allies and Germany's Kurt Student and his staff were appalled as the casualty reports came in to his HQ in Athens. Refusing to give up, Student focused his efforts on Maleme's airfield and after a fierce bombardment early on May 21, his surviving Paratroopers pushed the New Zealand defenders off Hill 107. Despite their losses, Student's men had created a foothold and the general rushed transports in carrying the remainder of GEN Ringel's 5th Mountain troops.

Back in Berlin, however, Hitler was furious at the losses on Crete and ordered Student removed from command. Ringel got right to work and after several days of fighting, the Allies knew that while Germany could resupply and reinforce their troops, the combined British, Australian, New Zealand and Greek forces were on their own. The Royal Navy would eventually evacuate 15,000 of them to safety. The rest would be captured and spend four years in captivity.

Over 3,500 Cretans would be shot in reprisal for resistance activities.

On May 25, GEN Student was allowed to visit what was left of his

Paratroopers at Maleme (and watch his rival, GEN Ringel, claim the pyrrhic victory). It was gut-wrenching experience for the formerly-confident Student. His forces which until then had successfully waged *bewegungskrieg* (the war of movement) suffered 6,698 casualties on Crete, including 3,352 killed. Hitler would swear off large-scale airborne operations from then on and Student himself would later mourn that Crete was "the graveyard of the German airborne force."

Nearly two months later, on July 17 at a reception held in honor of the bearers of the Ritterkreuz (Knight's Cross) Hitler would confirm Student's deepest fears when he told the commander, "Crete proved that the days of the parachute troops are over."

Student's mighty *Fallschirmjägers* would make several more small jumps in Europe and even participate in the Battle of the Bulge, but for the rest of the war they were mostly used as ground infantry.

## The Airborne Lives On

Like many of der Führer's decisions, Hitler's choice to close the door on Germany's airborne troops was more reactionary than visionary.

While the German casualties had been high, many in America's growing airborne program had an entirely different viewpoint of Student's Crete operation. Back at the Fort Benning headquarters of the 502nd PIB, COL Howell and his officers, including CPT Orin Haugen, studied reports of the operation like scientists analyzing another's experiment.

One thing they noticed was that Germany's Operation Mercury displayed the tactical prowess of airborne troops. Their ability to drop at key points on the battlefield could be utilized by ground commanders to disrupt the enemy's cohesion and defensive disposition, not to mention take and hold key strategic positions to facilitate victory in an operation.

Crete also showed secrecy was paramount to an airborne campaign's success, as was proper intelligence regarding the drop zone and the enemy forces in the area. The wide dispersal of GEN Student's troops kept Allied defenders on their toes and prevented a massing of manpower to repel the invaders, but the lack of a full understanding of the Allies' anti-air capabilities led to disastrous German losses.

The speed of Germany's planning was also a factor. GEN Student's staff only had a few weeks to plan, which undoubtedly led to errors in effecting the operation. In comparison, D-Day planners would have 18 months to prepare for the Normandy drops and one the main lessons implemented was that Germany had tried to spread their strength across Crete (by direct action and by mistake). Thus, in attempting to be strong "everywhere", they were strong nowhere. When planning the Normandy operations, Allied planners worked to select specific dropzones and send sufficient manpower to them.

Linking up with and reinforcing airborne units on the ground with additional forces proved critical to Germany's success on Crete. It was only after the Maleme airfield was taken and Germany could fly in reinforcements (as costly as that was) that the tide of the battle shifted. Standard American doctrine, then, became to plan to link up with airborne troops via an amphibious landing or larger ground campaign, usually within 24-48 hours.

Studying the reports and firsthand accounts, America's airborne officers noticed that Germany's parachutes were inferior and created tremendous problems for GEN Student's men. Based on old Italian designs, the *Fallschirmjäger*'s parachutes were hard to slip (they lacked risers) and tended to drop the Paratroopers at a faster rate, thus increasing the number of broken ankles or legs.

Their parachutes also lacked a quickrelease harness, so many Paratroopers who landed on Crete's trees were quickly assaulted by Allied defenders and local Cretans who killed the hanging Germans.

Another problem the Americans quickly observed was that the German Paratroopers seemed to only jump with pistols and knives. Their rifles and other weapons were dropped in bundles which meant they had to be recovered on the ground, an action that was made increasingly difficult by the heavy fire which left some German troops nigh-defenseless (some Cretans even recovered German rifles and fought the invaders with them).

GEN Kurt Student later pointed out that Crete had used up Germany's sole parachute division, sole glider division and the 5th Mountain Division which was unaccustomed to air transport. There was no backup airborne force, a factor which would affect the makeup of America's airborne divisions in the future.

All these lessons and more were taken into consideration for the

502nd PIB's limited roles in the Lousiana Maneuvers of September of 1941 and the Carolina Maneuvers that November. When the 502nd PIB's was given orders to participate, as mentioned they barely had any time to prepare and the ground commanders of both the Blue and Red Forces failed to fully utilize the Paratroopers' full capabilities, yet the 127 men of A-502 commandeered vehicles, captured "enemy" troops and blew up a bridge. One platoon raided the Second Army HQ at Winnfield, then withdrew to Clarence where they captured a Red Army division HQ before being surrounded.

Just how involved the 502nd PIB's CPT Orin Haugen was with the planning for and perhaps even participation in the Louisana Maneuvers is unknown. But given the 502nd's results, many ground commanders had their eyes opened to the full capacity of utilizing airborne troops in the field. It was a great milestone in the airborne's development, one that further demonstrated the need for America to expand her airborne forces.

On August 31, 1941, the War Department had authorized the activation of America's third parachute battalions, the 503rd PIB, which would form at Fort Benning using troopers from the 501st and 502nd PIBs as cadre. Continuing to study and implement the lessons learned from Crete and to train new parachute volunteers, the 501st, 502nd and 503rd PIBs kept busy as the country as a whole wondered if she would indeed be dragged into another world war.

We must remember that CPT Orin Haugen and all the other airborne pioneers were soldiers serving in a *peacetime* army, one in which the airborne was fighting for a piece of the very limited financial pie. As such, the Arkansas, Lousiana and Carolinas Manueuvers were all test exercises to see how prepared the United States' military forces were for such a war and luckily more and more general officers were warming to the idea of utilizing parachute troops in future conflicts.

After studying the results of the maneuvers, plus Germany and Russia's uses of airborne forces, and with war now officially declared post-Pearl Habor, the first quarter of 1942 was a hive of accelerated activity at nearly every level for America's military. The War Department realized that parachute *battalions* lacked the strength to survive a real engagement with the enemy so it authorized the creation of an additional four parachute *regiments*, but a severe lack of qualified men and equipment slowed the plans (MAJ Howell and CPT Haugen had been struggling with the same problems for months).

*A training group for the 502nd PIB. Photo taken at Fort Benning on July 28, 1941*

Even so, the 502 Parachute Infantry Battalion was redesignated the 502 Parachute Infantry Regiment on March 2, 1942. MAJ Howell was promoted to Colonel, but departed after a month to take command of Fort Benning's parachute school. Howell's former Executive Officer LTC George Van Horn Moseley, Jr. was given command of the 502nd PIR and one of his first actions was to make Orin Haugen his new XO. Moseley and Haugen labored to turn the 502nd into an elite fighting unit, one that would go on to fight in Italy, Normandy, Holland and the Battle of the Bulge.

Orin had been promoted to Major on February 1, 1942, and was making quite a name for himself when in July of 1942 now-BG William C. Lee went to England to discuss British airborne doctrines, plans and achievements. Lee learned that England planned to form entire airborne divisions and upon his return to the States, Lee recommended to GEN Lesley McNair that America do the same.

As a result, the Army Ground Forces ordered the activation of two full-fledged airborne divisions by August 15, 1942. On that date, the 101st Infantry Division was reorganized as an airborne division and the 502nd PIR made the move from Fort Benning to Fort Bragg, NC where GEN Lee gave his famous "Rendevouz With Destiny" speech on August 19. Lee said, "we shall be called upon to carry out operations of far-reaching military importance and we shall habitually go into action when the need is immediate and extreme."

It was a speech that MAJ Orin Haugen would not hear in person. Instead, when the 505th PIR was activated on July 28, 1942, Haugen was there to help the fledgling unit, under Airborne Command, get off the ground. His new CO was an old friend from Haugen's earliest days in the parachutes, the legendary LTC James M. Gavin who only three months earlier literally wrote the book on airborne doctrine at the time, *FM 31-30: Tactics and Technique of Air-Borne Troops*.

Exactly when Gavin and Haugen met is unclear as neither made

# 1. Airborne All the Way

note of it before their deaths. Both were serving at Camp Ord, CA in 1940 in the newly reactivated 7th Infantry Division (Orin in the 132nd Regiment), so that is one early possibility. Gavin also arrived at Fort Benning in the summer of 1941 for jump training, roughly a year after Orin did the same. At the time, Haugen was serving in the 502nd PIB which was posted at Benning and provided some of the instructors at the time.

*James M. "Jumping Jim" Gavin*

Regardless, LTC Gavin was only thirty-five years old at the time (Haugen was thirty-four) that he handpicked Orin to serve as his Executive Officer. Orin himself would be promoted to Lieutenant Colonel on September 25, 1942, but I am still researching whether or not he made the regimental move to Alabama on October 1, 1942. All evidence seems to point to the negative.

While Orin's time serving with Gavin in the 505th would only last a few months, the 505th PIR provided the two with the perfect opportunity to implement the procedures, practices and doctrines that their small airborne community had been developing. The 505th would be America's first parachute regiment built from the ground up which allowed Gavin and Haugen to mold the unit from its inception.

Orin and "Jumping Jim" shared similar thoughts on leadership, specifically that airborne officers (especially junior ones) should lead by example, put their men first, and fight as hard as any enlisted man. Haugen and Gavin believed in the value of intense training and were careful to only let the very best into their regiment, a tradition Haugen would continue throughout his own career.

After taking command, Gavin and a few of his staff who had been junior officers a year earlier got together to discuss what they had learned and how they could develop and train the 505th into finest fighting unit in the army. Orin was likely a participant and its outcome certainly influenced his future role as an airborne commander.

Gavin said they discussed that Paratroopers needed to be superbly physically trained, that their mental condition was equally important, that individuality was not to be crushed, that their men were to repeatedly reminded that they were the best of the best, and lastly that Paratroopers needed to be as thoroughly trained as possible.

It is interesting to note that several of America's existing parachute regiments were now under the command of a friend or former colleague of LTC Orin Haugen. The 502nd was commanded by LTC George Van Horn Moseley, Jr. whom Orin had served with there; the 503rd had been commanded by Orin's old CO from the 501st PIB, COL William M. Miley, and was now under LTC Kenneth Kinsler (upon Kinsler's death in October 1943, Orin's good friend George Jones would take command); the 505th was still under Orin's friend and former CO LTC James M. Gavin; the 506th by Orin's old friend from the 501st PIB COL Robert F. Sink; and lastly, the 508th by LTC Roy E. Lindquist, also a colleague from the 501st PIB.

For two years, Orin Haugen had served with some of the biggest names in Airborne history and helped develop this new school of America's warfighting doctrine. No wonder when BG William C. Lee and Airborne Command considered who to entrust with the new 511th PIR, one name stood out from all the rest of the candidates: LTC Orin Doughty Haugen.

As the 511th's MAJ Henry Burgess pointed out in 1988, "The excellent combat records of practically all of the regimental commanders of parachute infantry regiments (in World War II) prove that each was carefully selected."

On November 12, 1942 the Department of the Army issued orders constituting America's 511th Parachute Infantry Regiment which initially would form at the now over crowded Fort Benning before moving to "a little camp outside a little town far off the beaten path" that would become a sacred pilgrimage stop for airborne enthusiasts: Camp Toccoa, Georgia.

Initially the 511th PIR was constituted as a separate regiment that would head to the European theater as either an independent parachute unit or a regimental combat team. LTC Edward H. Lahti, who would soon

# 1. Airborne All the Way

join the new 511th at Camp Toccoa, would write decades later, "Little did we realize...the Regiment was going to become one of the elite parachute organizations in the U.S Army, making a record unmatched in history."

Before we delve further into that record and history, now that we have followed the initial story of America's parachute program, let us switch gears to quickly recount the story of the airborne's other half, the iconic gliders which would play such huge roles in airborne operations through the end of the war.

# 2: Glider Wars

Germany & United States – 1931-1943

*"I'll tell you straight out. If you've got to go into combat, don't go by glider. Walk, crawl, parachute, swim, float – anything! But don't go by glider!'*
-Walter Cronkite, War Correspondant

When I speak with people about the 11th *Airborne* Division, many are so focused on the division's Paratroopers that they forget the other half of the equation, the gliders.

Gliders are engine-less aircraft that in World War II were used to transport troops, vehicles, equipment, artillery, supplies, etc., usually during combat operations. When I asked some of the 11th Airborne Division's World War II-era Paratroopers what they thought of the gliders, they all said, in one form or another, that they would rather jump into combat than crash into it. Many Paratroopers felt bad for the gliderists and thought they were nuts which is ironic since many across America's military thought that Parachutists were the ones who needed mental help.

The history of America's glider program really begins at the end of World War I with the Treaty of Versaille. As one of the many punitive restrictions placed on Germany for their responsibility for the war, the country was forbidden from having an air force and from training pilots in anything beyond a glider. Taking full advantage of this loophole, German glider programs and clubs sprang up all across the country and as the nation became more and more militarily-focused, the glider clubs and sport programs began to attract Germany's youth who were thrilled to be trained by World War I pilots.

During the Opening Ceremonies of the 1936 Olympic Games in Berlin, made famous in part for Jesse Owen's dominance of the track and field events, Adolf Hitler watched proudly as German gliders flew overhead as the world watched his Reich's growing air power, many with concern. Having trained in the sport of bobsled myself, that crazy winter Olympic sport, I was interested to learn that the glider demonstrations held at the 1936 Games were under the

## 2. Glider Wars

direction of the International Olympic Committee (IOC) which was displaying the sport of glider soaring at the Berlin-Staaken airfield.

Three years later, Hitler's gliders would effectively take part in the country's blitzkrieg tactics in Poland then again in May of 1940 when the Luftwaffe landed troops in gliders to quickly overtake Belgium's Eben Emael fortress. In just 24 hours, the French garrison of 800 surrendered to 78 German glider troops. This operation really got the attention of flyers in militaries around the world and seeing the successes of Germany's early programs, in 1932 Russia got onboard as part of their "peasants to pilots" program and began developing their own gliders which could hold 18 troops and heavy equipment.

England followed suit, as did Imperial Japan whose glider initiatives exploded after inviting two German glider pilots, Wolf Hirth and Karl Baur, to visit in 1935. Under Hirth's and Baur's tutelage, Japan's glider program was based on Germany's format which was fortuitous as Japan was concerned about Russia's growing air power after the takeover of Manchuria. Japan called their growing enthusiasm for gliders *guraidā netsu* ("glider fever") while Germany's was called *Fluggedanke* or "air-mindedness."

Despite the growing glider programs in other countries around the world, those in America's Air Corps remained skeptical of their value and tactical usage. It wasn't until Germany's successful airborne assault on Crete in May of 1941 (which we discussed in the last chapter) that the United States really began to take gliders seriously.

That is not to say that gliders were ignored completely in the States. A few months earlier, in February of 1941, the Chief of the Army Air Forces GEN Henry "Hap" Arnold had ordered a study out of Wright Field, Ohio about the feasibility of gliders and their potential usage in what was becoming the increasingly likely war with either Germany or Imperial Japan, or both.

Gliders were originally seen as cheaper options to move more troops that could travel with heavier equipment and weapons than parachutists. In addition, while Paratroopers could be spread over the map due to winds or timing of jumps, gliders could land in numbers in a relatively small area, thus providing a concentration of strength instead of a dispersal.

Originally the Air Corps planned to train 70,000 glider pilots should war break out, though ultimately only about 5,500 received their wings. In October of 1941, just two months before the attack on Pearl Harbor, GEN Arnold placed America's fledgling glider program under the direction of glider pioneer MAJ Lewin Barringer and at first the military could only find a handful of glider pilots in the United States that could be used to teach future volunteers.

Even before GEN Arnold's study was completed, on March 8, 1941, engineering requirements for gliders were sent to eleven American companies for consideration, of which only four responded: Frankfort Sailplane Company; the Waco Aircraft Company; Howlus Sailplanes, Incorporated; and the St. Louis Aircraft Corporation.

While the other companies were larger, the Weaver Aircraft Company out of Ohio (W-A-C-O) was seen as more promising since it had experience with commercial manufacturing of aircraft. It should be noted that some of America's aircraft manufactures were far from keen on the idea of the gliders and either said their sites were too small for the project or simply stated their fears that the gliders were too untested for their taste.

Later in March of 1941, under Francis Arcier, a Waco vice-president and chief designer, the company was contracted to build one static test and one flight test model of an eight-seat glider (XCG-3) and one static test and two flight test models of a fifteen place (XCG-4) glider.

On 28 April 1942, Waco impressively delivered one fifteen seat (place) XCG-4 static test glider and later on May 14 the flight test glider to Wright Field. Under the direction of MAJ Barringer's Flight Research Unit, the first test flight for the XCG-4 static glider was held at Wright Field on June 20 and was deemed a satisfactory success. A subsequent test was held when the XCG-4 was towed 220 miles from Wright Field to Chanute Field, Illinois, complete with fifteen passengers and a pilot and co-pilot.

Two months later, the Army's first air-landing unit was activated on July 1, 1941 at Fort Kobbe, Canal Zone (the Marine Corps also planned for 75 gliders and 150 pilots but abandoned their program in May 1943.) Designated the 550th Infantry Airborne Battalion, with an authorized strength of 22 officers and 550 enlisted men, the 550th was created by inviting Canal Zone troops to volunteer.

Under LTC Harry M. Melasky, the men of the 550th were trained as an air landing unit and not a separate parachute or glider regiment. Kept in the Canal Zone in case they were called upon to land somewhere in Central America or the Caribbean (Germany was showing increased interest in the area), the 550th was reinforced by Company C of the historic 501st PIB out of Fort Benning.

With things progressing, in August the War Department G-3 called on the Air Corps to develop new cargo aircraft for a complete airborne combat team to consist of an infantry battalion, an antitank company, a field artillery battery, and a medical detachment.

After the attack on Pearl Harbor and America's entrance into the war, her glider program accelerated which exposed a rather high rate of casualties both during training and combat. This earned the gliders their famous nickname, "The Flying Coffins" and led to the saying that the "G" on their pilots' wings stood for "Guts".

After experimenting with numerous models, the War Department officially accepted Waco's CG-4A combat glider (C-for cargo, G-for glider) and about 14,000 were built during the war at a cost of between $15,000-20,000 a piece (the British called the CG-4As "Hadrians"). 70,000 individual parts made up the glider

During October of 1942 the first CG-4A gliders were delivered to Laurenburg-Maxton Air Field, N.C. and troops there learned to lift the transport's nose to allow the loading of jeeps and other equipment. The gliders also arrived packaged, unlike other aircraft which were ferried by live pilots. This meant that receiving units had to learn to safely assemble the gliders which, of course, allowed for human error, some of which led to early in-flight failures.

While both the new parachute and glider programs were struggling due to America's lack of air power, the first glider unit to be officially

*A CG-4A sits at Wright Field, OH - 1942*

activated was the 88th Infantry Airborne Battalion on October 10, 1941 at Fort Benning. Under LTC Eldrige G. Chapman, the 88th's 27 officers and 500 enlisted men spent six months testing and experimenting new methods of loading troops and equipment for Airborne missions (again, they had no gliders to "fly" in yet).

Just as the Test Platoon and the 501st PIB are recognized as pioneers in parachuting techniques, the 88th rightly deserves respect for helping lay the groundwork for America's glider programs and operations during the war. By the end of World War II America had formed eleven glider regiments and one glider battalion, of which the 11th Airborne Division's 187th and the 188th GIRs were part. I have been asked in the past if the 88th GIB and the 11th Airborne's 188th GIR have any relation, but their numerical designations are simply coincidental.

The 88th's successes led to the unit being expanded to full battalion strength (1,000+) in April of 1942. COL Robert C. Aloe was given command when COL Chapman was sent to the new Airborne Command (formed March 23, 1942) to serve as GEN William C. Lee's Executive Officer. Under COL Aloe's direction, the 88th GIB moved from Fort Benning to Fort Bragg, N.C. then one month later the battalion was expanded again to become the 88th Glider Infantry Regiment with a T/O of 1,600.

Ironically, while the 88th was America's first stateside glider unit, there were still no gliders available to use, so the 88th's mission was to continue testing and refining air-landing techniques and to instruct others on how to load, lash and so forth in America's new Airborne divisions that were being formed at a rapid pace.

Whether or not these glider troops got "enough" time training in actual loading, riding and landing in gliders is up for debate. They were "glider troops", but their mode of transportation did not require as much specialized training as did their brothers in the Paratroops. And while the gliders certainly were dangerous, their soldiers did not qualify for "hazard pay" like the Paratroopers and their jump pay.

On the ground, both would fight as infantry (the glider artillery, of course, were trained as cannon-cockers, the engineers as engineers, etc.) so for a time it seemed as though the glider troops needed only a small amount of training in actual gliders. The rest of their instruction could be dedicated to ground combat tactics, or their other areas of specialty, which is why glider troopers could be volun*told* they were airborne while Paratroopers were volunteers who could admit themselves in (and out) of Parachute training.

Thankfully these discrepancies would be corrected later in the war, but countless 11th Airborne Paratroopers who took glider rides for training per GEN Swing's orders said that "landing" in a glider was far worse than parachuting and that gliderists certainly deserved more pay than they were getting. Initially, however, Paratroopers, often viewed Gliderists as "lesser-soldiers" and joked that the glider infantry should be correctly labeled "The Towed-Target Infantry."

With the arrival of the first gliders to Laurenburg-Maxton Air Field in October of 1942, the training of glider troops could begin in earnest and by the war's end gliders would be used in combat operations around the world.

To put those first gliders' arrival into context with the 11th Airborne Division's history, the first CG-4As were delivered in October of 1942 and the 11th Airborne Division's 187th and 188th Glider Infantry Regiments were constituted just one month later on November 12. When these two glider regiments were formed in March of 1943, America's glider program had only been training with the CG-4As for six months and many in their cadres had never ridden in one.

The officer cadre for the 11th Airborne's two glider regiments, 187th and 188th, came from the 76th Infantry Division at Fort Meade, MD, except for the regimental commanders and their executive officers who joined the cadre at Laurenburg-Maxton Airfield, NC for a two week Airborne orientation in January of 1943. They then attended a month-long refresher course known as the New Division Officers' Class at Fort Benning, GA.

The 187th and 188th GIRs' enlisted cadre (which had zero airborne training) came from the 88th Infantry out of Camp Gruber, OK, and joined the officers at the as yet unnamed camp outside Hoffman, NC.

But let's leave the gliders for now and return to the parachutes with a move south to Camp Toccoa, Georgia, the home of the 11th Airborne Division's first tactical unit: the 511th Parachute Infantry Regiment.

# 3: Haugen's Heroes

Camp Toccoa, Georgia –January-March 1943

*"While not being from the samurai class, none-the-less I do recognize great warriors when I see them, and I take great pride in having served with the best fighting men of World War II."*
-1LT Ralph E. Ermatinger, 511 PIR, F Company

Nestled on the southern edge of the Blue Ridge Mountains, Camp Toccoa has been described as "a little camp outside a little town far off the beaten path." Located five miles outside Toccoa, Georgia, the 17,530-acre camp sat an average 935 feet above sea level.

Toccoa itself is a beautiful area, full of green pines, rolling hills ("mountains"), friendly people and a long history which is kept alive by the city of Toccoa. In World War II, over 18,000 men would train there to fight in Africa, Europe, and the Pacific.

Originally named for Confederate general Robert Toombs, Camp Toombs began construction in 1938 and originally housed Georgia's National Guard until Japan attacked Pearl Harbor. With war officially declared and America's airborne program ramping up to full-speed, Fort Benning was becoming overcrowded and Airborne Command needed somewhere else to train its Paratroopers.

As a result, the Army took over and began expanding Camp Toombs in 1942. The first parachute regiment to be activated at the camp was the 506th PIR on July 26, 1942 under 37-year-old COL Robert F. Sink. One of the first actions Sink took was to have the name changed from *Toombs* to *Toccoa* because he felt a Confederate did not deserve the honor. Sink also disliked the idea of new recruits detraining in town only to travel down Highway 12 past the Toccoa *Casket* Company then past the Zebulon Baptist Church *Cemetery* before arriving at a camp called *Toombs*.

One resulting problem was that when intoxicated soldiers got lost and asked for help locating "Camp Toccoa", townspeople initially directed them to the *other* Camp Toccoa, a nearby Girl Scouts site which is still in use today, so if you visit Toccoa be sure to specify which camp you want to explore.

# 3. Haugen's Heroes

COL Sink also had two World War I tanks removed from the camp's front entrance, saying he was running an outfit for Paratroopers, not tankers (their cement footings are still visible today).

Sink's 506th PIR was actually the first to test a new concept: forming a parachute regiment out of *civilian* volunteers, not active duty personnel, who would undergo a strenuous Basic Training program before attending Jump School to become airborne qualified.

In July of 1942, 5,000 men arrived at Toccoa's front gate and as the first of nearly 18,000 "Toccoa men", these volunteers would train hard at the camp then head to Fort Benning to learn how to "jump out of a perfectly good airplane."

The 501st PIR was then activated at Toccoa in November of 1942, just as Sink's 506th PIR was making their historic march to Atlanta and then Fort Benning. The 501st was lucky as they inherited the 506th's now-established barracks, mess halls, support buildings, etc.

But when Colonel Orin D. Haugen arrived from Fort Benning in December of 1942, he found that the 511th's area still under construction. Like the men who would soon arrive via trains in town, the 511th's area was fresh, raw and would need work to develop.

Haugen saw the potential and gave a rare smile.

## Forming The Cadre

"He was mean as a hornet," said PVT William "Billy the Kid" Pettit, who would soon be the youngest man in Haugen's regiment at age 16. Pettit frequently served as the Colonel's Orderly and told me, "He had a darn good regiment, so he must have been a good officer."

Haugen's new regimental dentist 1LT Ross J. Riley said, "Haugen was stickler for conditioning, and I cannot state too firmly that he was an admirable man, a soldier's soldier. To him, an order was an order, whether he gave it or received it. His primary concern was results -- and he got them!"

B-511's resident Texan (and one tall Paratrooper!) PFC James Wilson told me, "He was quite a leader. A good soldier."

Jim went on to recount a story from their Luzon campaign to retake Manila in 1945. Haugen was up front with B Company when a Filipino guerilla said to Orin, "Colonel, don't you think we rank a

*The 511th Parachute Infantry Regiment's area at Camp Toccoa - 1943*

little high to be out here?"

COL Haugen stared at the Filipino officer and growled, "Colonel, if you want to go back to another place to be comfortable, you go ahead. My place is here leading my men."

Jim Wilson then told me, "He was where he wanted to be, up front."

D-511's CPL Wilbur Wilcox, who served under Haugen all the way from Toccoa to Luzon, paid the ultimate compliment by saying, "Colonel Haugen was an enlisted man's officer."

MAJ Henry Burgess, who would have a bright history with the 511th PIR and the 11th Airborne as a whole, said, "Haugen was a remarkable man. He was a real soldier. He could outrun everyone in the 511th except (1LT Robert) Foss, the G-1 who had been the intercollegiate champion cross country racer."

Burgess added, "(Orin) could pick up rifle and fire it at two and three hundred yards offhand and shoot eight consecutive bull's-eyes. "

Years later, William E. Lindau, a war correspondent for YANK magazine who saw Haugen in action the Pacific Theater, said, "He was one of the bravest and best soldiers I have ever seen."

When asked in 1949 what commendations Orin had received, his old West Point classmate LTC Robert Allen Ports responded: "(He) should have had everything the Army could give him."

On November 12, 1942, Orin began laying the foundation for his new command while at Fort Benning. Airborne Command notified the commanders of the 504th PIB and 502nd, 503rd and 505th PIRs to provide the cadre for Haugen's new 511th PIR and making the move from the 505th with Haugen was MAJ Glenn McGowan.

Like Haugen, McGowan had years of service and was an incredible athlete, having run track and played basketball and football in high school. Glenn attended the University of Illinois-Urbana and DePaul University in Chicago under football scholarships and played against future US President Ronald Reagan whom he described as being "long legged and easy to block".

McGowan enlisted in 1930 and served for nearly a decade in the Civilian Conservation Corps (CCC) as a company officer and commander. After serving in the 2nd Armored Division under then-COL George S. Patton, Glenn volunteered for the new parachutes and joined COL Haugen in the initial 501st Parachute Infantry Battalion.

*MAJ Glenn J. McGowan*

The two then served together in the 502nd PIB before Glenn was promoted to Major and assigned as Assistant Executive Officer and Test Officer in Airborne Command. When COL Haugen was given command of the new 511th PIR, he asked his friend to come with him.

One of their first tasks was to personally interview every man on the list for the regiment's senior and cadre officers. McGowan noted that it was a "conglomeration (from the 502nd, 503rd, 504th and 505th), but all good men." The officers who passed Haugen and McGowan's interviews (mainly from the 505th) moved into a handful of buildings recently vacated by the 502nd PIR which had moved into the 29th Infantry's old buildings.

The fifth officer to report at Fort Benning, and pass the interview process, was a young 2nd Lieutenant from San Diego, California, Stephen "Rusty" Cavanaugh (his men called him "Rusty" due to his reddish hair). Rusty had participated in UCLA's ROTC then was commissioned a $2^{nd}$ Lieutenant in the Coast Artillery. 2LT Cavanaugh was sent to active duty on July 15, 1942 with the $201^{st}$ Ordnance Ammunition Company at Indio, California's Camp Young.

"I hated it," he told me. "I quickly concluded (Ordnance) did not appear to offer the kind of excitement I had hoped to find in a wartime army."

After a few weeks, Cavanaugh had had enough since, he said with a smile, he "was not going to be able to proudly announce after the war how (he) had single-handedly defeated the enemy."

While at the Benicia Arsenal Rusty's company watched a captured German propaganda film about their own Paratroopers, the *Fallschirmjäger*, and decided that the airborne was more his speed. After completing Jump School, 2LT Cavanaugh was assigned to the 501st PIR pending the 511th PIR's activation.

2LT Stephen "Rusty" Cavanaugh

Steve recalled: "By this time, I was becoming aware that I had bitten off a big chunk to chew, and that my role was to become what was considered by many a member of an elite band of men not expected to survive many battles. We were told that in parachute units, two lieutenants were assigned to each parachute platoon because the survival rate of officers was considered to be very poor."

"Each man had to carry his own share of the load," Cavanaugh added. "And in many cases do the duties of two men in a standard infantry division under the toughest conditions."

When he first arrived at the 511th's "area" at Benning, Rusty wore his "Flaming Piss Pot" Ordnance insignia to which COL Haugen thundered, "What the hell are *you* doing here?"

After Cavanaugh sheepishly explained (and promised to fill out the paperwork to transfer to the Infantry), the day after Thanksgiving, Haugen and McGowan led Rusty and the 511th's small cadre to the train station for the short ride to Toccoa where they found the camp "unfinished, dank and a sea of mud."

Shortly after arrival, Haugen gave 2LT Cavanaugh, the former engineering-student a test, I mean, a task: to build a bridge over a nearby fifteen-foot ditch. Rusty quickly "liberated" planks from Supply then took a small detail to cut down trees for supports.

A few cold, Georgia wintery weeks later when LTC Haugen asked, "When the hell are you going to get the bridge built?" Rusty responded that it was done. Dubious, Haugen ordered Rusty into his Jeep to show him. Upon inspecting the new footbridge, Haugen announced his satisfaction and 2LT Cavanaugh found himself promoted to Platoon Leader, 3rd Platoon, A Company.

Rusty added: "My personal recollections of those days (at Camp Toccoa) as a very green second lieutenant are of the long marches, disastrous encounters with Colonel Haugen and trying desperately to keep from screwing up my short-lived military career by displeasing the powers that be."

Some of those powers that be were LTC Haugen's three handpicked battalion commanders: MAJ Ernie LaFlamme (West Point, Class of 1937) of the 1st Battalion cadre; LTC Norman Shipley of 2nd Battalion; and MAJ McGowan whom Haugen placed in command of 3rd Battalion. MAJ Frank S. "Hacksaw" Holcombe would serve as Haugen's S-3. LTC Shipley had actually served under COL Haugen in the 501st PIB just two years earlier.

After MAJ McGowan became Haugen's XO, Genn's own XO, MAJ Edward H. Lahti, was made commander of 3rd Battalion. Lahti was more than a little surprised to even find himself in the 511th. In September of 1942, Ed was sent to the Battalion Commander and Staff Officer course at Fort Benning and while there, he ran into his old friend, and at the time COL Haugen's CO, LTC Jim Gavin of the 505th PIR. Lahti, who was also known as "Big Ed" or "Slugger", told Gavin that he had volunteered for and was rejected for parachute duty. Knowing that Lahti was a fine officer, Gavin told him to try again and to send him a copy of the request. This time Lahti was accepted and Gavin promised to have him ordered to the 505th.

Instead, when Lahti graduated Jump School, he found himself reporting to COL Haugen and his XO, MAJ Glenn McGowan at Camp Toccoa. While there, Big Ed discovered that it was McGowan who had lobbied so hard to have the respected West Pointer sent to the new 511th PIR instead of Gavin's 505th.

Despite his initial disappointment, Lahti quickly found that Haugen and McGowan shared his tennant of leadership, one that Haugen drilled into his officers time and time again: "If you are loyal to your troops, they will be loyal to you. Loyalty is a two-way street."

Indeed, discipline and excellence were to be the guiding philosophies of the 511th and LTC Haugen led the way, literally. When the first group of officers arrived at Camp Toccoa just before New Years, Hard Rock met them at the Toccoa train station. Although they were still in their Class A "Pinks and Greens" dress uniforms, Haugen ordered them to follow him on Currahee Mountain's six-mile roundtrip "hike", declaring, "You guys are gonna run that every day."

The officers later collapsed on their cots in the school auditorium as the 511th's barracks were not completed. Since COL Robert F. Sink's 506th PIR had left Toccoa for Fort Benning and the 501st PIR had moved in to their area, LTC Haugen found himself battling everyday to get his regiment's still-under-construction area finished on time.

The day after their Currahee "hike", Haugen began giving the small group of NCOs and officers "less than inspiring jobs" like KP or driving trucks into camp to fill their two-ton coal bins.

"Not the exact picture I had of a glamorous parachute unit," A-511's 2LT Stephen E. Cavanaugh dryly noted, although he added, "We all pitched in one way or another to get things ready for our recruits."

Rusty would retire a full-bird Colonel after serving in MACSOG in Vietnam. Having spent so many decades around the airborne, Steve joked of his early days in the 511th, "Parachute officers were an eccentric, resilient, tough and a non-conformist bunch to say the least. In other words, they were crazy."

After Rusty and the small group of the 511th's "crazy" officers celebrated New Years, LTC Haugen sent LTC McGowan, who was now acting as Orin's XO, back to Fort Benning to harvest more junior officers from among the existing parachute units and various Infantry Training Centers (he also visited the Artillery center as the 457th Parachute Field Artillery Battalion would soon form at Toccoa as well). Taking a handful of others with him on his "tour", Glenn showed the movie, *Parachute Battalion*, before giving his sales pitch to the gathered troops. When conditions permitted, McGowan and the others even gave demonstration jumps to show interetested soldiers how it was done.

McGowan, who had just been promoted to Lieutenant Colonel,

would later lament with some humor, "(Robert) Sink and (Jim) Gavin were there first and as a new lieutenant colonel I had to take what (officers were) left."

Given the 511th PIR's superb combat record, "what was left" must have been of high quality. So high, in fact, that word was already spreading throughout Airborne Command that LTC Haugen's barely-there 511th PIR was shaping up to be a fine unit. Indeed, as LTC Glenn McGowan would later write, "The record showed that we built a fine team that was later the envy of the division."

This fact would soon change the path of the 511th's future.

Having been told that his regiment would quickly head to Europe as an independent Regimental Combat Team, Haugen taught his officers to put the welfare of their men foremost and to lead by example. They would jump out the door first, eat last, share the load by occasionally carrying machine guns or mortar tubes on marches and check their men's feet for blisters. Haugen instructed those leaders to learn their men's names by heart so they could be recognized in the dark and gave them a sobering reminder: "When you leaders fail to accomplish your mission, you are responsible for all the men you lose."

"He set high standards," 2LT Cavanaugh recalled. "At the end of each phase of training, he'd get up on a podium and give his famous crossroads speech. 'You men are at a cross-roads,' he would say. He was always setting the example and insisting that we had to do better."

And he expected better, even if he was silent when it was achieved. One month after filling the regiment's T/O, Haugen held a race among his junior officers up Mt. Currahee in which Cavanaugh came in third out of about 40 participants.

"He didn't say anything," Rusty remembered. "He was never one to tell you you'd done a good job, but he noticed. He was determined to have the best regiment in the army."

## Only the Very Best

To achieve his goals, LTC Haugen spoke with another of his handpicked cadre officers, Henry "Hank" J. Muller, a young captain from Philadelphia, Pennsylvania who would have a tremendous impact on the 11th Airborne Division's history.

Hank told me that he and LTC Haugen were good friends and when Orin received orders to form the new 511th PIR, he found Henry at Fort Benning and said, "I've just been given a regiment. Would you like to come join me?"

While MAJ McGowan was on his "recruiting tour" to find new junior officers, LTC Haugen was busy getting the regiment's uncompleted area ready and preparing his plans to process their fillers. He put CPT Muller, now his S-1, in charge of developing a plan to process the influx of parachute volunteers that would soon be coming their way.

*Henry J. Muller*

Muller noted, "(Orin) wanted it to be a masterpiece of administrative efficiency and, under his close control, it was..."

COL Haugen made it crystal clear to Muller, McGowan, and all his regimental and battalion officers that only the very best would do. Anyone who did not meet his standards should be sent back to their original units or to processing centers.

Haugen felt, as did General Robert L. Eichelberger under whom Orin's regiment would later serve, that "Many are worth their weight in gold--a large percentage are liability."

Some of Haugen's standards included a superb level of physical fitness (former athletes were considered more promising), a keen intelligence (an I.Q. of 100 or higher was required), and a willingness to fight. Haugen fully believed the American proverb, "Train hard, fight easy." His philosophy was that it was ok to be afraid, but it was never okay to run from a confrontation out of fear. Again, as a child Haugen was often teased by bullies, but the late bloomer never backed down, no matter how big his opponent was.

Orin wanted his Paratroopers to possess the same willingness to stand firm in the face of opposition, and with good reason. As one of America's pioneer parachute officers, Orin fully understood the missions and conditions that he would be leading his men through.

He also corresponded with parachute officers in other units which further reinforced Orin's desires to cultivate excellence within the 511th. It is my belief that one of those officers was likely with the first American airborne unit to go overseas, the 509th PIR (formerly the 504th PIB which joined the 503rd PIR and was then separated as the 509th). I feel this way because the 509th was the only parachute unit training overseas at the time (the 509th was in England training with the British 1st Parachute Brigade), something the writer mentions.

Although the full letter has been lost to history, this officer wrote to Orin, "Boy, you better enjoy that soft life (and it is soft no matter what you are doing) while you can, because it is too good to last long. Whoever joins us had better be in shape for this place has licked plenty of good men."

Sharing the words of his friend, on January 29, 1943 Hard Rock wrote to the officers and men who had begun arriving at Toccoa (the fillers began arriving in late January and early February):

"This is a challenge to every man in this Regiment to meet the tests and so called hardships you will undergo here in preparing yourselves for combat. When the bullets start flying you will know that you are physically tough and mentally prepared for the shocks and real hardships of War."

To further help his men prepare for combat, while CPT Henry Muller was finalizing his processing procedure, LTC Haugen directed his new supply officer 2LT Miles Gale to purchase fifty pairs of boxing gloves to increase athleticism and unit morale. Haugen believed that boxing would teach his men to face their opponent with courage and he wanted his Paratroopers to follow the words of Shakespeare's King Henry V who told his own soldiers, "when the blast of war blows in our ears, Then imitate the action of the tiger..."

But first they had to pass Haugen's tests.

## Joining the 511th Parachute Infantry

Most of the 511th's potential Paratroopers were between 18 and their early twenties and weighed at least 140 pounds. A number had been drafted into regular units but volunteered for the airborne, the only way to enter parachute training. Most were "fresh from the farm" and had been lured by recruiters' unique Paratrooper uniforms, bloused over polished Corcoran jump boots, with matching garrison caps and silver jump wings pinned over the left breast. Recruiters declared that Paratroopers were the best of the best and that only the toughest and bravest men would be accepted. This notoriety was one of the true draws and to further emphasize the dangers, Paratroopers received an extra $50 a month (officers received $100) which doubled what the average Private made.

Even the 5' 5" Audie Murphy, who became the Army's most decorated soldier in the war, was enthused by the paratroops, but was rejected for not meeting size and weight requirements.

Each of the volunteers signed the famous sheet that said:

"I, (name of soldier) hereby volunteer for duty with parachute troops. I understand fully that in performance of such duty, I will be required to jump from an airplane and land via parachute."

CPL William R. Walter of Philadelphia, Pennsylvania who would soon join the 511th's Company D remembers seeing two Paratroopers at the local train station. He declared, "They were IT! I loved the uniforms and boots, the cocky way they wore their hats. I thought, 'This is what I want to be.'"

HQ3-511's PVT George Doherty, whose desire to become a paratrooper began when he watched the movie, *Parachute Battalion*, volunteered for parachute duty at San Pedro's Fort MacArthur. After being accepted, George boarded a train for Camp Toccoa, saying, "United States Paratroops here we come, 15 young brash and arrogant Paratroopers to be...God help anyone that would get in our way."

*CPL William R. Walter*

Another D Company trooper, PVT William L. Dubes of Aberdeen, South Dakota, dreamed of joining the Paratroopers since his former junior high teacher came home on furlough from the newly-established 82$^{nd}$ Airborne Division.

"I was greatly impressed and thought (the parachutes) would be a great adventure," Dubes said of his transfer from Ft. Snelling to join the 511th PIR at Toccoa. "About a dozen of we 'airborne volunteers' shipped out in January 1943 to Camp Toccoa where we began our training in the Georgia mud."

That reddish Georgia mud was one of the first things new arrivals noticed. At Toccoa's train station, booming cadre sergeants boarded the trains and bellowed for the prospective Paratroopers to do twenty-five pushups and then load into waiting trucks. After reaching camp, the sergeants shouted for the recruits to get out and PVT Billy Pettit of Texas told me he remembers everyone tossing their barracks bag over the trucks' sides only to watch them splash into Toccoa's ankle-deep mud. Billy then dropped off the truck and felt mud ooze into his service shoes.

He told me that one new arrival saw the red Georgia mud and mistook it for blood. Several troopers explained that at first Toccoa's mud would be frozen when the men woke up, turn into a quagmire during the day only to freeze again at night.

"By this time, being a paratrooper didn't seem to be a glamorous as had been previously presented," Billy said.

In addition to the frequent bone-chilling rains, the new arrivals were given several "dashes of cold water" when the cadre emphatically let the recruits know there would be no weak links in the 511$^{th}$. As acting-Sergeant CPL Robert R. Kennedy announced to a group of new volunteers, the regiment planned to accept only 30% of the new "Jockos" and of those, 25% would quit before the regiment headed to Fort Benning's jump school.

G-511's 2LT William L. Miley, whose father was the famous GEN William M. Miley who now commanded the 17th Airborne, told a group of recruits, "When you guys become troopers, you'll own the world and you'll never let things stand in your way."

One group of volunteers were met at Toccoa's train station by a larger-than-life paratrooper from A-511's 3rd Platoon who boomed, "I'm Sergeant Joe Chitwood. Before this war I was a daredevil stunt man. I traveled all over the country performing in fairs and shows, crashing cars into flaming walls, and jumping them over impossible hurdles. I thought I was a pretty good man when I joined the Paratroops. Well, I *was*, but not anywhere near as good a man as I am now after one year in the Paratroops."

PVT Murray M. Hale of D Company noted, "Their pre-planned psychology really worked, as it heightened our desire to become a trooper in the 511th. So much so that I didn't sleep too well and included in my prayers that I be accepted."

After arriving in camp, the newcomers underwent a series of initial tests to help the cadre and officers select who would train for the regiment. This included standing naked, or nearly naked, in front of an acceptance panel that was often led by a battalion commander, or at times by LTC Orin Haugen himself.

3rd Battalion's MAJ Edward Lahti explained, "The interview for the selection process was under rules strictly laid down by Haugen."

When Haugen personally interviewed PVT Donald "DJ" Hyatt and his friend, Orin asked DJ's friend if he could do twenty-four pushups. He responded, "No, sir."

Haugen then turned to Hyatt and asked the same question. "I don't know, sir, but I'll try," DJ replied. Donald's willingness to try led to his acceptance; his friend was rejected.

When an acceptance board consisting of one major and two lieutenants asked why Minnesota's Twin Cities-native PVT Murray Hale why wanted to join the 511th, Murray responded, "I volunteered for induction into the Army with the sole purpose of getting into the Parachute Troops. I knew they needed good men, so here I am."

And there he stayed; a staff sergeant later announced that Hale and half the men in his barracks had been accepted. Murray noted, "To have been one of those selected, I thought was a great compliment..."

Murray's future comrade PVT Chauncey S. Poole of Seattle, WA remembers standing naked before 2nd Battalion's MAJ Norman Shipley on January 25, 1943. Shipley asked Poole and a handful of other new arrivals things like, "How many three cent stamps in a dozen?" "What is the hair style in Washington?" "Why do you want to be a Paratrooper?" "How can I be sure that you will make that first jump?" "How many pushups can you give me?"

LTC Haugen's battalion commanders were studying the men to see who had the mental potential to become Paratroopers. Many of the 511th's original Toccoa-men said that *attitude* was the first qualification for the regiment. If a man displayed any timidity or weakness of spirit, the 511th shipped them out.

CPL Edwin Sorenson certainly portrayed the level of grit LTC Haugen was looking for. When Ed arrived at Toccoa fresh from graduating Fort Benning's jump school, the new Paratrooper proudly wore his silver jump wings. However, thinking the new "Jocko" (trainee) had stolen or simply purchased the honored badge, one of the 505th PIR cadre ordered Ed to take it off.

"He thought I had never jumped," Sorenson explained. "So, he threatened to remove my shiny new wings." Ed calmly stood his ground and declared that "any such attempt would result in his backside meeting the floor."

There were no more challenges by "Fearless Phil".

The second attribute LTC Haugen wanted in his men was physical fitness. While this was initially evaluated by having the men stand naked before acceptance panels, those who made it past this first hurdle were subjected to fitness tests with timed runs up Toccoa's famous Mt. Currahee which LTC Haugen was thrilled to find located so close to his camp. When he arrived in Toccoa prior to New Year's, Orin took one look at Currahee and knew it would prove to be the perfect test of a parachute volunteers' athletic abilities.

Anyone who has attempted the "running of Currahee" mountain's "three miles up, three miles down" will agree.

Likely derived from the Cherokee word *gurahiyi*, "currahee" is often interpreted as "stands alone" or "apart" which is appropriate since it is the last of the Blue Ridge Mountains. Currahee rises 800 feet

*Troopers running up and down "That Damn Mountain"*

above Camp Toccoa which required the men to run on a road that varied between dust-cloud inducing dirt, slippery rock and energy-sucking mud. As I can personally attest, the first mile and a half are easy enough, but after that the incline steadily increased until the last mile left many men able to only perform a brisk walk at first.

These runs up and down what one trooper called "that damn mountain" were often led by LTC Haugen himself who used his long cross-country strides and rarely the "paratrooper shuffle."

Haugen quickly became known as the toughest man in the regiment, although by now he was smoking two packs of cigarettes a day. His XO, LTC Glenn McGowan, who was Haugen's roommate for over a year, pointed out that while Orin smoked, he never inhaled the smoke. "It only stained his teeth and fingers," McGowan stated.

Even so, Haugen was in incredible shape himself and wanted to set both the pace and, more importantly, the example. As his wife, Marion Sargent, once told their young son William, "He never asks the men to do something he isn't willing to do himself."

This led several of the 511th's troopers to declare on Haugen-led runs on Currahee, "If that old bastard can make it up this hill, so can I!"

PVT Stanley Young of HQ1-511 told me, "I was a track athlete. I said, 'If that old S.O.B. can do it, I can!'"

Initially the men took over an hour to run The Hill, and those who fell out of formation were allowed to try again the next day. If they couldn't make it on the second attempt, they were bounced.

As weeks went by, the 511th's men began running Currahee in just over forty-five minutes, then thirty. While this certainly made LTC Haugen happy, when E-511's CPL Harry Yazzie, a former wrestler from Thoreau, NM, took part in a race among the 511th's NCOs earlier on January 23, he set a Haugen-pleasing regimental record of just forty minutes, five seconds. To honor his accomplishments, Haugen

*CPL Harry Yazzie*

awarded the Diné with $15 cash and a ten day furlough. Harry, who was already a qualified Paratrooper, would go on to say that his hardest battle had been "conquering fear" and that "nothing but willpower drove (him) through the door" to make a jump.

Yazzie, who came to the Paratroops from Fort Bliss's cavalry units, added, "It was worth it and I'm with the swellest group of men and officers in the world."

Many in that "swellest group" remember just how cold it was at Toccoa and as one put it, after a hard day of running up, down and around Currahee, plus all the other P.T., their barracks' "sounded like a tuberculosis sanitarium at night."

Since the regiment was forming just after New Years, Toccoa was often covered by clouds which frequently doused the troopers.

"The rain was awful," PVT Billy Pettit noted. "It was never quite freezing, but there was mud up to your ankles everywhere."

Running Currahee was just the beginning of LTC Haugen's physical exams. Potential volunteers also had to pass a flight physical and color blindness tests as Paratroopers needed to distinguish between red and green jump lights and set up colored signaling panels.

The next attribute that LTC Haugen wanted to test for was intelligence. As a pioneer in America's parachute program, Orin knew that Paratroopers needed courage, stamina and intellect. So, when CPT Henry Muller designed the regiment's processing plan, he included the Army's General Classification Test (AGCT) which the 511th's potential Paratroopers had to pass with a score of 110 or higher, the same requirement for Officer Candidate School (OCS).

This meant that the lowliest Private in the 511 could have been an officer in "the regular Army". That said, 2LT Edward Flanagan of the 674th Glider Field Artillery Battalion, which would later fight alongside the 511th, pointed out with the humor of an officer who went up through the ranks, "...it must be admitted that the higher a man's inteligence, the cleverer are his misdeeds and gripes, and at times it seemed a division of morons would have been preferable from the commander's viewpoints."

It also meant that many of the 511th's troopers picked up on things fairly quickly and grew tired with the monotony of training. As CPL Murray Hale noted, "Army Regulations are designed for all intellects so there is a lot of repetition. The IQ level for our Regiment was much higher than average so our training progressed and the repetitive part of it was extremely boring."

Murray then added, "The officers did their best to keep the classes as interesting as possible, and I thought they did a rather good job."

3rd Battalion's CO LTC Edward H. Lahti proudly testified that, "The 511th Regiment probably contained the finest group of prospective soldiers of any regiment ever assembled in one unit."

He was not exaggerating. By February of 1943, those who remained in the regiment's Dog Company, for example, had an AGCT score of 115 or higher. As one Paratrooper put it, Haugen and the 511th were looking for men smart enough for OCS, but dumb enough to jump out of a perfectly good airplane.

## The Hardrock of Toccoa

After the 511th PIR was officially formed on January 5, 1943, LTC Haugen's acceptance boards, runs of Currahee, fitness tests and additional test given by the cadre were quickly weeding out the wheat from the chaff. Hard Rock himself would frequently tell his men, "If any one of you want out of this outfit, come see me."

"But no one ever got to see him," laughed PFC James Wilson. Jim told me that with all the staff officers and secretaries and HQ red tape, no one could get in to see "The Boss".

When I asked what led him to volunteer for the airborne, Jim told me prior to us celebrating his 100th birthday, "I wanted to go to the Paratroops because if something happened to me, I could only blame myself. I never regreted one minute of it."

*PFC James Wilson*

Those who could not meet Haugen's requirements, or those who *did* regret it and quit on their own, were transferred to "Cow Company" where they were required to wear blue denim

## 3. Haugen's Heroes

and sleep in the soggiest part of camp. Cow Company's tents frequently flooded, and cots sank into the mud. New recruits began there as well which led to the moniker of W Company for "Welcome or Washout". The *Washouts* were usually transferred within 48 hours while *Welcomes* were quickly sent to their new companies.

Word began to spread that the 511th had incredibly high requirements for acceptance. So high, in fact, that inspector reports about LTC Haugen's washout rate (1 in 3 of those accepted were already expected to later wash or "un-volunteer" themselves) caused concern in Washington. The War Department wired Orin stating that his selection process was *too* stringent as it was taking 12,000 men to fill 3,000 slots. The message told Haugen to quit being so critical of the recruits, but by then Orin had filled his T/O so he laughed and told his staff, "They're too late!"

It was a rare display of emotion by their well-respected commander. Some of the first to arrive at Toccoa originally called Haugen The Great Stone Face because he never smiled.

"But never to his face!" 2LT Stephen Cavanaugh pointed out. Rusty noted that while he was surrounded by incoming officers and the existing cadre, some of whom he already knew, Orin was not a social commander.

"He didn't socialize much," 2LT Cavanaugh explained, although Orin was extremely fond of his own family. "He selected some old timers he was familiar with to be company commanders, people he respected. He may have had close friends, but I never knew of any."

In the coming months, the Paratroopers of the 511th PIR would come to know just how much their commander cared for their wellbeing and to respect his stern, yet respectful manner and discipline.

For example, to encourage his men during especially difficult exercises, Orin's friend COL Robert Sink of the 506th PIR shouted to his own men at Toccoa, "We want the best!". Not to be outdone, Orin would bellow to his own men in the 511th, "We *are* the best!"

That said, given how hard he pushed his regiment at Toccoa, LTC Orin D. Haugen would become known among his men (and even officers) as "The Hard Rock of Toccoa", or simply, "The Rock."

The young boys of the 511th PIR were lucky. They were not being led by someone who simply studied or only trained in parachute principles and doctrines. COL Haugen had helped *develop* many of them and as such he knew what it would really take to succeed. And even those who had been accepted into The Rock's unit still had a long way to go to prove that they deserved to wear The Silver Badge of Courage.

Haugen's XO LTC Glenn McGowan said, "When we got the fillers in at Toccoa we started right in on modified unit training as we were still under Airborne Command and at that tine we did not know that we were to be a part of the llth (Airborne) Division."

As part of that training, Hard Rock Haugen wanted his new troops to be in the best shape of their lives before they went to Fort Benning for Jump School, so daily life at Toccoa started early in the morning. After breakfast the physical training (PT) began with the Daily/Army Dozen: side benders, toe touches, side straddle hops, windmills, squat thrusts, six-inch leg lifts, flutter kicks, crunches, lunges, knee bends, eight-count pushups, and jogging in place (some recruits and platoons began the day by running around the camp). It was not uncommon for units to repeat the Daily Dozen several times in cold temperatures, chilling winds and the occasional icy rain.

"It was pushups all the time in elbow deep mud," D-511's PVT Billy Pettit said. As another trooper noted, it was always "double-quick. We never walked anywhere."

One 511th trooper added, "Our non-coms said the training would make us so ornery we'd be able to chew razor blades and spit nails."

The motto of the 511th's cadre was, "Run 'em until they think they can't go another step, then run 'em five more miles just to prove they can." This fierce training was in line with the time-old tradition of pushing recruits to see who really wanted to be there and to find out who would meet expectations to prove it.

"They were separating the men from the boys," explained PVT Pettit. "They did everything they could to make you quit. Those that were left wanted to stay."

As another trooper put it, the boys of the 511th spent their time at Camp Toccoa "hurting and hungry."

Hard Rock continued to emphasize basic soldiering skills as well, since according to D Company's CPT Lyman Faulkner, "Haugen wasn't interested in experimental parachuting ... he saw the parachute as a vehicle to get to the fight."

Hard Rock knew that once his troopers hit the ground, they would be fighting as infantry, albeit highly trained infantry. Physical fitness and mastering the basics of soldiering were the goals and while his passion for the airborne never left, D-511's PVT Bill Dubes' enthusiasm for LTC Haugen's strict fitness regime did.

"I don't recall just how long we toiled in Toccoa and Mt. Currahee, but I was happy when we left...", he noted. Even the 511$^{th}$'s 1943 yearbook states, "Currahee is okay: as a memory..."

F Company's PFC Ray Brennaman told me that his company commander, CPT Charles A. "Baldy" Morgan, told them during a Judo class he was teaching, "'Bitch you guys-that's the only right you have!' We liked him. He was a nice guy."

When I asked if he ever regretted volunteering for the Paratroops, 2LT Stephen "Rusty" Cavanaugh, at the time a retired colonel with decades of service, chuckled and replied, "I was young. We all were."

Hard Rock's S-1 MAJ Henry Muller agreed. When we were discussing those early days at Camp Toccoa, he told me, "We were all young. Everyone was young."

By March of 1943, the average age for the 511th was just 21.

2LT Cavanaugh remembered the results of the 511th's young status:

"I look back now and remember how we junior officers use to criticize (to put it mildly) some of the actions of our company, battalion and regimental-level commanders and I recognize now how really young and inexperienced they all were and how naïve we were to complain about them. The battalion commander of the 1st Battalion, LTC Ernest La Flamme, would have been a junior captain, if that, in the pre-war army with many years ahead of him before he became a major. LTC Haugen would probably have been a senior major instead of commanding a regiment. They were assuming ranks and positions far beyond their level of experience but that was the acceleration in rank necessary for a rapidly expanding war time army, they were bound to make mistakes yet they led us well."

Indeed, these young officers enforced Hard Rock's decrees that obedience, competence and excellence were the way of life in the regiment and the smallest infraction or error made would provoke

*The 511th PIR's first review held at Camp Toccoa, Jaunary 1943*

commands to "drop and give me twenty-five" for the perpetrator or even the entire platoon.

While the 511th' cadre and officers were extremely professional as a whole, one unforgettable influence was from Hard Rock's Regimental Sergeant, the tough-as-nails Master Sergeant Major Frederick Thomas.Thomas, like LTC Haugen and many in the cadre, was an early volunteer for parachute training having made his first parachute jump in September of 1941. He had served in the 503rd PIB at Fort Benning before joining the 505th PIR in November of 1942. It was here in the 505th, Hard Rock's old regiment, that Orin found then-S/SGT Thomas and asked him to come with him to his new 511th PIR as Acting-Master Sergeant of the regiment's cadre.

A few weeks later, Thomas was told to drop the "Acting" part. At just twenty years old, M/SGT Fredrick Thomas was the youngest Regimental Sergeant Major in the U.S. Airborne Forces during World War II (and probably the entire U.S. Army).

Surrounded by officers and NCOs of such high quality, CPL Murray Hale recalled, "These were tough and impressionable days. And a fitting introduction to our forthcoming Basic Training to become troopers of the 511th..."

One NCO who gives us an example of the quality of the regiment's non-coms was Dog Company's 1SGT Louis E. Filippelli. Chauncey Poole explained, "(Filippelli) was something to contend with. I admired him so much, because he would give orders as if they were his, as much as he personally might have disliked it. He was hard as nails, a spit and polished soldier. He ran the company as far as we were concerned."

Later, during the battle for Manila on February 8, 1945 a Japanese knee mortar shell exploded near the Italian-born Filippelli, sending shrapnel across his entire body. The medics wrapped the tough Italian "like a mummy" and after stumbling to his feet, Filippelli approached D Company's CPT Stephen Cavanaugh and in an apologetic fashion said, "Sir, I think I've got to go to the rear."

Back at Toccoa, the 511th's young troopers were given ninety-minutes for lunch and the tired "Jockos" often ate quickly then took naps in their barracks. Warmed by pot-belly coal-fed stoves, the hutments held sixteen men in double bunks with electrical outlets and overhead lighting. Each trooper was given a small shelf and footlocker and told to keep his area clean.

Meals were served in the mess hall "family style" with ten men to a table. One or two men from each table would bring food from the kitchen and whoever scooped up the last of a dish had to go back for more. As the cadre and staff wanted the men to put on muscle, seconds were given without question (unless an extra tasty dessert was served) and while it was not exactly gourmet quality, Toccoa's food was generally enjoyed.

Eating was a bit of an experience, at least at first. B-511's PVT Sidney Smithson wrote, "This is a new camp so we have very few luxuries. We have no metal trays for food so we have a six course meal piled on one plate. No forks, no coffee, no milk, very few cups so we usually drink cocoa out of a soup bowl."

In addition to limited marksmanship training (the nearest rifle range was thirty-miles away at Clemson College), the men were subject to frequent lectures on a never-ending list of subjects relating to military life and protocols before running through the camp's challenging obstacle course or participating in the ever-present close order drill and formations.

Afternoons were usually spent training for parachute deployment beginning with the boxy mockups of C-47 fuselages where the men divided into "sticks" of 16. The term "stick" denotes one load of 14-20 Paratroopers and is connected to the word "chalk" which describes a group of troopers gathered for an operation (white chalk often marked the side of their aircraft). When actual airborne jumps began, many officers in the 511th wisely placed their largest man in the back of the stick to act as a bull rusher.

As HQ1-511's PFC Rod Serling, the future creator of the famous *Twilight Zone* television series, explained, "If you didn't jump in time, you'd be five miles beyond where you were supposed to go with the comparative comfort of your own colleagues; so, it behooved you to get out that door as fast as you could."

2LT Stephen Cavanaugh added that, "If a man failed to jump, it was our fault, and some platoon leaders were relieved after their men froze in the door of the plane."

Training officers taught recruits how to sit on mock fuselages' benches and listen for commands to "Stand up!" "Hook up!" "Equipment check!" "Stand in the door!" "Go, go, go!" The men learned to plant their left foot and pivot out the door with their right, thus allowing their backs to take the brunt of their aircraft's propwash. The jumper would then count "one-thousand, two-thousand, three-thousand!" at which point either the static line would deploy their canopy, or they would tug the handle for the reserve chute on their chest.

After fuselage training, the 511th's Jockos quick-timed to a collection of five-foot high platforms where they practiced landing in sawdust pits or over to the loathed "nut-crackers" where they hung in parachute harnesses to practice "slipping" by pulling on the risers. Slipping changes the canopy's shape which provided a Paratrooper

a small amount of "steering" in the air. It was a necessary skill to acquire, but an uncomfortable way to learn it.

"You better get your family jewels in the right place," PFC Billy Pettit told me with a laugh.

Next the men quick-timed over to a 34-foot jump tower, "The Widow Maker" or "The Great Separator" which had originally been designed by PFC John Swetish of the historic 501st PIB's Company B (many sources incorrectly attribute this feat to airborne legend CPT Willam M. Ryder). My grandfather, Dog Company's 1LT Andrew Carrico, pointed out that this tower washed out more recruits than any other exercise. After climbing the stairs and hooking their harness onto a pulley, the men performed a "leap of faith" out the "door" before sliding down a 200-foot cable.

H-511's PVT Albert Roe told me that when he climbed the tower for the first time and looked down at the ground, he instantly grew nervous. "A size twelve boot kicked me in the ass and out I went!" he said with a laugh. "I was Five-feet seven-inches and weighed 127 pounds. I was a little shit!"

He then added that at the time of discharge he was 5' 11" and weighed 155 pounds. "I grew quite a bit," he said with another laugh. Albert then told me that because he joined the regiment as a replacement much later, he was able to serve in the Honor Guard that transported President Roosevelt's body from Warm Springs, GA to Washington, DC before he joined the 511th on Luzon in 1945.

The days at Toccoa back in 1943 ended with the Buglers' Regimental Retreat Formation followed by evening chow before lights out.

Saturday afternoons were spent in parade review on the athletic grounds, after which most of the 511th had the rest of the weekend off. Those *very* few who were lucky enough to get passes ventured into nearby Gainesville or even Atlanta (especially Peachtree Avenue), while others stayed in camp to enjoy the peace and quiet (and extra helpings of dessert). The enlisted men enjoyed beers at John Lathan's Wagon Wheel right outside the camp's gate while the officers preferred the Hi-De-Ho closer to town.

As the weeks went on the cadre accepted that the remaining Jockos were beginning to talk, move and think like potential Paratroopers. As entertainer Bob Hope joked during a visit to Toccoa, "You guys are so rugged you look like Wheaties with legs."

On January 22, COL Haugen's forming regiment had a special guest in the way of Congressman J. Parnell Thomas of New Jersey. A member of the House Military Affairs Committe, Thomas was there to inspect the camp, as well as the troops of Haugen's 511th PIR as well as COL Howard R. Johnson's 501st PIR. Haugen and Johnson accompanied Thomas on his tour of the camp where they watched troopers training on the obstacle course, doing PT, etc.

Thomas, whose son Silas was a Private in the 501st PIR, said:

"Uncle Sam's parachute troops are, man for man, the finest troops in the world... Each man is a finely trained athlete with a mental attitude and eagerness to learn that speaks highly for their training program. They are individualists while working with their comrades as a team. This sort of thinking is unbeatable."

Hard Rock and his boys completely agreed.

Haugen also whole-heartedly agreed with Airborne Command's Training Memorandum No. 2, dated May 15, 1942, which outlined the objectives and procedure of parachute training. Its first stated objective was "To train the qualified. parachutist in those basic subjects necessary to produce an aggressive, resourceful, and effective individual soldier."

Haugen had successfully created a regiment full of such soldiers.

The 511th's routine changed little until March 21, 1943, seventy-five days after the 511$^{th}$ was activated, when the regiment's 3rd Battalion, the last to be fully formed, boarded a train for Hoffman, NC, Airborne Command's new HQ. LTC Orin D. Haugen's men were headed to join America's newest airborne unit, the 11th Airborne Division.

*Aerial view of Camp Toccoa, GA*

It was a development that Hard Rock himself was probably still processing, and I wish he made a record of his emotions regarding

## 3. Haugen's Heroes

the change. Again, when he was given command of the new 511th PIR in November of 1942, he had been told that his regiment would most likely remain independent and be sent to fight in Europe as a regimental combat team.

That all changed when Brooklyn, NY's BG Albert Pierson arrived from Fort Benning in late February. Pierson was the designated assistant division commander for the new 11th Airborne Division and spent several days studying Hard Rock's process of training his new recruits (Pierson was also impressed by the way Haugen's officers evaluated and eliminated those who would not measure up).

Orin's XO LTC Glenn McGowan remembers, "General Pierson told us in confidence that he understood that we were to be the Parachute Regiment in a newly formed airborne division, the 11th.... That was not good news as we thought we would be a part of a Parachutes brigade and go to Europe. However, everything worked out OK for us."

Ever since he was given command of the new 11th Airborne Division, Pierson's senior MG Joseph May Swing had been busy looking over the records and statuses of the 501st, 502nd, 504th and 505th PIRs. While they were impressive, Swing discussed things with GEN William C. Lee who had just taken command of the 101st Airborne Division. Lee gave COL Haugen's 511th PIR "high marks" which was enough for MG Swing who selected the 511th to become the first fully-formed unit in his new 11th Airborne Division.

It was a decision that would give Swing immense satisfaction in the years to come... and an infinite numbers of headaches. The general would declare, with a mixture of fatherly pride and frustration, that COL Orin D. Haugen's 511th PIR was full of "The greatest men in the world to go to war with and the last people in the world I'd take home to date my baby sister!"

COL Haugen's S-1 MAJ Henry Muller remembered that, "Swing, who had heard terrible reports about the alleged rowdyness and unprofessionalism, determined to 'make us right.'"

In the middle of 1st Battalion's final preparations before boarding their trains for Hoffman, B Company's CPT William Bostwick asked his men if any of them would like to run Currahee one last time. They were surprised when he let them know that it was an invitation, not an order and roughly thirty men decided to go.

Departing at 0800, 2nd Platoon's PVT Bert W. Marshall made the run with his brother George, saying, "When we got to the top, we had a little rest, then we ran all the way back down to Toccoa into the camp. When we reached the camp there were only about six of us left, besides Captain Bostwick."

When the Marshall brothers initially volunteered for the paratroops at Fort MacArthur, California, they stood before a lieutenant who asked, "Do you know what you are getting into?"

I imagine Bert was smiling when he wrote years later, "We told him yes, even though we did *not* know what we were getting into."

Roughly 3,000 such troopers remained in COL Haugen's regiment, yet Hard Rock and his officers knew that number would have to be further whittled down. While each company currently had 180 men in it, the authorized strength of a parachute rifle company was 8 officers and 115 enlisted men. This meant that over the next few months the 511th would have to eliminate almost a thousand of the best men that the Army had to offer, men who beat out 9,000 others to be there.

As my grandfather's good friend in D Company 2LT Leo E. Crawford pointed out, "This allowed the retention of only the *very* best."

19 year old PVT Leland J. Ranier echoed the notion, telling the people of his hometown of Cayuga, NY, "I wouldn't change to any other branch of service in the world. I think the Paratroopers is the best outfit of them all."

A-511's 2LT Stephen Cavanaugh noted, "Colonel Haugen, 'The Rock', saw too it that any officer that failed to measure up was handed a quick trip out of the outfit and many were."

ORIN D. HAUGEN,
Lt. Col., 511th Prcht. Inf.,
Commanding.

# 4: Forming the 11th Airborne

Camp Mackall, North Carolina – November 1942 – December 1943

*"Often neglected in our later tales of battle are the stories of how we honed our skills in the sand hills of North Carolina and the swamps of Louisiana." -2LT Stephen "Rusty" Cavanaugh, D-511*

If we were to travel back in time and arrive at the new camp outside Hoffman, NC, in late 1942, we would probably find ourselves less than impressed. Amongst the tall Carolina pines, Hoffman was a cold, dreary hive of construction: roads were still being bulldozed, tarpaper barracks were half completed and many support buildings remained nothing more than drawings on engineering blueprints.

Career officers who would soon arrive at Hoffman noticed the stark difference between their former posts whose structures were built to last (some are even in use today). Hoffman's buildings were hasty, cheap and only held to the "theater of operations" standards. The barracks themselves held double the number of bunks, but engineers had only built half the required number of toilets!

And yet, located just forty miles west of Fort Bragg, the yet unnamed camp would become an important part of America's airborne efforts in World War II. After all, Fort Benning, "the birthplace of the airborne", was becoming far too crowded to solely bear the weight of the quickly expanding airborne program of 1942-1943. Some airborne units had already moved to Fort Bragg itself to make room, but even Bragg was filling up quickly.

On November 8, 1942, the chief of engineers decided that a new camp would be built, one that would be exclusively for airborne units and would be home to America's Airborne Command. Plans were drawn up for a cantonment that would house three divisions and six months later, it would cover nearly 60,000 acres and consist of over 1,750 buildings. These included a 1,200 bed hospital, seven service clubs, two guesthouses, three libraries, sixteen post exchanges, twelve chapels, five movie theaters, six beer gardens, and three 5,000 foot runways which are still used today.

With the 82nd and 101st Airborne Divisions already established (both were currently at Fort Bragg), on November 24, just two weeks after construction began in the "Sandhills Recreation Area" near Hoffman, the War Department authorized the creation of a third airborne division to be numbered the 11th under forty-seven-year-old then-Brigadier Geneneral Joseph May Swing.

Hailing from Jersey City, NJ, the Hollywood-looking Swing graduated 38th in his class at the United States Military Academy in 1915, "the class the stars fell on." His roommate and football teammate at The Point was Dwight Eisenhower (Omar Bradley also played with them under head coach Charles Dudley Daly).

*Major General Joseph May Swing*

Swing served as a 2nd Lieutenant under GEN "Black Jack" Pershing in Mexico during the "Punitive Expedition" against Pancho Villa in the 4th Field Artillery. When America entered World War I, he served in France with the 8th Field Artillery under GEN Payton C. March before returning stateside where he married GEN March's daughter, Josephine Mary March, on July 8, 1918. Three years later the couple would set sail for Hawaii where Swing would take command of lst Battalion, 11th Field Artillery at Schofield Barracks.

In 1925, the Swings returned to the States where then-Major Swing assumed command of the 9th Field Artillery at Fort Des Moines, Iowa. The following year he graduated with honors from the Field Artillery School at Fort Sill, and in 1927 he graduated from the Command and Staff School at Fort Leavenworth, Kansas.

For the next four years, MAJ Swing was on duty in the Office of the Chief of Field Artillery in Washington, DC, and in 1933 he became chief of its war plans section. In 1935, he graduated from the Army War College in Washington and then joined the 6th Field Artillery at Fort Hoyle, Maryland and was promoted to Lieutenant Colonel.

Next, LTC Swing went to Fort Sam Houston where he was the chief of staff of the 2nd Division from 1938 to 1940. Later, as a full-colonel he commanded the 82nd Horse Artillery Regiment of the 1st Cavalry Division at Fort Bliss, Texas, then oversaw its division artillery.

## 4. Forming the 11th Airborne

Swing's next move would allow him to participate in the historic re-activation of the 82nd Infantry Division, the All-Americans from World War I, at Camp Claiborne, Louisiana, on March 25, 1942. The 82nd's CO was now-Brigadier General Swing's old West Point roommate, GEN Omar Bradley who asked Swing to come organize the division's new artillery units.

A few months later, on May 7, Swing and Bradley listened as Sergeant Alvin C. York, who won the Medal of Honor in World War I for his actions as a member of the 82nd Division, addressed the 15,000 gathered men of his old unit in their first retreat ceremony. York, now a Major, gave the All-Americans a rousing speech and told them in his southern drawl, "Freedom is not a thing that you can win once and for all. We never owned freedom; we only got a lease on it. A payment came due in '17-'18. Now another one is due, but this time we're going to make such a big payment that it will be many a' year before another one is demanded of us."

GEN Bradley and his commanders like Swing did such a good job training their men to make MAJ York's "payment" for freedom that when the War Department reviewed records to see which division was in the best position to become airborne, the 82nd was selected.

On August 15, 1942 the 82nd Infantry conducted its final parade then listened as their new commander, MG Mathew Ridgeway read orders stating that the 82nd Infantry Division was now deactivated and was thereby reactivated as the 82nd Airborne Division.

It was here that Swing's future in the airborne was cemented as the 82nd became America's first airborne division and BG Swing spent the next three months working hard to get the 82nd's division artillery units airborne ready.

Then, given his penchant for daring leadership and understanding of airborne tactics, when the War Department ordered the formation of its third airborne division, Swing was given command of the new 11th Airborne at the planned airborne camp outside Hoffman in November of 1942 and promoted to Major General.

His new command came as no surprise to those who knew the general. As MAJ Douglas Quandt, who would later serve as Swing's G-3, noted, "He thinks big, and has amazing perspective which, to a large extent, is derived from a great respect for, and an encyclopedic knowledge of, the traditions, precedents, and accomplishments of

*The new 82nd Airborne Division's generals on their first jump. From left to right: MG Mathew Ridgeway, BG Joseph Swing, BG William M. Miley, jumpmaster MAJ Warren Williams of the 504th PIR and 1LT Don Faith, Ridgeway's aide*

the service, as well as a remarkably accurate and infallible memory."

Thus began for General Swing a tenure of service which was unique then and still remains a record, one that has for far too long been overlooked by airborne historians who focus, perhaps myopically, on Lee, Ridgeway, Taylor and Gavin. Major General Joseph Swing was division commander of one division for five consecutive years, during which he activated the division, trained it, and commanded it in combat and during its subsequent occupation of Japan. No other airborne commander in the war can boast of such a resume.

Unlike many other airborne "brass", the piercingly blue-eyed Swing elected to complete all five of his training jumps (Generals Ridgeway and Taylor, for example, only completed one or two before their first jumps into combat).

During a meeting in Washington, D.C., Swing presented his idea for the new division's shoulder patch, a blue shield with white wings crested around a red circle and the number 11, to COL Francis W. Farrell, his Chief of Staff, and BG Albert Pierson, his assistant division commander, and BG Wyburn D. Brown, the division's artillery commander. All enthusiastically approved and the 11th Airborne's iconic "Angel" emblem was created.

What some troopers came to call the insignia when Swing wasn't around, however, is unprintable.

## Swing's "Royal Family"

As is often said, leadership can be isolating and cause leaders to rely on a small group of trusted subordinates. General Swing's subordinates would become known as his "Royal Family."

Swing and some of his "Royal Family" traveled to Washington at the request of GEN Lesley McNair, commander of Army Ground Forces. McNair greeted the officers in his office and then they began four days of briefings and orientations followed by four days at Fort Holabird, MD where they underwent "refresher" courses on the operation and maintenance of the Army's motorized vehicles. Swing's staff then traveled to the nearby Aberdeen Proving grounds for weapons orientation, after which the general and COL Farrell went to Fort Leavenworth, KS to select the division's original chiefs of staff before returning to the 11th Airborne's camp.

Let us briefly learn about those division officers before moving on:

**COL Francis W. Farrell**:
MG Swing's Chief of Staff was born in Chicago and graduated from the United States Military Academy at West Point, Class of 1920. Upon commission, 2LT Farrell selected the infantry and completed the Infantry Officer Course in 1921. After several assignments, including postings to Hawaii and China, 1LT Farrell transferred to the Field Artillery on July 7, 1926. He completed the Field Artillery Officer Course in 1928 then spent the next few years teaching at West Point. In 1939 he graduated from the Command and General Staff College  and in 1942 COL Farrell was selected for the 11th Airborne where some officers referred to him as "Fearless Frank."

Swing's future G-2 MAJ Henry Muller said, "Farrell, to my mind, had to be the Army's best Division Chief of Staff... He was brilliant, dedicated, incisive, energetic, and always very fair."

**BG Albert Pierson:**

MG Swing's assistant division commander was born in Brooklyn, NY at Cornell College, where he was in the ROTC, in 1918 to participate in World War I. He graduated from Camp Perry Small Arms School in September of 1918 and was commissioned a 2nd Lieutenant, but the war ended before he was shipped to Europe. Pierson became a company officer in Puerto Rico with the 42nd Infantry and Panama, then taught military science at Cornell College and served at Fort Benning, Georgia; Fort Devens, Massachusetts; Washington and the Philippines where he served several months on Corregidor in beach defense training.

Pierson then attended the Army War College in 1933 alongside his classmates Omar Bradley and Maxwell Taylor before graduating from the Command and General Staff School 1940. Pierson was then selected for the 11th Airborne in 1942 where he became affectionately known as "Parade Rest Al" for his habit of standing at Parade Rest when talking to other troopers.

**BG Wyburn D. Brown:**

The 11th Airborne's division artillery commander was born in Marion, SC, and attended The Citadel Military College. He then graduated from West Point in 1919 and went on to serve in the Philippines and as a mathematics instructor at West Point through 1938. From 1939 to 1941, Brown was assigned to the Artillery Center at Fort Sill, OK, where he developed new artillery tactics and literally wrote the book on the topic, the Army's Field Artillery Firing Manual, that defined the techniques that would

## 4. Forming the 11th Airborne

be used by American forces in the war. Then, in 1942, Brown was selected to oversee the new 11th Airborne Division's artillery units.

The division's Assistants Chiefs of Staff for G-1 would be LTC James W. Smyly, Jr.; G-2 was MAJ Clifford L. Dier; G-3 was MAJ Robert A. Ports; and G-4 was LTC Glenn A. Ross.

With his headquarters shaping up, MG Swing immediately set out to organize the 11th Airborne into America's finest fighting unit. His first challenge was, of course, the cantonment itself.

As a side note, if you want to see what the camp looked like at the time the 11th Airborne was there, watch MGM's movie *See Here, Private Hargrove* which was filmed on location.

The Hoffman camp was still expanding when Swing finalized his staff in November of 1942. In the 11th Airborne's area the roads were unpaved, several support buildings were uncompleted, and plumbing was spotty (although leaky roofs "provided water"). They had work to do and since Swing believed the maxim, "Give a man a job and let him do it", he told his assistant division commander, BG Al Pierson to call the chief of engineers in Washington to report on Hoffman's deplorable conditions. Swing wanted things improved, and he wanted it done *now*.

The message was received and the engineers got to work, although their projects were not totally completed when Swing's men began arriving in mid-February of 1943.

We should note that like COL Haugen was doing with his 511th PIR at Camp Toccoa, much of the 11th Airborne was being created "from scratch." This made the 11th the first airborne division to be formed that way since both the 82nd and 101st Airborne Divisions had been born from existing Organized Reserve units, the 82nd and 101st Divisions. This new structure added an extra layer of challenge for MG Swing and while it was an exhausting job at times, Swing handled the pressures through humor and taking limited downtime when he could. The general was known for his quick wit and enjoyed reading several paperbacks from cover to cover, then returned to the division's needs with a sharp mind and clear eye.

To help get things moving, the 11th Airborne's officer cadre for their four glider regiments (the 187th and 188th GIRs and the 674th and 675th GFABs) was provided initially by the 76th Infantry Division

*The 11th Airborne's camp outside Hoffman, North Carolina*

out of Fort Meade, MD. The enlisted men's cadre came from 88th Infantry Division out of Camp Gruber, OK, and the cadres for the division's remaining units such as medical detachments, parachute artillery, engineers, ordnance, etc. would be provided by their appropriate training schools and organizations.

Again, the 11th Airborne's tactical parachute regiment, the 511th PIR, was still at Camp Toccoa and would join the division in March as the first fully-formed regiment in MG Swing's command.

When many of the division's young "fillers" began arriving (fillers for the glider units would begin on March 2 at 0200), Swing's staff organized Basic Training for those fresh from civilian life (which was most of them). The recruits were met at the train station by a "casual detachment" led by MAJ Ernest Massad and trucked to camp for classification. There *were* volunteers for parachute duty which were assigned to the additional parachute units, including medical, signals, etc., while all others were sent to the gliders or glider field artillery. More than one set of blurry eyes shot open on the trains when the casual detachment welcomed the new arrivals, most still in civilian clothes, to the 11th *Airborne*.

This led to a central distinction between the parachute troops and glider soldiers. The first were hand-picked volunteers who had already completed basic and specialized unit training, while the second, the division's glider troops, were volun-told that they were now airborne troops. As 3/511's MAJ Edward Lahti pointed out that, "The men in the Glider Regiments did not choose to be members, they were simply collected and put there."

# 4. Forming the 11th Airborne

The 188th GIR's PFC Edward A. Hammrich, who would become HQ1's "Message Center Chief", wrote decades later:

"My first realization that I was a Gliderman, *drafted* into the Airborne army, was when I disembarked from the train at Hoffman, N.C.... My first impression on seeing camp was one of surprise, thinking that these tar-paper shacks must be the temporary buildings until the regular barracks are put up. It did not take us long to find out otherwise... It was nice being able to see what was going on outside of the buildings without going to a window; just look through the cracks."

Hammrich noted what would prove to be a problem in countless of the division's buildings. The builders had used wood that was too green causing it to shrink and leave gaps that allowed wind, rain and even weeds and other foliage to creep through.

CPT Luis "Lou" Burris of the 457th Parachute Field Artillery Battalion (who was a pioneer of airborne artillery) described the post as "a freshly drained swamp 20 miles west of Fort Bragg..."

As such, the divisions glidermen and parachutists both agreed the post was a disaster and cursed the desk jockeys who chose this miserable unfinished camp for their assignment. Many later said they would rather be in combat than at Hoffman.

Of those disgruntled troopers, whose average age was 20, MAJ Henry Burgess observed, "When the 11th Airborne was formed...the draft age had been dropped from 21 to 18 and most of the personnel were within that age bracket. When the 1944 election was held, only 40% of the division could vote."

As PVT Thomas Armstrong of H-511 observed, "I quit school, lied about my age, volunteered for the Paratroopers, and never knew what it was to be a teenager."

MAJ Burgess went on to explain that "The standards for being assigned to the 11th Airborne as to size, weight, and intelligence, both for enlisted men and officers, were quite high. As I recall, initially the soldiers had to be 5'6", but not over 6'0", and not more than 200 pounds, but all of those standards went out with the growth and development of the physique and strength of the men and officers."

Again, the original enlisted cadre for the glider regiments came mostly from the 88th Infantry which had no airborne training. The cadre included battalion commanders, their executive officers and company commanders. All other junior officers came mainly from Fort Benning's Officer Candidate School. The non—commissioned officers' cadre included some headquarters personnel, first sergeants, supply sergeants, mess sergeants and platoon sergeants. All the others, squad leaders, radio operators, etc. were carefully selected from among the new recruits.

One tremendous benefit that the 11th Airborne enjoyed is that it would never have to provide cadres for other forming units. This allowed MG Swing to retain nearly all of his high-quality troops all the way through training into their later combat operations.

On February 25, 1945, the 11th Airborne Division was officially activated by Second Army, though several division officers remarked that the "ceremony" was rather uneventful, just a small luncheon whose main guest was Denver, Colorado's MG Elbridge Gerry Chapman Jr. of Airborne Command.

Eventually the 11th Airborne' Division's T/O came to include:

- 11th Airborne Division, Headquarters
- 11th Airborne Division, Headquarters Company
- 11th Airborne Division, Military Police Platoon
- 408th Airborne Quartermaster Company
- 511th Airborne Signal Company
- 511th Parachute Infantry Regiment
- 711th Airborne Ordinance Maintenance Company
- 221st Airborne Medical Company
- 127th Airborne Engineer Battalion
- 152nd Airborne Antiaircraft Battalion
- 457th Parachute Field Artillery Battalion
- 674th Glider Field Artillery Battalion
- 675th Glider Field Artillery Battalion
- 187th Glider Infantry Regiment
- 188th Glider Infantry Regiment

When COL Haugen's 511th PIR arrived in March from Camp Toccoa,

## 4. Forming the 11th Airborne

they found their new beds spotlessly made by the barrack's previous tenants, the 82nd Airborne's 504 and 505 PIRs. The luxuries did not last as "Hard Rock" ordered their clean, white sheets replaced with rough wool blankets. His Paratroopers thought the actions harsh until they discovered that their small coal-fed heaters were less-than-adequate against the night's chill. Those who slept far from the barrack's stoves would frequently stoke them red hot at night which singed the eyebrows of the closer men.

I even heard the (likely tall) tale of one frozen 511th platoon's return from a blustery night exercise only to use an M15 white phosphorous grenade to light their stove with expectedly combustible results.

2LT Stephen Cavanaugh of A-511 opined that, "To this day I'm convinced the non-jumpers in G-3 at Division Headquarters, who I'm sure disliked our cocky attitude, assigned us the most remote training areas they could find." This meant that the 511th's Paratroopers had to traverse the camp's famous "Range Road" every day which Rusty compared to the Bataan Death March.

Cavanaugh's fellow A Company comrade SGT Steven Hegedus pointed out, "Don't forget: wherever we marched TO, we had to march BACK from. We all knew the scenery by heart, and only the pain of our shin-splints, or blisters, or the effort to cough up and/or spit out the dust in our eyes and nose and mouth, kept us from total boredom."

## The Battle of the Coal Bins

I would be remiss if I did not at least mention one humorous episode that many in the new 11th Airborne experienced (or rather, endured) upon arrival at the Hoffman camp.

Since each of the barracks was heated by small coal-fed stoves, the coal used for fuel was stored in large bins located just outside each building along the street as seen in the photo to the right. At first, the bins were placed according to each company or battery commander's preference. Then, battalion and regimental commanders got involved with their opinions. Next came division staff officers followed by General Swing himself.

Whenever a new directive came down, the men (mostly of the 511th PIR and 457th PFAB as they were the first to arrive) had to go out and move the "several-ton" bins to the now-proper location through North Carolina's sweat-inducing, energy-sucking sand.

*A typical company street, complete with the much-hated coal bins*

1LT John S. Conable of the 457th PFAB noted, "If only one of our individuals had asked General Swing where he wanted them placed before they were filled the first time! Another Army rule—if there is any doubt check with the highest ranking officer before you act."

To make matters worse, several groups of practical jokers (fingers usually pointed to COL Haugen's 511th PIR) would sneak out at night to move random coal bins from their spot which meant that the barrack's occupants had to move them back with an equal amount of physical labor and verbal cursing in the morning.

In addition to their coal-bin exercises, MG Swing's troops spent their chilly initial weeks at Mackall doing pushups, burpees, close order drills and runs long enough to get their wind up (and cause new recruits to vomit along the way). The division's cadres were putting most of the men through Basic Training and like COL Hard Rock Haugen had done at Toccoa, Swing set high standards. He expected his subordinates to see those values achieved, though many 511th officers maintained that Hard Rock's standards were *always* higher.

Of their physical training, PVT George Doherty of HQ3-511 remarked, "I remember the calisthenics every morning; they were tough and painful."

Some sessions involved climbing up and down ropes and one day D-511's PFC Charles Douglas got tired on a climb and just hung there. A British training officer with the last name of Kirkland grew disgusted and bellowed loud enough for everyone to hear, "Douglas, what in the 'orrible 'ell are you doing there – bivouacking?"

D-11's CPL William Walter remembered with a laugh, "After that episode, we kidded him when he couldn't go one way or another, 'Douglas, you're bivouacking!'"

PVT Clifton Jones of the 187th GIR wrote home to his family a few days after his arrival, "Although we haven't started on the real tough training yet, my day looks something like this. Get up at 5:45, dress, make bed, wash, eat and be ready for roll call at 7:15. Then we have 1 hour of calisthenics and then three 1 hour classes in different army tactics such as bayonet, rifles, marching, etc. The afternoon is generally the same. Very quick we start taking long hikes."

Those "long hikes" grew in length from three to twelve miles, then eighteen and finally twenty-five miles which was eventually completed in six and a half hours with full gear. After such treks, the PX was especially valued for its cold bottles of soda (the men also prized the beer halls, or "slop chutes") and the new issue of *Yank* magazine.

The enlisted men often took their drinks outside to watch General Swing's famous "Swing Sessions" or "The General's Walk" every Friday afternoon. At first, Swing's officers had been ordered to run with the enlisted men every morning, but when the general found that officers were taking turns as to who would run each day, he got angry and posted the route for the officers' mandatory "new run" so the enlisted men could come watch.

With the athletic Swing in the lead followed by the division's two brigadier generals, the 11th Airborne's officers were led on six-mile jogs that often left those who had not yet physically measured up red in the face with heaving lungs, especially after ending on the obstacle course. For Swing, all his men, officers included, would meet the physical standards and the Brass who could not keep up were quickly bounced to other units. The enlisted men, of course, greatly enjoyed watching the officers struggle in their own "rat races".

"He always put the 511th officers at the end, because that's the toughest place to run," A-511's 2LT Stephen Cavanaugh recalled before adding: "When it was over, and the rest of the (Division's) pudgy officers were huffing and puffing, dragging their posteriors, we'd take off and sprint back to our regimental area, Colonel Haugen leading the way, to begin a real run."

It was not uncommon for Haugen's young son William, or "Billy", to run alongside the 511th's troopers during their own pre-breakfast

*MG Swing (far left) leading a "Swing Session"*

five-mile jogs. Billy affectionately became known throughout the division as "Pebble", the son of "Hard Rock."

During these initial weeks while the division's other units were trying to organize and flesh themselves out, Haugen's 511th PIR moved throughout the camp as if they owned the place. Truth be told, many of the future-Paratroopers looked down on the other non-jump qualified units in their division.

2LT Stephen Cavanaugh noted that while Swing had his ideas, COL Haugen "wasn't afraid to follow his own instincts" in training his men. His methods, however, were frequently criticized by the division's other unit commanders who felt that the 511th PIR was too cohesive and independent (in all fairness, the 511th *had* formed and trained under the impression it would be independently sent to Europe to fight as a regimental combat team).

Touching on the level of cohesion 2LT Cavanaugh mentioned, HQ3-511's PVT George Doherty explained that Swing's troopers, "were tuff (sic), they were smart, they were kind and forgiving, they were caring, and they faced the future for whatever that future was destined to be with determination and selflessness..."

While the 82nd and 101st Airborne Divisions had two tactical parachute regiments, MG Swing's 11th Airborne only had one, the 511th PIR, whose men felt that they were the best fighters in the division. After all, they had made it through COL Haugen's strenuous requirements to make it into the regiment, after which they were constantly told by the cadre and their officers that as Paratroopers they were the elite of the elite in the United States Army.

"Our regiment was not beloved by Division Staff..." 2LT Stephen Cavanaugh noted. "We were felt to be mavericks and troublemakers and prone to feel superior to the rest of the Division. Which of course, we were."

When I asked about the 511th's mavericks and troublemakers, D Company's PFC Billy "The Kid" Pettit, who would later serve under Cavanaugh, laughed and said, "There were a lot of them."

One "troublemaker" was RHQ-511's SGT John B. Muntz who, after the mess hall staff repeatedly gave the troopers poor food, and even poorer service, pulled one of the cooks over the counter and "stomped his teeth out."

Muntz's buddy PVT Frank Lewis noted, "Manners improved considerably." Lewis and Mince were members of the demolitions platoon under 1LT Robert Keyes who were ordered to stop carrying around demolition charges in their packs on marches. Keyes ordered his platoon to dig a hole and put all their extra demo charges in. When the collection was detonated, it broke windows for miles.

It requires very little imagination to see that by April the situation with the 511th was causing headaches for MG Swing. Swing realized that he would have to reign in the cocky future-Paratroopers to maintain command control, yet he knew he would also have to allow them to retain unit morale and individual self-confidence.

It would require a balancing-act that, for now, would have to wait. After all, Swing's division had a historic ceremony to prepare for.

## Camp Mackall

On May 1, 1943, nearly 10,000 spectators and troops crowded around the Mackall Airport for a special dedication of the camp as America's first large-scale airborne training facility.

It was decided that the post should bear the name of the first American airborne trooper to be killed in the war, Wellsville, Ohio's PVT John T. "Tommy" Mackall of the 503rd PIR's E Company. Tommy died on November 12, 1942, in Algeria during Operation Torch, the first combat operations for America's airborne. Unknown to many, Tommy was actually the *second* paratrooper to be killed in the operation; his name was just the first to be released. PVT Mackall was initially wounded when a French Vichy fighter attacked his transport as it landed near Oran. Seven Paratroopers were killed in the attack and the wounded, like Tommy, were evacuated to a British hospital on Gibraltar where PVT Mackall died four days later.

As such, General Order Number 6 was issued on February 8, 1943, naming Camp Mackall in honor of PVT Mackall. MG Swing's troopers were relegated to "crowd control" as the spectators and soldiers poured in. Everyone listened intently as MG Gerry Chapman, commander of the newly relocated Airborne Command, dedicated the camp. After paying an emotional tribute to PVT Mackall, Chapman said, "local conditions have indeed changed, save one - the ideals of American life for which we live, and if need be, for which we offer all."

While the 11th and 17th Airborne Divisions listened to MG Chapman's words, so did Tommy's mother, Ada May Toland Newton and his sister June and his younger brothers Robert and Gerald. Gerald would later be killed in action on July 7, 1944 near St. Lo, France. After Chapman's speech, as well as remarks by post commander COL Vernon G. Olsmith, a bronze plaque was unveiled dedicated to PVT Mackall. The plaque was lost in 1970 and has never been recovered.

Then, on a signal from HQ-511's bugler PVT Billy J. Horn, the entire 11th Airborne passed in review for MG Joseph Swing, Post Commander COL Olsmith, MG Chapman, and Tommy's family.

The 11th Airborne took twenty minutes to pass the stand and Swing's troopers solemnly saluted Tommy's mother.

*Division Review at dedication of Camp Mackall. L-to-R front: BG Albert Pierson, MG Joseph Swing, Ada May Toland Newton and COL Vernon G. Olsmith*

## 4. Forming the 11th Airborne

# From Boys to Men

After the dedication ceremony, MG Swing issued an order that all of his battalions were to be on the same level of training on June 1, 1943 at which time everyone would take the Airborne Command basic training test. This left some of the newer units with roughly nine weeks to prepare.

"Classes" were held when the men gathered around chalkboards or easels as junior officers and their NCOs explained map reading, first aid, military protocol, hygiene and more.

All in the division would eventually watch the then-new training filmes such as:

- "Airborne Mission", a training film for air-transorted units.
- FS 7-79 - General Information of the C-47 Airplane.
- FS 7-80 - Loading and lashing the 37mm AT Gun in the C-47 Airplane.
- FS 7-81 - Loading and Lashing the 75mm Pack Howitzer in the C-47 Airpane.
- FS 7-82 - Loading and Lashing the 1-ton Trailer ir the C-47 Airplane.
- FS 7-83 - Loading and Lashing the 1-ton Truck in the C-47 Airplane.

In addition to closer-order drill, long marches, and endless PT, the 11th Airborne's troopers erected field fortifications and foxholes in Mackall's dirt during training exercises among the tall Carolina pines. Later, when crates of personal weapons arrived packed in Cosmoline, the sticky black substance evoked curses as the troopers tried to clean their new rifles. Some laughed years after the war, saying that they ended up covered in the stubborn "goo" and the rifle had just as much Cosmoline on it as before.

The troopers next underwent Preliminary Rifle Instruction (PRI) before practicing firing on the Transition Course and learning to execute "snap shots" at the Close Combat Range. They were reminded that their rifles were life itself and E-511 demonstrated their understanding by earning a 100% qualification rating.

Mackall's Infiltration Course was quite a memorable exercise. After crawling across a field with live machine gun fire racing overhead, Swing's troopers slid into a deep hole while dynamite was detonated nearby to simulate artillery barrages. The troopers then had to sprint for one-mile, rifles in hand, through a course complete with trip-wired explosives, a house they had to toss a hand grenade in, a mud pit to cross and finally dummies for bayoneting after hearing, "If you can't shoot him, stick him."

## Athletic Angels

That is not to say that life at Camp Mackall was all work, however. While training took up most of their time, the division's troopers enjoyed the post's beer gardens (where the 511$^{th}$ PIR's regimental band often played) and Range Road Lake which they relished on sweltering summer weekends.

Unfortunately, the area's famous golf courses were off-limits (unless you were a staff officer, of course). HQ3-511's PFC George Doherty noted with some humor, "We arrived at the large metropolis of Hoffman N.C. population 22 in the heart of the pine tree country and the golf capital of the world. In the next six months we saw a lot of the pine trees…, but very little of the golf courses."

Full of former athletes, the 11th Airborne organized leagues and unit competitions for swimming, boxing, touch-football, and basketball. Boxing matches were especially well-attended and in the Division's semi-weekly tournaments, the glider troops in the 187th and 188th GIRs traded jabs, and standings, with the Paratroopers in the 511th PIR and the 127th Airborne Engineers.

Later, when the division held a boxing match with the visiting 84th Infantry, the real showstopper was four-year-old "Private First Class" Ray Davis, son of E-511's PFC Andrew C. Davis. The 11th Airborne's PVT Albert Gualtierir had just defeated the 84th's PFC Eugene McLaughlin when little Ray stepped into the ring in dress uniform, complete with little jump boots, to shake Eugene's hand. The crowd roared approval and young "Private First Class" Ray Davis won the hearts of both divisions.

Formal and informal foot races were also common around Mackall, both within and between units. One Saturday when many wives and girlfriends were visiting, D-511 pitted their resident champion runner PFC Alex "The Chief" Village Center of South Dakota's Standing Rock Sioux against a prized runner from Easy Company, CPL Harry Yazzie who had set the 511's record for running Mt. Currahee at Camp Toccoa.

## 4. Forming the 11th Airborne

D Company's CPL William Walter and PFC D. J. Hyatt knew exactly how to get Alex riled up and egged him on when Village Center worried about running with his ingrown toenails. Walter derogatorily asked who Jim Thorpe was then promised Alex a case of beer if he won. Sufficiently fired up, Alex raced and their platoon leader 1LT Andrew Carrico noted, "He won by a respectable margin."

*PFC Alex "Chief" Village Center*

At the finish line CPL Walter exclaimed, "Damn, I owe him a case of beer." Willie later noted, "(Alex) could do everything. He could shoot, run, he could do anything you name athletically."

Tragically, Village Center would later be killed during the Vietnam war in a training accident.

With a field right behind the 511th's chapel, baseball was another favorite, a focus that was encouraged by 3/511's MAJ Edward Lahti whose first-year batting average at West Point was .522. In 1936, Lahti faced the Yankees and played against Joe DiMaggio, then a rookie, and Lou Gehrig in one of the final games for "The Iron Horse" (Ed even caught Gehrig's long fly ball). The Portland, Oregon-native earned the nickname "Slugger" when he went four for four in the Army-Syracuse game of 1937 then stole bases in the year's Army-Navy game.

CPT Henry Burgess, who would later serve under Lahti as 1st Battalion's commander, said, "He was probably the finest combat infantry officer it was my privilege ever to serve under. He was thorough, a great planner, and conservative, but also very aggressive in the execution of his plans."

Lahti's influence, as well as all the 11th Airborne's West Point graduates, was felt across the division throughout their training. G-511's 2LT Melvin Garten, who would retire as America's

*Edward H. Lahti*

"most decorated colonel" in 1968, noted there was a "flow of vitality, energy, and duty-honor-country that spread from the West Pointers to the rest of the regiment... I know that I felt it, and I'm sure that the others did as well."

Garten, Lahti, and the 11th Airborne's other West Pointers, including MG Swing himself, provided the division's newer soldiers with role models to emulate and leadership to follow.

They even found occasion to show their troopers what it meant to be an officer and a gentleman.

## Southern Belles

Mackall's newly-finished dance halls, or All-Purpose Recreation Buildings (APRs), were places of refuge for General Swings troopers. On Friday evenings, the stage filled with the 511th PIR's eighteen-piece orchestra under WO Robert M. Berglund (whom some called Blue Barron), along with vocalist PFC Joseph "Joe" Sartori, which meant one very important thing: the "Victory Girls" were coming (Sartori had an audition with Glen Miller's Orchestra prior to his enlistment).

On weekends the Special Service Dance Partner unit gathered young women from all over Hamlet, Greensboro, Southern Pines, Pinehurst, and Rockingham to attend the dances. After their parents gave stern lectures about their patriotic duty to attend (complete with warnings about being *too* patriotic with the servicemen), the girls loaded onto trucks bound for Mackall. Dressed in long gowns, the girls were whisked inside and hardly had a chance to sit down before the dance ended at eleven o'clock and they boarded the trucks for home.

*One of the division's APRs, or All-Purpose Recreation buildings*

Not everyone was invited to the first few dances. As RHQ-187th GIR's PVT Clifton Evans complained, "They had a swell dance here last night – we didn't get to go though as it was just for Paratroopers." When he was finally able to attend one, Evans told his family that the 511th's band was "the best army band in the country" He then added, "Gee those southern women, they sure sound funny the way they talk…. These girls are very sociable however."

2LT Edward M. Flanagan of the 457th PFAB expressed the feelings of all the Division's troopers when he said, "God bless the Southern belles who came to dance with us in the APRs of Mackall!"

## Changes of Address

General Swing could see that the division's hard work was beginning to pay off, and just in time, too. In three months, his men had completed their Basic Training and would now begin their UTP, or Unit Training Period beginning June 21, 1943.

Of the division's growth, D-511's 2LT Leo Crawford noted, "At Mackall, a fantastic esprit de corps developed. The loyalty within platoons, companies, battalions, and regiments was fantastic."

To give one example of the many beliefs expressed by 11th Airborne troopers who felt that *their* unit was now the best, HQ3-511's PFC George Doherty declared, "SGT (R. T.) Suess and 2LT (Evan W.) Redmon developed the communications platoon into the finest communications platoon in the 11th ABN DIV."

Four months after the 11th Airborne's activation at Mackall, the men of each "finest" unit were sent to their various schools and courses for more specialized training and exercises.

It was soon tallied that due to the strict requirements for entrance into the 11th Airborne's parachute units, a wopping 65% of volunteers were sent back to infantry training centers. Those who remained in the 511th PIR, 457th PFAB and 127th AEBs were sent to Fort Benning's Jump School between May and June. No member of the 511th refused to exit the plane and nearly all of Hard Rock's boys would earn their parachutist's badge. We will cover more of their experiences at "The Benning School for Boys" in the next chapter.

In July the 187th and 188th Glider Infantry Regiments headed to Laurinburg-Maxton Air Base to begin their formal glider training (the

187th under COL Harry Hildebrand and the 188th under COL Robert "Shorty" Soule). Here the glidermen would learn to properly load into gliders, effective lashing techniques, slide-rule manipulation, and how to load and tie-down vehicles and equipment.

One unknown trooper from the 188th GIR provided great insight into the makeup of each glider regiment:

"The glider regiment was a new breed, designed to travel light, and, of course meant to be transported in gliders which could carry an 11 man squad with no heavy equipment or jeep with two or three men, etc. Most were armed with carbine rifles, rather than M1's. The regiment had only two battalions, in contrast to three in the infantry and parachute regiments. Each battalion had HQ and HQ Company, and rifle companies; no heavy weapons company. HQ Company contained one platoon of water cooled .30 cal. machine guns (4 guns) and one platoon of 81 mm mortars (4 mortars). Rifle companies had light air cooled .30 cal. MGs and 60 mm mortars. That is the way we fought the war."

Similarly, the division's Glider Artillery Battalions had only two gun batteries instead of three. The 457th Parachute Field Artillery and the 674th and 675th Glider Field Artilleries headed east to Fort Bragg to practice on the camp's expansive ranges, the 457th under MAJ Douglas Quandt, the 674th under LTC Lucas E. Hoska Jr. and the 675th under LTC Ernest "Ernie" Massad).

*A group of still-fresh 11th Airborne glider troops at Mackall*

The 457th PFAB's CPT Luis Burris had been in the first class of artillerymen to attend Jump School at Fort Benning in 1942. He noted, "We grumbled together, swearing we would kill some of those instructors if they ever came to a unit of ours." Burris was humorously surprised to find some of those instructors serving alongside him in the 457th: MAJ Douglass Quandt, the battalion's CO, and CPTs Norman J. Martin and Nick Stadtherr, CO of Burris's Battery D. Burris and his 1942 classmates had gone on to form the test parachute artillery battery, the 456th, which formed at Fort Bragg on September 18, 1942 to devise techniques of packing and dropping 75mm pieces from transports.

The core of this group had then formed the cadre for the 457th PFAB which received their fillers at Camp Toccoa in mid-February of 1943, the same time the 511th PIR was there. Similar to COL Haugen's processing of volunteers for his 511th PIR, the 457th's Battalion commander MAJ Douglas Quandt personally interviewed each man sent to his battalion to evaluate their intelligence, physical fitness, character and grit. As H-511's PVT Albert Roe declared, "If you weren't fit, you wouldn't make it in the parachutes."

Upon activation at Camp Mackall, Quandt's 457th was comprised of three parachute batteries and Battery D which was comprised of one anti-aircraft platoon and a glider-riding anti-tank platoon armed with antique 37mm anti-tank guns. They were cannon-cockers with no lanyards to pull and after the battalion's first batteries attended Jump School at Fort Benning in May and June, morale declined for D Battery until MG Swing decided he wanted the battalion brought up to its full 12-gun strength.

Battery D's CPT Burris noted, "We were instantly transformed from an unwanted, orphaned, bastard battery into a regular firing battery…"

2LT John S. Conable of the 457th's Battery B had also been a member of the parachute artillery Test Battalion which had been tasked with finding a way to drop 75mm pieces from transports (Conable himself would later design the standard 2900# tensile strength webbing).

He provides us with great insight into this piece of airborne history:

"Lieutenants Bert Locke and Bob Goldsmith were carpenters who were putting together plywood containers to drop the 75 Pack Howitzers. 1st Lieutenant Herb Armstrong had been running the

*The "Red Legs" of D Battery, 457th PFAB at work at Camp Mackall*

rigger's section without benefit of any training and had been making harnesses. Vic Toffany and I immediately joined in this latter task. Some days we had kindling but gradually the plywood and the harnesses stayed together. We were primarily interested only in proving it could be done. The designs we came up with were used until mid-1945 when someone finally replaced our buckles with quick release devices."

After his move to the new 457th PFAB, 2LT Conable noted that one evening at Mackall the battalion's CO MAJ Douglas Quandt decided that it was time for a night march of about ten miles. John later described the interesting results that this, and all of the other division marches, had among the men. He writes:

"The Howitzers were to be pulled by the men of the gun sections, radios back-packed, etc.... That march made the Battalion. The men for the first time helped each other—first one carrying part of the machine gun, then the other. They were going to show that they could do it and as the march progressed they realized that to accomplish it they had to help each other. I had virtually no business at the end of the column. The men were very tired but very proud the next day. They were much more tolerant of each other and realized that everyone had to help everyone else. Different groups remained but they all were now part of one organization."

Thinking back on their time at Camp Mackall, the 457th's SSGT Paul S. Childers humorously bemoaned, "Who could forget the long road marches, pulling those howitzers through the sand…"

While the artillery units marched and trained at Bragg, the 11th

## 4. Forming the 11th Airborne

Airborne's 152nd Airborne Antiaircraft Battalion went to nearby Fort Fisher Firing Range for their own training. When its troopers prepared to board their trucks for the move, however, General Swing arrived for a surprise inspection and began tossing contraband items such as beer and unauthorized civilian clothing out of their bags.

"He had a sharp eye for any kind of dereliction" noted acting G-2 MAJ Henry Muller. "And an equally sharp tongue with reprimands."

Chagrined by Swing's gruff (and loud) chastening, the battalion spent four hours repacking and word spread through the division that the Old Man meant business. As B-511's PFC Eli Bernheim noted, "That remarkable and indefatigable man who had to be at least 50 (Swing was only 49) had more energy than anyone."

One division officer pointed out that Swing was never desk bound and loved to be in the thick of it, whether in training or combat.

Swing had made MAJ Muller his "Acting G-2" after his original G-2 was injured in a training jump and was reassigned. Muller, "the only Leavenworth G-2 type in the division" said that Swing emphasized the "acting" part as he was wary of anyone who was an "unrepentant paratrooper." Impressed by his work, the general told Hank to drop the "Acting" part of his title six months later.

Hank told of once experience with Swing when the General was in a heated argument with his Chief of Staff, COL Francis Farrell. Frustrated, Swing blurted out, "Frank, how can you be so dumb?" COL Farrell calmly replied, "General, I have never established a reputation for brilliance, but in this instance, I happen to be correct."

Swing bust out laughing and admitted the colonel was right.

It is to be expected in a combat unit, especially an airborne one, that heads *would* roll. COL Orin Haugen's XO MAJ Glenn McGowan related an illustrative experience he had with Swing at Mackall just a few months later:

"I had a good crew (in RHQ-511). We were the first to get our (Mackall) area cleaned up and messes organized. I also had a nice Shack for Colonel Haugen with beer in the fridge. The story goes that (LTC Ernest Louis) Massad goofed off and did a piss-poor job in organizing Divivion Headquarters (at Mackall). Particularly facilities for General Joe (Swing). When the general arrived his shack was not in very good shape, so he chewed Fearless Frank (Farrel) out who in turn chewed Mike (Massad) out and recommended that he be sacked. At the same time (Swing) recommended that I be made Division G-1. I was somewhat disappointed in leaving the outfit that I had grown-up with (the 511th PIR), but took it and did the best I could."

McGowan would be made Acting G-1 on January 1, 1944, although MG Swing told him he would let the Paratrooper go back to the 511th once a suitable G-1 was found. Glenn noted, "That never happened, so I was made the G-l on March 16, 1944."

COL Haugen protested McGowan's permanent move as he wanted Glenn back in the 511th before combat operations began, but Swing kept the former XO where he was. LTC Massad, however, was sent to the division's 675th Glider Field Artillery Battalion.

Swing's future G-3 MAJ Douglas Quandt explained:

"General Swing is impatient with mediocrity and with denseness, and this is putting it mildly. Moreover, he has a temper which complements this impatience and does it full justice, though its displays are of the flash—flood type: brief and devastating."

It was his keen eye for tactics and deep understanding of airborne tactics that would soon require MG Swing to make a move of his own. While his various units went to their schools and programs for specialized training, Swing found himself heading to North Africa at the behest of his friend and old West Point roommate, General Dwight D. Eisenhower. Operation Husky was about to begin.

We will follow Swing to Africa in a later chapter. For now, let us head to Fort Benning, GA, to join the division's 511th Parachute Infantry Regiment for Jump School to better understand the experiences of the 511th PIR, the 457th PFAB, the 127th AEB and the division's additional parachute troops, including medics and chaplains.

Of note, the 127th AEB was the second such airborne engineering battalion in America's military and one of the only AEBs in existence after the end of the war, so the airborne portion of the engineers' training was still new for the branch and led to a tight-knit bond amongst the engineers, similar to that of the tactical Paratroopers. We will see the results of the 11th Airborne engineers' courage and skill as we pursue the Angels' history.

But for now, let's head to Fort Benning's Jump School.

# 5: Jump School & Camp Mackall

Fort Benning & Camp Mackall – May 1943 – November 1943

*"To those who have sacrificed their lives in the line of duty, To those who have been injured, To those who train hard, work hard and pray, there is a day to come. A day on earth perhaps, possibly a day in the beyond, but there shall be a day of reward..."*
-511th PIR yearbook, 1943

Nestled east of the Chattahoochee River, Fort Benning sits within the "Tri-Community" area comprised of Columbus and Fort Benning, Georgia, and Phenix City, Alabama. Benning grew to cover 197,159 acres during the war, and it was to these proving grounds that COL Haugen's 511th PIR arrived by battalion in May and June of 1943. The 511th's original cadre, most of whom were already parachute qualified, were sent to specialisation schools such as for demolitions, communications or rigger training.

Hard Rock was pleased; after his regiment had moved to Camp Mackall in March, a team from Airborne Command arrived to observe his men and evaluate their fitness levels. Sufficiently impressed with their readiness and status, the Airborne Command team told Haugen's regiment that they could skip their first week of Jump School, the physically-intensive Phase A as did the 457th PFAB.

But Haugen decided to give his men another test. CPL Murray Hale of D-511 remembered:

"One of our final activities for basic training was a two-week bivouac We marched out twenty-five miles and spent two weeks living in our pup tents and running through all kinds of combat simulations. We spent the last night of our two weeks in a forced march back to camp. So far in our training, this was the toughest challenge. Under the threat of disqualification from Jump School if you fell out of the march, everybody made it! I don't remember the exact time, but we averaged nearly five miles an hour, carrying all our field equipment, including mortars, machine guns, etc. Several of the men were suffering from dysentery, so it turned out to be quite a challenge. Colonel Haugen and his staff stood at our Regimental Headquarters building, and as we passed them on our route to the barracks, he voiced his congratulations for a job well done. It almost made it worthwhile! We were ready!"

Hard Rock led his men to Benning's famous Frying Pan where the 1st Parachute Training Regiment (PTR) instructors found devious ways to push recruits. However, COL Haugen's boys often frustrated the instructors by smirking when asked to do pushups or run as punishment. The Toccoa Men simply ran further or did double the number of pushups asked.

I-511's PFC Charles Muse thought back to their PTR instructors and noted, "Physically we could easily have matched most of them."

Not that the instructors let them off easy.

RHQ-511's PVT John Kuntz noted with some humor, "Every afternoon I'd vow that I'd ask the C.O. for a transfer that evening; and every evening I was too tired to walk to the orderly room."

D-511's CPL Morris "Morry" Bryant joked that he spent Parachute Training, "Sweating blood!"

## Week 1: Phase B

To Benning's Jump School instructors of the 1$^{st}$ Parachute Training Regiment (PTR), the young men of the 511th were still "Legs" (since Paratroopers blouse their trousers over their boots, regular infantry units are Straight-Legs). They were officially "Jockos" (recruits) and would remain Jockos until they qualified as parachutists.

Like the 511th's cadre had told them at Camp Tocoa, the PTR instructors declared that the airborne only wanted the best and that they could drop out at any time by completing a Quit Slip. Sometimes their words alone, describing the training that awaited or the dangerous missions that airborne units would be assigned was enough to cause men to request transfers.

"I think they wanted to make us quit, that's my opinion," my grandfather, 1LT Andrew Carrico of D-511, told me.

Pushups became second nature as did sit-ups, squat thrusts, windmills, time on the obstacle or live-fire machine gun courses and whatever additional torture practices the instructors concocted. Jump School attendees double-quick-timed everywhere and

# 5. Jump School

*Fort Benning's famous "Plumber's Nightmare"*

everybody ran daily. It was at Benning that the 511th's troopers first sang "Blood on the Risers" to the tune of the Battle Hymn of the Republic. In a somewhat grisly fashion, the song refers to a new Paratrooper whose main and reserve chutes fail to open, leading to a plunging death. Other cadences included *"Beautiful Streamer"*, set to Foster's *"Beautiful Dreamer"*, as well as *"Oh, How I Hate to Jump Out of a Transport,"* set to Irving Berlin's *"Oh, How I Hate to Get Up in the Morning."*

Much of the training during Phase B consisted of dropping off 2-, 3-, and 5-foot platforms into sawdust pits to practice Parachute Landing Falls (PLFs). The men also used mock C-47 fuselages to follow a jumpmaster's commands then position themselves in the door for a strong exit. They then practiced oscillation checking before using the Swing Landing Trainer to learn proper body position for landing.

There was also a return to the "Widow Maker", the 34-foot jump tower which the 457th PFAB's 2LT John S. Conable of Battery B described: "There was a slack metal cable with a car on it above and to one side of the tower. We put on a standard parachute harness which was fastened to the car. The cable was so rigged that you had a 12- to 16-foot free fall before the slack came out of the cable. You then had a Coney Island ride into a large sawdust pile."

In addition to training for knife, bayonet and pistol attacks, the Judo that the 511th and 457th PFAB studied focused on delivering quick and ruthless strikes to incapacitate and leave opponents *hors de combat*, exposed to a killing stroke (Fairbairn's "Shanghai Method" later proved more effective). One trooper even testified with a smile that the instructors suggested the Jockos use their newfound knowledge against the armored force personnel around Benning.

The Jockos reviewed marksmanship and practiced on the light weapons a parachute unit would have access to. COL Haugen wanted all of his Paratroopers to qualify as, at the minimum, "Marksman" (160 points) if not "Sharpshooter" (187 points). "Expert" (212 points) was, of course, celebrated and Hard Rock elected to promote the 511th's enlisted men who did so by one rank.

The 511th and 457th PFAB spent two days in Benning's Rigger Shed learning about canopies, risers, suspension lines and reserve chutes. Instructors taught the men to look for weakened or torn seams in their panels and harnesses then properly fold and pack the assembly.

Packing was a process they all respected, and the Rigger Shed remained a place of gravity with heavy rules. When SGT Elmer Small caught D-511's CPL William Walter leaning on a table, a major infraction, to watch his buddy pack his chute, Small said, "Sergeant Small was on the ball, he caught Walter leaning on the wall."

Small ordered Walter to load his shoulders with shot bags (BB-filled sacks used for packing) then waddle around the massive edifice like a duck, shouting, "Sergeant Small was on the ball, he caught me leaning against the wall!"

B-511's PFC Bert Marshall was also in the massive Rigging Shed and saw the whole thing. When Walter got to the far side of the building, Bert said SGT Small bellowed, "I can't heeeaarr you!" so Willie had to shout even louder.

"Boy, that straightened everybody up," Bert noted.

"That hanger must have been eighteen miles long," Willie chuckled years later as he thought of his punishment. "It sure felt like it!"

Watching their friend waddle, PFCs David M. "Red" Iles of Louisiana and Richard A. Goff, the ladies' man from Buffalo, NY, began to laugh.

"Oh, you think that's funny?" SGT Small asked before ordering them to join Walter's "march." To twist the knife, Ball told the trio to quack like ducks as they waddled.

"It's your own fault," Willie told his buddies. "You shouldn't have laughed at me."

The enlisted men, of course, thoroughly enjoyed watching officers subject to the same level of expectation. When a major couldn't land properly from the Swing Landing Trainer, everyone tried to keep a straight face when the PTR sergeant made him hold his risers over his head and run around the field, shouting, "I'm a bad little major!"

## Week 2: Phase C

The 511th's and 457th's second weeks, or what some called "Carnival Week", involved official drops from Fort Benning's famous 250-foot towers. They also practiced packing their parachutes which they would soon use for an actual jump. As HQ3-511's PFC Robert "Bob" Leroy noted, this allowed the troopers to build "confidence in our chutes, ourselves and our God!"

*Training on Fort Benning's 250-foot jump towers*

The trooper's first "jump" from the tower was a controlled decent on a two-person "buddy-seat" while the second was done solo (still controlled). On their third jump, each trooper's harness was connected to a special 38-foot parachute before he was hoisted 250 feet in the air then released (uncontrolled) so he could practice guiding himself to a clean landing. PFC Billy Pettit of D-511 remembered, "My gosh, you would just float to the ground like a feather."

2LT John S. Conable of Battery B, 457th PFAB, explained that the Paratroopers were given a subtle test in this phase:

"The harness was so arranged that you were face down in a horizontal position. There was a rip cord which, when pulled, let you fall with your face down for about ten feet. You then fell to a vertical position and were lowered to the ground. While you were falling face down you were required to move your rip cord from your right to your left hand. This was designed to sort out those who froze while falling. A paratrooper should always be thinking."

During Phase C the 511th's and 457th's troopers also practiced deflating worn-out T-5 reserve canopies in high gusts with the help of a Sioux City-made Windcharger wind-machine used on Hollywood movie sets. The men did so by quickly rising to their feet, running around the inflated canopy, then pulling on the suspension lines to collapse it ("only civilians call them shroud lines!"). More than one trooper ate Georgia dust as he struggled to get off the ground.

Week 2 also included forced marches with full combat gear, including forty-pound pack, steel helmet with jump liner, personal and squad weapons, canteens, entrenching tools, bayonets and gas masks.

# Week 3: Phase D

"This week we made our final five jumps from a plane," D-511's 1LT Andrew Carrico recalled. "One jump each day. Scared? Yes, I was! But also, glad to get out of that plane with all the weight we carried."

The 511th's and 457th's first and second jumps were made individually with the third done in "sticks" as the men quickly rushed out the door together. It is of note that these were not tandem jumps and that for many jump school attendees, these flights were their first time ever in an airplane (some in the 511th and 457th had never even seen an airplane until they arrived at Fort Benning).

After retrieving their T-7 harnesses and parachutes (which they had packed) at about 0745, the 511th's and 457th's troopers grouped into sticks and entered a large room called The Sweat Box where PTR riggers made sure to tighten everything. At Lawson Field they loaded into a C-47 Douglas Skytrain, or "Gooney Bird", which held twenty-four jumpers each jump. Flown by a crew of four, the C-47s, or "Workhorses of the Sky" had a wingspan of 95 feet 6 inches. Powered by two Pratt & Whitney R-1830-90C Twin Wasp 14-cylinder radial engines, over 10,000 of the planes would be built during the war and it was an aircraft the 11th Airborne's Paratroopers would become very familiar with over the next two years.

Over the "DZ", the Jump Master would yell, "Is everyone happy?' to which the Paratroopers would respond, "Hell yes!" The Jump Master would then below, "You damn liars!"

"We had the officers jump out first," 1LT Carrico remembered. "And behind you were enlisted men also going through Jump School. So, it is up to the officer, to you, to show you weren't afraid."

The troopers jumped first at 1,200 feet then counted "one-thousand,

# 5. Jump School

two-thousand, three-thousand" before his canopy opened with a jolting shock. Shaking off the momentary stars, the trooper would then go through his list: check the 28 silk panels, check descent, check surrounding air for other parachutes, prepare to land when about one-hundred feet from the ground, and finally, land. At that height, he had roughly eight seconds of free-fall, so he had to quickly pull his reserve chute if necessary.

When asked what he thought about on his first jump, 1LT Carrico said, "It was scary, but when you moved to the door you had so much to think about. The steps and procedures, the stance, the jump out the door, checking your parachute, all that."

*Last minute instructions*

Many of the 11th Airborne's Paratroopers said that their *second* and *third* jumps were the hardest since they only conceptually knew what to expect on the first. Some were also quite clear that most of the 511$^{th}$ PIR did not shout "Geronimo!" during exits, although some jokingly cried out, "I don't wanna go!"

D-511's PFC Jorge Varella was famous for what would prove to be an especially painful "second or third jump" when he became the only man in the division to land, painfully, on a split-rail fence, with one booted foot on one side and one on the other.

The 511th's and 457th's fourth jumps included a full combat load weighing between 60-70 pounds and the troopers more shuffled than walked to the plane's door then struggled to climb the ladder's three steps (broken legs frequently occurred in these jumps).

"You ended up black and blue from the opening shock," remembered D-511's PFC Billy Pettit.

Phase D's fifth and final jump was made at night, with combat gear, and included a small "tactical assembly" mission on the ground. Everyone sided with extreme caution as no one wanted to be disqualified (or dismembered) on the last jump and countless troopers prayed they would not land in the Chattachoochee River which looked like a road in the dark.

Upon completing their fifth and final jump, the 511th's sticks would assemble on the Drop Zone (DZ) before heading back to the Mess Hall to celebrate. They were now officially United States Army Paratroopers.

D-511's CPL Murray M. Hale exclaimed, "We had climbed the mountain. We were now qualified Paratroopers of the United States Army! We were members of the elite."

B-511's SGT Jim Wilson told me, "I felt like I could whip the world after Jump School! My

*"Down From Heaven"*

"And we no longer had to worry about packing our own chutes," several in the 511 and 457th pointed out with relief.

'It was such a proud feeling to have that behind me and a whopping $100 dollars a month added to my paycheck," exclaimed D-511's 1LT Andrew Carrico. CPL Murray Hale was in Carrico's platoon and remembered, "We celebrated together in Phoenix City, Alabama before leaving Fort Benning. We received our wings at a formal Regimental Review when we returned to Camp Mackall."

After moving back to Mackall, the Jump School "graduates" wore their new Paratrooper uniforms with confidence and gave their Corcoran jump boots a glowing polish. For most of the 11th Airborne's Paratroopers, the "formal" ceremony for the awarding of their jumps wings occured at battalion formations at Mackall since they were moved back to the camp so quickly. Even so, the division's Paratroopers famously made sure their garrison caps sat tilted on their heads and often weighed down the front by talking the PX tailor into sewing a heavy coin behind their Paratrooper patches highlighted blue for infantry, red for artillery and gold for medical.

The parachutists' swagger continued to annoy the rest of the 11th Airborne. 100% of the 511th PIR had qualified and alongside the parachute-qualified artillerymen, engineers, surgeons, etc. they were now cocky, dangerous Paratroopers, "tougher than a 30-cent steak" as one stated. And they were not about to let some other unit, even within their division, rain on their parade, nor were they shy about pointing out the silver Parachutist Badge pinned on their chests.

But General Swing, who commanded a complete airborne *division,* knew that his units needed to work, train and fight as one. He and his staff were well aware of the potential dangers that could result from the widening rift between the glidermen and the Paratroopers who had begun calling the glider troopes "Haimans" after RHQ-511's MAJ Joseph Fagan's dog "Herman" nearly bit General Swing. To be fair, the dog thought Swing was attacking Fagan after the General lectured Joe rather fiercely. Fagan was an Irishman from Brooklyn so "Herman" sounded like "Haiman" and after this incident, the 511th's Paratroopers took to calling the glidermen "Haimans."

Something had to be done about the 11th Airborne's rift and it started with Camp Mackall's famous Battle of the Boots.

## The Battle of the Boots

While at Mackall, 86% of the 11th Airborne earned the blue Expert Infantryman's badge which only added to the division's Paratroopers' seemingly-limitless confidence, an attribute that was starting to be viewed as a problem by some within Division HQ.

2LT John Conable of the 457th PFAB noted, "The boys were a sharp looking, cocky bunch by the time they completed their training. There was something about a pair of shiny jump boots and silver wings that lifted a young man's spirit and his opinion of himself."

Perhaps with a desire to take the Paratroopers down a notch, someone higher-up issued orders that their jump boots were to be worn on parachute drops *only*. The official reason, (i.e. excuse) was that the jump boots would wear out too quickly and needed to be preserved for jumps only. No one believed it.

Scuttlebutt said this new mandate was initiated by senior *glider* officers and the order went over as well as can be expected. Anyone who knows anything about the Paratroops knows what an offense this was to qualified parachutists. Indeed, while the men of the 511th had been issued jump boots at Camp Mackall prior to Jump School, COL Haugen had stood before them and very clearly stated, "Until you earn those boots you only have the privilege of shining them."

*Proud Paratroopers of D-511: Left to right - PFCs Elmer Hudson, Joseph Miller and James Kennedy*

HQ3-511's PFC George Doherty noted that after they had their boots, "we shined them, shined them to the point that if a fly were to lite on the toe of the boot, he would very likely slip and break his ass."

Having earned the right to do more than just shine them, the 511th's Paratroopers, whose officers had already been ordered to ditch their distinctive leather flight jackets by GEN Swing, responded by obediently wearing GI service shoes but cut five inches off their M38 knee-high leggings. Calling their new attire "Glider Boots", the cocky Paratroopers bloused their trousers over the tops.

The division's other Paratroopers in the 457th PFAB, the 127th Airborne Engineers, and their other jump qualified specialists were frustrated as well. They had joined the elite and earned their jump boots and now were being told that they could not wear this distinctive part of their uniform.

Given the rebellions, the officers who issued the original orders were furious and rumor has it General Swing (now Acting Commanding Officer of Airborne Command) was irked as well. The displeasure flowed downstream and one day G-511's CPT James Lorio of Baton Rouge, LA, appeared on the firing range with 3rd Battalion's MAJ Ed Lahti in tow. With the stickler for discipline Lahti watching, Lorio ordered CPL David L. Webb, PFCs. James F. Massey and George K. Emerson, and PVT Stephen Conger to attention and proceeded to chew them out about their cut off leggings. Threatening court martial, Lorio told the four to be in his office at 1900.

# 5. Jump School

That night, in a much lower voice Lorio explained that their punishment would be a two-week restriction to 3rd Battalion's area. The four troopers stifled grins when Lorio moved out from behind his desk and lifted his leg onto his desk to display folded leggings and bloused trousers.

"And the punishment," CPL Webb of Earlington, KY laughed, "Well there wasn't any because the entire 3rd Battalion was already restricted to its designated area."

With similar acts of defiance spreading throughout the division, the ridiculous jump boot restriction was soon lifted. Some say that MG Swing had made his point, while others claim that the 11th Airborne's Paratroopers won the day (and their first "battle") and that the jealous glider officers turned tail against the mighty paratroops. The "truth" probably depended on if you were wearing Jump Wings or not.

*Two cocky 511th Paratroopers: PVT Gilberto Sepulveda (L) and CPL George Cushwa (R)*

In addition to the Battle of the Boots, the division began experiencing ten-day tactical bivouacs that provided ample time to practice the techniques and principles in the field that they had been learning over the past several months.

The division's parachute units also began holding regular drops, including a battalion drop where everyone in 1/511 got airsick.

B-511's PFC Bert Marshall remembered, "When you would look out the window the planes were going up then down. Pretty soon a plane next to you would drop out of sight, and then it would come up and go on by and then it would get into formation again. It was just like the bottom would drop out. Pretty soon one guy got sick, then another, and soon everybody was sick and throwing up in buckets they had on the planes. Even the plane crews were sick."

Some of their drops occured on the fields of the area's farmers. On one such jump, the Paratroopers were given a squad problem and had to find their azimuth before rushing to the assembly point through a watermelon patch that they reaped clean, much to the farmer's consternation (the Army reimbursed him for the 11th Airborne's "procurements"). At first, the farmer had enjoyed the division's presence when the Paratroopers of the 457th PFAB *purchased* their watermelons as they marched. But as more serials dropped, especially the 511th PIR's, the Paratroopers saw the fields picked clean and thought, "I want one!" and would branch out to grab more distant watermelons before moving on.

PFC Marshall remembered, "You could see where the squads had jumped before us, as they had kicked the watermelons, grabbed the hearts out of them, and kept on going."

"We lived off the economy," joked PFC Billy Pettit of D-511.

The areas farmers were understandably angry about their losses and one day A-511's CPT Tom Brady, whose men had done plenty of the stealing, found himself confronted by both a farmer and a captain from General Swing's HQ. SGT Steven Hegedus was listening outside the office and heard CPT Brady bellow, "Thiry-nine watermelons?!"

A Company was lucky. Division had yet to discover the company's stolen machine gun or the case of "appropriated" whiskey.

Other training exercises proved to be far less thrilling. With many transport and glider pilots, not to mention transports themselves, being called to meet the anticipated demands for the war in Europe, for some exercises the 11th Airborne's Paratroopers were simply trucked out and spread all over the "DZ". Their biggest jump, or drop, on those days was out the back of the truck.

## Betty Hutton

One unexpected surprise lifted the division's spirits on July 20, 1943. The 17th Airborne Division, also at Camp mackall, received a USO Camp Show courtesy of the American Theater Wing while the entire 11th Airborne was in the field for more training exercises.

When American film star Betty Hutton learned that the 11th Airborne was unable to attend the show, the determined actress organized a personal tour of the Division's units in the field and won the 11th Airborne's hearts with her wit, charm and beauty.

## Fire in the Sky

Some of the division's experiences, however, were far less pleasant

On September 16 during a routine training exercise, one of the gliders carrying artillerymen from the 674th GFAB crashed after the tow cable was released. The glider's two pilots were killed as were four men from the 674th: CPL Myer J. Needle, PFC Carlton L. Mumford, and PVTs Laurence V. Leusch and Harold Hirsch.

Then during a night jump on October 29, a C-47 carrying Headquarters Battery of the 457th PFAB developed engine problems as it flew right over the 511th PIR's 2nd Battalion area and clipped the tops of the area's pine trees.

D-511 was close nearby and CPL Murray Hale remembered, "Soon after the flight went over, we heard several emergency sirens that seemed to be going down Range Road. On investigation we found that they were not too far from us, so we all went out to check on them... We could not get back to the crash site, they kept us away while they removed the bodies."

**CRASH KILLS 4**
CAMP MACKALL, N.C., Oct. 30 — (AP) — Authorities at this army air-borne troop post announced tonight that 14 officers and men were killed and four seriously injured yesterday in the crash of a transport plane during a training flight. The dead included: Max J. Jonientz, father, Max Jonientz, Seattle, Wash.

The division's losses included CPT Joseph C. Utter; SGT Leroy A. Listug; 2LTs Kenneth R. Larson, Joseph T. Whitaker, Richard A. Christian, Charles C. Hinson; S/SGT James A. McCarthy; CPL Elmer L. Mchlum; T-4 Max J. Jonientz; T-5 James P. Atkins; T-5 Harold T. Nicholson; PFC Robert E. Cuskey; PVTs John Orloff and James B. Saint.

The 457th's CPT Luis "Lou" Burris explained, "During flight the plane developed engine trouble at a low altitude. The men of Headquarters Battery, under the command of Captain Joseph Unger, were hooked up ready to jump and could have saved themselves and the plane by lightening the load, but the (pilot a) young second lieutenant ordered them to unhook, sit and ride the plane down. The plane hit the trees with one wing and crashed in the pine forest and burned. Only two men survived."

Those two had been in the aircraft's tail section which broke off in the crash. One of the two would earn the Soldier's Medal for trying to rescue his comrades in the burning fore section of the plane.

For many of the division's young troopers, this event brought the realities of war close to home. CPT John S. Conable of the 457th, who had been on leave at the time of the crash, said, "I returned to a very sober outfit. It could have happened to any of us."

CPT Lou Burris expressed the feelings of many when he said, "The Division funeral was mournful and the slow depressing music the band played was no help. I was choked up so bad I couldn't see how the other men were doing."

On November 19, the 511th PIR experienced its own splash of reality during their first night jump when G Company's PVT Guilio DiPangrazio was killed due to a parachute malfunction (some noted that he seemed to have pulled his reserve chute in the door and became entangled). Guilio's death was the first the regiment had sustained and was a stark reminder for the cocky Paratroopers that contrary to their popular belief, there were *not* invincible.

That said, B-511's PFC Eli Bernheim explained that early experiences such as these allowed the men to confront the danger, and inherent fears, of their new airborne "career":

"Perhaps as important a factor in our preparation as either the technical or physical training we had undergone was the psychological benefit of our airborne instruction. Men who had slept through night-long tactical glider flights and pulled twisted tubing from the mangled bodies of pals killed in crashes had learned poise. Men who had jumped into hundreds of feet of space after seeing their pals trailed by streaming, unopened chutes, plummet to violent deaths, had learned nerve the hard way."

To distract their minds, the Paratroopers were told they could all make Recreational Jumps on Sundays simply by showing up to the Rigger Shed to pick up parachutes. Many in the division took advantage of this development and enjoyed numerous supplementary jumps.

B-511's PFC Bert Marshall remembers one of their night jumps:

"After I completed the jump, I noticed I was right next to the swampy area. I looked up and saw the next planes were coming right over me and dropping the men. I knew half of them were going to land in the swamp. This was a silent exercise: no yelling, no talking or anything. When they started landing in the swamp, you could hear them, and the old dead limbs were breaking off of the trees with the chutes. I then heard a big 'plop' and heard a guy say 'Son of a bitch!' and I knew he landed right in the middle of the swamp."

## 5. Jump School

*An 11th Airborne paratrooper among the Carolina pines*

RHQ-511's PVT John Kutnz noted, "The 511th marched, and the 511th jumped. We jumped early in the morning, late in the evening, at high noon and at midnight. "

B-511's PVT Sidney Smithson pointed out that the regiment's strict fitness regimes was passing off. He added, "There's quite a difference between Paras and Gliders. The Parachutists are all thin and usually small while the Gliders are all heavy and big. I've never seen such fat hind ends in my life as in a formation of Gliders. A couple miles of double-timing would kill them."

The 511's jumping also kept COL Orin Haugen's mind off his own loss. On October 17, COL Haugen woke up to find that his prized thoroughbred mare Black Diamond had been stolen. For such an accomplished rider who loved his horses, the loss was heartbreaking. The official story was that three thieves escaped from Mackall's stockade then stole the mare, but the truth hit closer to home. After A-511's PVT Ermino was found to be AWOL, a sheriff from Charlotte, NC called to say that a dirty, unshaven soldier had tried to sell a horse to a local farmer for $50, but wouldn't say where he got the animal.

Haugen called Ermino and A Company's CPT Thomas Brady before him. Instead of reading the young private the riot act, Hard Rock asked him why he joined the Paratroops and why he stole the horse.

"My family needs the money," was Ermino's humble answer to both. He explained that his father had been hurt and unable work, so he had quit school in the ninth grade to work in grocery store. Ermino told the Colonel that he had little three brothers and sisters back home and that his service wages were the only family income.

COL Haugen studied the young Paratrooper for a moment and then told CPT Brady to send him home on a two week furlough to see his family and to loan him the money for a bus ticket and flowers for his mother. When he returned, Ermino would have to do extra KP duty, but Hard Rock said he was not going to press any charges.

Haugen then put his arm around the shoulders of the stunned Paratrooper and said, "When you come back, I expect you to be the best damn soldier in your platoon. Work the hardest, do the most, be a help to your non-coms and to your officers. Tell your mother that we are taking good care of you so she won't worry. If you work real hard you'll make PFC when there is an opening. That's $12 more a month. Dismissed!"

He may have been called Hard Rock, but everyone in the 511th came to know that COL Orin D. Haugen had a soft heart for his boys.

## Dangers on the Horizon

While the summer of 1943 was full of training, the 11th Airborne also kept busy hosting several distinguished visitors who reviewed America's newest airborne unit. These included France's General Henri Giraud, the riding boots-wearing LTG Ben Lear from the Personnel Board of the Secretary of War (and bronze medalist in the 1912 Olympics) and MG Elbridge G. Chapman, Commanding General of Airborne Command who kept in frequent contact with MG Swing.

Chapman told the 11th's proud troopers, "Your Division, which was the first to activate at Camp Mackall, has set a high standard for future units which will come here to train."

Chapman then gave them a stark reminder, "This time next year you will be serving your country not at Camp Mackall, but on some foreign battlefield." His prophecy was only off by three months.

With six reviews in under five months, the 11th Airborne earned the title of "The most reviewed Division for its age." Even so, General Swing tried to keep the reviews to a minimum as he felt that they meant more time "polishing the brass" and less time in training.

That said, the visitors' praise for Swing's efforts to shape the 11th Airborne Division into an effectively lethal combat unit imbued a deep sense of pride in his officers and men.

It also led to Swing being sent to North Africa on June 10, 1943 as

## 5. Jump School

an observer for the War Department. Swing took his acting G-3 MAJ Douglas Quandt as an aide and upon arrival he quickly found his old West Point roommate LG Dwight Eisenhower to whom Swing would become a de facto American airborne advisor alongside BG James W. Coutts, Ike's official advisor who agreed with Swing's suggestions and insights. While Ike and England's General Sir Harold R.L.G. Alexander listened to Swing during the planning and coordination of the 82nd Airborne Division's role in *Operation Husky* (the invasion of Sicily), General Bernard Montgomery made several changes that Swing objected to, and that Coutts disagreed with.

US Eighth Army's General Robert Eichelberger who would become friends with Swing observed, "He spent quite a long time in Africa and in the Sicily landing on a very peculiar mission. . . . He saw a great deal of the interplay of personalities…"

According to MAJ Quandt, "In the Sicily assault, (Swing) foresaw and foretold the grave danger inherent in the combination of low-flying, slow-moving aircraft, unlighted and unarmed, with navy and ground units tensed to repel hostile air attacks."

As LTC John T. Ellis Jr. would later note in his famous *Airborne Command and Center Study Number 25*, "Many principles of employment, long advocated by airborne commanders and generally recognized as essential to the success of airborne operations, were violated in the planning and execution of this mission."

Montgomery also overruled Swing's plan to drop the 82nd as a *complete* unit; Monty wanted to drop the Americans stretched out across the line even though Britain's airborne troops experienced a rocky start to their own piece-meal drops. A forty mile an hour gale ("Mussolini's Wind") made following an overly complex flight plan in the dark problematic for many of the inexperienced transport pilots and out of 144 British gliders, only fifty-four reached Sicily. Of that only a dozen landed in their intended drop zones with ninety men. Nearly seventy crashed into the ocean when their sun-dried towropes broke, leaving two hundred and fifty dead.

The Americans did not fare much better and on July 10 the 505th PIR found themselves scattered across the map (their commander, COL Orin Haugen's old friend COL James Gavin, landed twenty miles outside his Gela DZ). Even so, the highly trained Paratroopers engaged enemy patrols, cut communication lines and otherwise created confusion for the Italian and German forces who believed the Americans were attacking in much larger numbers due to the ferocity and effectiveness of the 505th's tactics and fire.

General George S. Patton decided to reinforce the center with over 2,000 airborne troops and with the Husky Number Two drop scheduled that evening, Allied leadership emphasized strict fire discipline. Even so, after earlier attacks on their ships, when the C-47s and C-53s carrying the 82nd Airborne flew over the Gela beachheads from Tunisia at around 2300, overzealous Allied gunners opened fire. 23 aircraft were shot down and 37 others damaged, leading to the loss of 318 troopers and air crews.

In total, friendly fire and in-air disasters led to 570 Allied airborne deaths before they even reached the shoreline, a statistic that GEN Swing believed resulted from a lack of communication between the Navy and the Air Corps. And although Husky was ultimately a success, the problems associated with the airborne portions of the campaign would soon come back to haunt the 11$^{th}$ Airborne.

In early July, General Swing and MAJ Quandt returned to Camp Mackall sobered and pensive. Many of the 11th Airborne's officers had friends in the 82nd Airborne, some of whom had been killed or wounded in *Operation Husky*.

Swing and Quandt brought the news that given the mixed results of *Husky's* airborne operations, America's leadership was questioning the necessity of airborne *divisions*. After the War Department studied Axis airborne operations and the British and American actions in North Africa and Italy, the belief was circulating that small groups of Paratroopers in *battalions* or *regiments* or *regimental combat teams* were deemed more practical.

It was a mindset that GEN Swing and Airborne Command's GEN Lee Donovan fervently disagreed with. Swing felt that Husky was an airlift failure but an operational success, declaring that the airborne troops "proved their worth in Sicily".

Swing's acting G-3, MAJ Douglas Quandt, who earned his appointment to West Point from the enlisted ranks noted:

"In the inexperienced world of the early airborne, (Swing) accurately foresaw its problems as well as its possibilities and he became an outspoken advocate of division and corps assaults, as opposed to those of regimental and smaller size; the joint training and stationing

# 5. Jump School

*11th Airborne Paratroopers jumping over Camp Mackall*

of airborne and troop carrier units; the transfer from the airborne to the air force of the responsibility for accurate placement of the Paratroopers on the ground; and the softening of the strenuous qualification course in order to attract senior officers who, though past the weight lifting age, would add the sagacity and experience which new units so badly need. These were not popular views at the time but they have long since been accepted and adopted."

Adding clout to the pro-airborne division stance, GEN George C. Marshall, the Army's Chief of Staff, firmly believed that such units would play key roles in the outcome of the war, especially in the liberation of Europe. Even Secretary of War Henry Stimson seemed to be onboard. He wrote to GEN Swing just after Thanksgiving, "The Airborne Division will play a great part in our future successes, and I know that the 11th Airborne Division will render outstanding service to our country on some not too far distant D-Day."

And yet, while GEN Patton and Germany's legendary GEN Kurt Student supported the Airborne's contributions in Sicily, two men who remained unconvinced (and whose opinions carried tremendous weight) were Army Ground Forces Commander LTG Lesley McNair and GEN Swing's old friend, GEN Dwight Eisenhower, who had just been selected to lead the invasion of France.

After reviewing *Operation Husky*, Ike wrote in his report:

> "I believe that airborne troops should be reorganized in self-contained units, comprising infantry, artillery, and special

services, all about the strength of a regimental combat team... To employ at any time and place a whole division would require a dropping over such an extended area that I seriously doubt that a division commander could regain control and operate the scattered forces as one unit."

Given Ike's opinion, and GEN Swing's feelings once he returned from Africa, I wonder if the two old roommates discussed *Operation Husky* and the future of the airborne before Swing left for the States. Neither general mentioned such a discussion, but it could explain why Swing knew the airborne's trouble on the horizon so early on.

Swing's Acting G-2 MAJ Henry Muller noted, "The airborne people were always planning airborne corps, while others believed a battalion for quick in and out raiding missions made more sense."

General Swing took a break from debating the issue on September 18 when the 460th PFAB's PVT Richard R. Daley, a student of the airborne school, made Fort Bennning's 200,000th jump. Daley was gathering up his chute when to his surprise MG Joseph May Swing, acting commander of Airborne Command, and COL Ridgley Gaither, commander of the Airborne School, came up to congratulate him. Although it was only Daley's third jump, Swing smiled and pinned a special pair of gold, not silver, jump wings on Daley's chest.

Swing had temporarily taken over Airborne Command after General Elbridge Chapman was ordered to Europe as an observer. BG Leo Donovan would take command on November 16, allowing Swing to return full focus to his division who were now questioning their fate (at least those who even knew that it was in question).

Would their 11th Airborne, or even worse their regiments, be broken up and sent piecemeal to operate within regular "straight leg" units?

Everyone in America's military was about to find out and the 11th Airborne Division was going to help settle the debate once and for all.

# 6: Knollwood Maneuvers

Camp Mackall - Knollwood – November - December 1943

*"I wish to congratulate you personally and through all your ranks under your command on the oustanding condition of your division as to physical toughness and high degree of training."*
-Secretary of War Henry L. Stimson,
letter to MG Joseph May Swing

A special Thanksgiving service led by the 11th Airborne's CPT Lee E. "Chappie" Walker of Ohio, one of the Division's "Flying Parsons", was organized to lift the Division's spirits. A Presbyterian with only six years in the ministry, Walker would become one of America's first chaplains to earn their Jump Wings and one of the few to qualify as Jump Master. In 1995 the 11th Airborne Association named him "Trooper of the Decade."

After addresses by other division and regimental chaplains, the men sang hymns. A few days later on Thanksgiving itself the officers' wives and girlfriends joined them for a smile-filled dinner complete with all the trimmings followed by dancing until late.

The enlisted men enjoyed a similar feast as noted by PVT Clifton Evans of RHQ-187th GIR who wrote to his family, "Turkey – all we want – pie, spuds, cranberry sauce, ice cream and just about everything and plenty of it. I suppose these lousy cooks will torture the turkey but they better not, not on this day. I'm really hungry and I'm going to really dig in and eat today."

Although many in the division later suffered from the "GIs", the holiday festivities helped the 11th Airborne ignore the fact that the fate of theirs and America's four other airborne divisions would soon be decided.

## Saving the Airborne

As MG Swing kept busy with Airborne Command, a special panel of representatives from the War Department, the Army Air Forces and Airborne Command was conviened at the Pengaton to help study the successes and failures of earlier airborne operations. This first panel is known as "the Pierson Board" as the 11th Airborne's assistant

*11th Airborne troopers and their "Angelettes" enjoying a holiday dinner at Mackall*

division commander BG Albert Pierson chaired the study.

General Pierson noted, "My Board had come up with the conclusion that a division *could* be sustained by air for 3-5 days, but some of my supporting documents were rather sketchy."

While detractors continued to voice their opinions against continuing to form and train airborne *divisions*, Airborne Command called for a second panel to review the Pierson Board's findings and to come up with solutions to all the things that had gone wrong, or could go wrong, with large-scale airborne operations.

This second panel would be headed by MG Joseph Swing himself and include several other passionate airborne officers, glider pilots, trooper carrier pilots, and representatives from Airborne Command and the War Department. Swing was selected to chair this second board by GEN George C. Marshall himself and with his own report, GEN Swing asked for permission to hold a large-scale demonstration to prove the viability of the airborne division.

He proposed that in this test, an entire division be flown from multiple departure airfields at least 200 miles from the objective and resupplied by air for seventy-two hours. These early-December maneuvers would also give General Eisenhower time to decide whether to use airborne divisions in the invasion of Europe the following summer, smaller Regimental Combat Teams or none at all.

Swing received permission to hold the maneuvers, and the General said that if he could not prove his belief that airborne divisions were viable and necessary in the war effort, he would accept "Ridgeway's opinion" that airborne divisions should be done away with. This is a small hingepoint of airborne history and Major General Joseph May Swing is very rarely given proper credit for his Horatio-like stand.

Plans for Swing's maneuvers, submitted to LTG McNair and GEN George C. Marshall, followed a training circular published on October 9 titled, "War Department Training Circular 113, Employment of Airborne and Troop Carrier Forces" written by General Swing's historic "Swing Board".

Swing's panel stated that, "An appreciation of the powers and limitations of airborne and troop carrier forces is essential for their sound tactical deployment. Their maximum usefulness can be obtained only when employed to exploit their strongest characteristics and to minimize the effects of their inherent weaknesses."

The main questions that Swing's proposed war games, and the Swing Board circular, sought to answer were:

1. Can large airborne forces travel for several hours on instrument courses over large bodies of water to arrive at their selected Drop Zones on time?
2. Could those same forces land Paratroopers and gliders while maintaining a low casualty ratio?
3. Once on the ground, could such forces effectively engage in sustained combat?
4. Finally, could those forces be resupplied by air and air landings alone?

To find out, the Knollwood Maneuvers were scheduled to involve a reinforced 11th Airborne Division with the historic 501st PIR attached acting as the "Blue Army" attackers against the defending "Red Army" made up of a combat team from the 17th Airborne Division, the "Golden Talons", reinforced by the 541st PIR. The Red Army's task was to defend the Knollwood Army Auxiliary Airfield near Fort Bragg against the "attacking" 11th Airborne troops.

Participating Troop Carrier groups included:

53rd Troop Carrier Wing
Signal Company Wing
Pigeon Detachment Wing

436th Troop Carrier Group
437th Troop.Carrier Group
438th Troop Carrier Group
439th Troop Carrier Group
879th Airborne Engineer Aviation Battalion
Air Evacuation Unit

2LT Edward Flanagan of the 457$^{th}$ PFAB added, "The knowledge that we were testifying for or against our own future added a tension to our actions above and beyond the normal pre-drop tension..."

## The Knollwood Maneuvers

After two-days' delay due to freezing rain, on the night of December 6, 200 C-47s and later 234 Waco CG-4A gliders airlifted the anxious 11$^{th}$ Airborne Division to thirteen separate objectives. Their flights were divided into four groups, two carrying only Paratroopers and two towing gliders (double tow). To test Army planners' calculations, the flights took off from separate airfields across North and South Carolina to deliver 4,800 troops in the first wave, of which the 511$^{th}$ PIR took the lead from Laurinburg-Maxton Air Base.

The additional airfields included Mackall, Fort Bragg's Pope, Lumberton and Florence. The 11th Airborne Division's transports rendezvoused near the coast and set off on a two-hundred-mile circuitous route before turning inland towards Knollwood (the distance was a requirement of the test itself). The flights were cold as

*I foresee reenactor groups recreating this one*

## 6. Knollwood Maneuvers

the transports' doors were open and the Paratroopers found the dark "half the night" flights monotonous.

B-511's PFC Bert Marshall remembers talking to their pilot before take off. The former brick layer mentioned that he had never pulled two gliders at once before and told the Paratroopers, "If I am not off the ground by the second to the last light on the runway, I am going to cut the gliders loose, then climb to 400 feet and hit the bell. You all had better leave, because I will be going down."

Bert then added, "When we started down the runway, I thought it was going to fly apart. The pilot had the motors revved up wide open, and we took off, and just barely made it."

Renowed for his "Adonis-like" physique, H-511's 2LT Miles Gale recalls flying over towns where children waved and adults on main streets stopped their shopping. Gale, PFC Laverl D. Pierson and PVTs. Thomas H. Armstrong and Hellis E. Parent also studied a lone car parked with lights on in a dark field. They concluded that some guy was out with his girl and enviously wished him luck.

The flights would be guided to the proper Drop Zones, or DZs, by 11th Airborne pathfinders who were waiting on the ground (the 511th PIR's Demolitions Platoon joined them).

As the Division's assistant commander BG Albert Pierson noted:

"A group of parachute officers were selected to augment the regular (division) pathfinders. General Swing assembled them ahead of time and they spent a week at Laurinberg-Maxton for training. The pathfinders were jumped in the night before (I'm talking about those for the gliders), hid out during daylight hours—(one pathfinder told me he hid in a barn), laid out panels at the proper time had guiding lanterns on poles. Single lights at one end of field to show the pilot where to come in and double lights at the other end of the field for him to taxi his gliders. He was to circle the field in a proper direction and the pathfinders with the double lights would move to the flank to guide the following glider."

When the red jump lights flashed on board their C-47s, the Division's Paratroopers went through their pre-jump paces before the green light burned brightly and they rushed out the door. Jumping in full combat gear, many of the Paratroopers found that items in their jumpsuit pockets tore through the material upon landing. To

*11th Airborne Paratroopers waiting to load up*

solve the problem, the Division's riggers later added double and sometimes triple stitching to their pockets for future jumps before M42 reinforced jump suits became common.

85% of the 11th Airborne's troopers were delivered to their DZs and the 511th's Paratroopers (who dropped on the Pinehurst and Southern Pines golf courses) achieved their objective of seizing the Knollwood Army Auxiliary Airfield at 0330 from the 17th Airborne's RCT (-) defenders. GEN Swing's men were following the doctrine outlined in by the Swing Board Circular which states, "It is of utmost importance that all plans be simple and flexible."

With the area secured, the rest of the 11th Airborne landed on the Laurinburg-Maxton airfield (mainly in gliders) at dawn, two years to the day after the attack on Pearl Harbor, and immediately set out to "attack" a nearby reinforced infantry regiment along with performing assorted resupply drops and casualty evacuations.

And there were casualties, including two fatalities and over 50 jump injuries that occured due to the low altitude of the drops. The initial flights came in at 400 feet with successive transports increasing in elevations up to 750 feet. It was a lesson the Division would remember and General Swing rarely allowed jumps below 750 feet again.

Throughout the next five days, the 11th Airborne's troopers were "surrounded by Brass" with nearly 300 military observers and referees on hand. These included LTG Lesley McNair, Under Secretary of War Robert Patterson, and multiple teams from the

# 6. Knollwood Maneuvers

*"Airborne Brass" at Knollwood: From L to R:
General Henry Arnold, Chief, USAAF; MG Matthew Ridgway, 82nd Airborne; MG
Joseph Swing, 11th Airborne; MG William Lee, CG, 101st Airborne; MG William M.
Miley, 17th Airborne; and MG Elbridge G. Chapman, 13th Airborne*

Army and Army Air Corps (including Troop Carrier Command), all of whom were suitably impressed by General Swing's men.

Secretary of War Henry Stimson also flew back from Washington to attend and arrived to watch several 11th Airborne troopers from the 511th Signals land in a glider and then attempt to unload the Division's radio. When it became obvious that the radio was too unwieldy to move, the 11th's troopers simply took axes and hacked off the gliders wings, much to the pilot's dismay. When the frustrated flyer voiced his protest, one of General Swing's men pointed to the Secretary of War who was watching and replied, "Secretary Stimson doesn't seem to mind."

The signalmen then hooked the wingless glider to a Jeep and pulled it down the road to where General Swing had set up his CP.

Several officers and referees on the ground soon wondered if their ears were functioning properly when they heard the faint lilting strains of the 1943-hit "Coming in on a Wing and a Prayer." The music grew louder and louder until another glider came soaring in and the 11th Airborne Division's band rushed out and began playing, "Hail, Hail, the Gangs All Here". This helped convince the observers and referees that night glider operations were feasible indeed.

Everyone on the ground laughed at the Division's attempt to attach identifiable multi-colored lights to dropped loads during a jump made by the 457th PFAB. When the cargo was pushed out of 52 jump craft, many of the battery-powered lights ripped free and dropped like twinkling Christmas lights, perfect for the holiday season.

Given the problems associated with the wide-dispersion of the artillery drops during *Operation Husky*, General Lesley McNair was keenly interested in watching the 457th's drops during the Knollwood Maneuvers. When the battalion's guns were assembled, LTC Douglas Quandt turned to McNair and said excitedly, "Sir, the Battalion is assembled and I am ordering them to move foreward."

A machine gun section from the 457th's Battery B, however, landed far from the Drop Zone, so the artillerymen simply commandeered a bus, loaded it with their gear and were dropped off at the Assembly Point. When the 457th's officers worried about the consequences of this unsual mode of transportation, referees on the ground said they were impressed with the 457th's troopers' ingenuity and initiative.

Not all the observers were so friendly, however. The 11th's Acting G-2 MAJ Henry Muller pointed out:

"The woods were filled with those who opposed large airborne forces. The Air Corps feared that the Troop Carrier requirements would cut into their 'all important' strategic mission. The ground force people, particularly the armored officers, believed that airborne units would be too light to handle the heavy German divisions."

Despite the doubters, given the 11th Airborne's accomplishments, not to mention the superb flying of Troop Command, America's leaders deemed the Knollwood Maneuvers a success and after studying the 503rd PIR's September jump on Nadzab, New Guinea, the Brass changed its tune (the 17th Airborne held similar maneuvers in January of 1944 which only cemented the decision).

A proud General Swing grinned when General Lesley McNair sent a message stating that the 11th Airborne Division had corrected the leaderships' negative assessments of large-scale airborne operations, saying "The successful performance of your division has convinced me that we were wrong, and I shall now recommend that we continue our present schedule of activating, training, and committing airborne divisions."

3/511's MAJ Edward Lahti pointed out that "If the test had failed, it is likely that the War Department would have limited such Airborne operations to regimental combat team size."

Many in Swing's division felt as PFC Edward A. Hammrich of HQ-

188th GIR who wrote, "I now know and will be forever proud knowing that it was the 11th Airborne Division, who proved that an Airborne unit could go into combat and fight in division strength successfully, thus on 7th December 1943 all Airborne Divisions were saved."

And it *was* official: the 11th Airborne Division had saved the airborne's future in large-scale operations. Plus, as an additional bonus, they caused the War Department to eat crow, a feat General Swing and his men enjoyed immensely.

While some historians credit General Matthew Ridgeway with developing airborne operations for the United States (while overlooking the Swing Board's work), prior to the Knollwood Maneuvers he opposed utilizing such tactics on a large scale in contradiction to the Swing Board Circular. After the 11th Airborne's success in North Carolina, General McNair helped sway Ridgeway and Eisenhower to accept airborne operations on a grander scale.

And given the effectiveness of the 11th Airborne's drops, coordinated "attacks" and tactics, General Eisenhower was so impressed that much of the 11th Airborne's Knollwood strategy helped form the template for the D-Day airborne operations. As PFC Eli Bernheim of 2/187th GIR noted, "A few months later, the principles we had tested were successfully applied in the Normandy drop."

General Swing's foresight, the fruits and labors of the Swing Board and the men of the 11th Airborne Division helped save the existing structures of the 82nd, 101st, 13th and 17th Airborne Divisions and paved the way for the historic Normandy campaigns, plus helped formulate more effective airborne procedures.

So, when any publication gives such credit to General Mathew Ridgeway, the 11th Airborne's General Joseph May Swing wrote, "Our officers and men resent it to no end."

The Swing Board and the Knollwood Maneuvers were just additional examples of General Swing's capacity as an airborne leader. His Acting G-2 MAJ Henry Muller said, "I suppose there are two ways to lead a division: one is to 'drive' the other is to 'lead.' Both seem to work, but if you are going to drive, you have got to be awfully good, almost infallible… and General Swing was."

# The Finest Fighting Unit in the Army

Following another week of simulated combat in Knollwood's freezing rain, Swing's victorious 11th Airborne loaded into 2 1/2-ton trucks for the drive back to Camp Mackall. Many in the division celebrated with leaves back home or with Christmas shopping and partying in nearby towns like Charlotte. D-511's PFC William "Whiskey Bill" Dubes partied a bit too hard and the cab driver bringing him back simply dumped the inebriated trooper in a ditch outside Mackall's main gates (after stealing his money).

Witnessing the offense, an angry SGT George Thomas carried Dubes inside then asked for permission to go into town with an irate 1st Platoon which promptly overturned every one of the company's cabs.

While the Knollwood Maneuvers were over, the tests for GEN Swing's troopers did not end. Many in the 11th were given unique exams on their orientering skills, as explained by PVT Clifton Evans of RHQ-187th GIR:

"The past week was a killer test covering just about everything such as panoramic sketches, typographic sketches, map reading, binocular reading, radio procedures, field wire test, creeping and crawling, compass reading, and the worst of all a route march of 5 miles all alone, often looking at a map of the area. You had to end up in the right place and believe me it was hard because we had to walk

*An 11th Airborne Christmas service*

through the woods."

On Christmas Eve most of the division attended church then enjoyed a Christmas Day feast with Virginia baked ham, roasted turkey, snowflake potatoes, candied yams, buttered peas, hot rolls, cranberry sauce, and giblet gravy, all washed down with coffee and beer followed by pumpkin pie and spice cake. To state the obvious, the food tasted heavenly after weeks of field rations.

The 457th PFAB's CPT John Conable found himself Officer of the Day and was surprised when at around 2100 he heard the sound of firecrackers going off in the Battalion Headquarter's area.

Imagine his shock when John found that instead of firecrackers the sounds were coming from 11th Airborne troopers firing their .30 carbine's *at each other's barracks*! After calling for the shooting to stop, Conable discovered that the Division's 152nd Anti-Aircraft Battalion was angry at the 457th's theft of their Christmas Eve turkey and were attempting to "rescue" it.

"As a result we got rid of the man we felt was most responsible," Conable noted with what could only have been an officer's disgust.

No one ever did find the turkey.

The next day GEN Swing ordered the entire division to assemble for a special Christmas message. The troopers, all dressed in long winter coats, listened as Swing declared, "Men, you are different from every other branch of service. Only one percent of all servicemen volunteer for the paratroops, and only one percent of these make it through Basic, through Jump School, and this far. Be proud of yourselves."

To a man, they were. Swing's Acting G-2 MAJ Henry Muller noted that they were also proud of General Swing, saying, "He was the motion picture version of the American general… The excellence of the 11th Airborne was a reflection of this capable, driving leader."

CPT Thomas A. Nestor, Regimental Surgeon for the 511th PIR, observed, "You don't understand the extraordinary quality of the officers and men…. Our troopers were almost always quite young and were tough as nails. Almost every one of them possessed an indomitable spirit and an astonishing attitude."

Pleased with his own regiment's conduct during the Knollwood Maneuvers, the 511th PIR's COL Orin Haugen distributed a note that said, "It has been my idea from the start to make this unit the finest fighting unit in the Army. I feel that we have welded together a powerful fighting team of which we should all be proud."

Shortly after their Christmas festivities ended, the Division received word to prepare for a permanent move. This would be their first move as a complete division and the officers and enlisted men alike conversed over coffee or beers about whether they were finally headed overseas and if so which direction: east to battle Hitler or west to fight Japan. Everyone knew that the 82nd Airborne was still fighting in Italy and the 101st Airborne was training in England for the expected invasion of Europe. Most in the 11th Airborne's ranks wagered they would join the Screaming Eagles in liberating the Old World, but others "heard from a guy who heard from a guy in HQ" that China was their goal.

They were all wrong and word came down that their destination was Camp Polk near Leesville, Lousiana. This led to a rush of activity to pack equipment and clean their areas. It also left Supply Officers scrambling to tally things for their Post Property lists (few were against stealing items from other units to square things away).

After a raucous night of New Year's celebrations at Scottie's in Southern Pines (the Italian restaurant Green's Grill was now off-limits to *all* of Swing's troopers), the groggy men of the 11th Airborne awoke up to find their Mackall Headquarters Building burning to the ground on January 1, 1944 (and no one shed any tears over it).

*11th Airborne HQ building"*

## 6. Knollwood Maneuvers

*11th Airborne Paratroopers "invading" North Carolina"*

The next day the troopers boarded twenty-two troop trains, some comfortable Pullmans, some converted haulers with rattling canvas bunks, for the 960-mile trip south to Camp Polk. Their route took them through South Carolina to Atlanta, Georgia, then down to Montgomery, Alabama, through Mississippi, down to New Orleans and up to Camp Polk near Leesville, Lousiana.

Making the move with the division was many of the officer's wives and children. With so many looking to rent, it was a challenge for the families to find housing and many couples shared apartments or houses, leading the men to frequently sneak home after hours.

"We had to be at camp at four in the morning," 2LT Stephen "Rusty" Cavanaugh of A-511 explained "and weren't supposed to go home at night except on weekends. We worked until dark or even all night, but whenever possible, some of us would duck out."

Clearly General Swing's officers were putting their infiltration skills to good use. They would need them, too, since Camp Polk was to be the Division's final exam before they left for the front.

# 7: Les Bon Temps

Camp Polk, Louisiana – January-April 1944

*"It soon became apparent that the 11th Airborne was as welcome at Camp Polk at the bubonic plague."*
CPT John S. Conable, 457th PFAB

Located in Lousiana's Vernon Parish, Camp Polk was originally constructed in 1941 to help train America's growing mechanized forces. As such, when the 11th Airborne arrived, General Swing's troopers found the post swarmed by the men of the 8th and 9th Armored Divisions whom the 11th Airborne's 1LT Edward Flanagan called the "most arrogant branch of the Army", an ironic classification as the tankers felt the same about the 11th Airborne.

One Division publication later testified, "We found ourselves not too welcome." HQ3-511's PFC George Doherty explained, "When armored personnel and airborne personnel got together it was not to swap home-spun stories or a care package."

The 11th Airborne's Paratroopers were greatly offended by the "Gasoline Cowboys'" facsimile jump boots and boisterous tankers were frequently "relieved" of their boots and forced to walk or ride home from Lake Charles or Shreveport only to find their liberated boots sitting in the orderly room. It did not help that the Paratroopers of the 511th PIR, 127th AEB, or 457th PFAB grinned as they watched shoeless tankers hobble back to their barracks.

To make matters worse, many of the Division's Paratroopers had been issued M2 switchblade knives to carry in a pocket near the collar to cut risers in case their lines got caught on a plane's tail or they landed in a tree. The 511th PIR's Paratroopers became famous, or infamous, for using their switchblades for more...creative means. While forbidden, the knives were frequently carried off post to "tailor" non-airborne units' jump boots down to "proper size".

"Angels we were not," 2LT Stephen Cavanaugh of A-511 laughed. The parachute unit commanders had to explain to their men that the boots were *not* jump boots but rather part of the tankers' uniform.

The 11th Airborne quickly gained a reputation at Polk as "General

Swing's Hell's Angels" and officers on both sides maintained a constant vigilance to avoid bloodshed (although some carefully turned a blind eye at times to let their men blow off steam and build morale).

"511th troopers were really not the rowdies," G-511's CPT James Lorio insisted, defending his regiment against the criticism that is was always Hard Rock's Boys causing the trouble. Lorio added that it only happened, "when their combat training-induced Airborne fighting spirit spilled over, usually when provoked. Most leaders could reconcile with this psychological phenomenon."

Lorio also pointed out that "Amongst the tankers it was said, 'If you get into a fight with a paratrooper, you had better bring your lunch. Those guys never quit.'"

This belief was exemplified when the Paratroopers of the 457th PFAB's Battery B got in a fight in a bar near Polk and made quite a mess of it. The battalion's CO LTC Douglas Quandt was called and made the necessary arrangements to have the damages paid and read his men the riot act for all the damages they had caused.

Quandt then concluded with "I don't want to ever see this again."

As his artillerymen were filing by on the way out the door, they heard Quandt say in a soft voice that only they, and not the bartenders nor MPs, could hear: "Next time use coke bottles. They won't break."

The Battalion's Acting 1SGT Paul Childers noted, "Some of the men had a little extra combact training, fighting with our next door neighbors and at the PX. Some were even taken prisoner by the MPs and had to spend the night in the brig..."

"Some people complained that the soldiers of the 11th Airborne thought they were tough," the 457th PFAB's 1LT Edward Flanagan wrote. "The people were absolutely right for the Angels knew they were tough and took occasion to prove it. People complained that we were cocky; again, they were correct for we knew there was no other outfit like our Division, and we were spoiling for combat to prove it."

Flanagan added that after strict commands by the Brass, the 11th Airborne's troopers and the tankers "felt, and acted like hostile dogs in the same room, ordered to lie down by our masters."

There was one positive result of the Camp Polk shennanagins: it brought the Division together, united against a "real", not assigned, common enemy. At Camp Mackall the 11th Airborne's Paratroopers and Glidermen fought each other, but at Polk both groups came together to battle the area's mechanized troops.

However, even with the orders to leave the tankers alone, it did not take long for COL Haugen's Paratroopers to begin raising more hell. One day a group started a "snowball" fight at one of Polk's large PXs using crushed ice from the soft drink cooler. The "battle" escalated to include bottles and as demolitions man PFC Frank J. Lewis of HQ3-511 said, "it ended with the PX being surrounded by the Provost Marshall and troops, plus MPs with a tank destroyer."

Frank may have been exaggerating a bit, but then again, maybe not. I couldn't get any of the old troopers to confirm or deny.

Either way, the story goes that the undeterred Paratroopers commandeered the PX and defiantly stacked food crates and large sacks of sugar against the door in anticipation of a siege. COL Haugen soon arrived and dismissed the Provost Marshall and his troops before firmly ordering his Paratroopers to open the door. The young troopers sheepishly "opened the gate" and after surveying the minimal damage Hard Rock reminded them that as members of his regiment, he expected better. And their punishment? The normal ten-mile night run around the post perimeter.

It was another example of the true character of the 511th's "Hard Rock of Toccoa". His men knew he was "Tough, but fair."

GEN Swing frequently found himself dealing with similar problems, and he always tried to handle them with the same mixture of firmness and fairness. During one late night craps game in an MP's office after payday as the beer flowed, some of Swing's troopers grew quite rowdy. The door flew open and a loud voice boomed, "What's going on in here?!"

An inebriated lieutenant tried to slam the door, shouting, "Who the hell wants to know?" and GEN Swing himself, who played football at West Point, shoved the door back open and thundered, "You call yourself an officer and a gentleman?!"

Well, the room cleared in a hurry and Swing ordered the now quite sober officer to report to his office at 0700 the next morning where he was sorely chastised for gambling with enlisted men.

But Swing let the humbled man stay. The lieutenant eventually saw combat overseas, but never forgot The General's "talk."

## Let the Good Times Role

The 11th Airborne Division's troopers quickly decided that Camp Polk was a major upgrade after the still under construction Camp Mackall. For one, Polk provided two-story heated barracks with connecting latrines and the excited troopers discovered that each company had their own mess hall and kitchen. Polk also boasted bowling alleys, movie theaters, portrait studios, barbers, athletic facilities, beer gardens, PXs, officer's clubs and more.

Knowing that their regiments and battalions would soon head overseas, and that their men needed to let off steam, the 11th Airborne's unit commanders were liberal with three-day passes and the troopers happily learned to *laisser les bon temps rouler* ("let the good times roll"). As PFC Clifton Evans of RHQ-187th GIR discovered, "A guy can have 3 times as much fun around here than he can in North Carolina (Camp Mackall) and on less money, too."

G-511's CPT James Lorio divided the troopers into five main groups. The *fighters and drinkers* favored Leesville and DeRidder where MPs were scarce, bars plentiful, and the areas' tanker units ready to brawl. The *lovers* headed east to Lafayette, Opelousas, and Ville Platte where young ladies invited the Paratroopers to picnic or home for dinner before they walked arm-in-arm to night clubs for true Cajun music. The *intellectuals* made for New Orleans with its potpourri of culture, cuisine and sight-seeing and the last group, the *undecideds*, simply followed the other four.

*11th Airborne troopers "out on patrol"*

Albert Dunn, a high school student from nearby Leesville, remembered the 11th Airborne:

"They were really cocky and they looked good. Each one of them believed they could whip five or six other people. That's what they were taught. They were kind of like the Three Musketeers, 'one for all and all for one.' They might fight among themselves and have problems, but the minute something happened they all joined together."

Impressed by their example, Dunn later joined the Army and applied for the parachutes.

## "Krauts"

One facet of life at Polk that caught everyone's attention were the German POWs held near Drowning Creek just south of the parade grounds. The prisoners were from Erwin Rommel's Afrika Korps and curious 11th Airborne troopers frequently found one reason or another to go take a look at "the Krauts" in the "Fritz Ritz".

General Swing's men had to admit that although incarcerated, the disciplined Germans adhered to a strict schedule and maintained martial hierarchy. They often sang Wehrmacht anthems, believing that Hitler would free them after he invaded America and played soccer. The Division's troopers even laughed when the Germans told stories of their work details filling in the trenches dug during the 1941 Louisiana Maneuvers. Believing that Hitler had indeed invaded, local farmers rushed to their fields with arms when they first saw German uniforms and their guards had to defend the very men who they would be fighting against if all were back in Europe.

Not everyone agreed with the way the POWs were treated. One Paratrooper who had especially strong feelings was HQ1-511's SGT R. Paulus (some records show Pawlos), a Polish refugee. After Germany overran his home country, Paulus escaped to England then America where he joined the Army and volunteered for the parachutes where he hoped to fight to free his homeland.

When the 511th passed the POWs on their daily runs, Paulus, who supposed the Nazis had killed his family back home, shouted as loudly as he could, "Deutschland kaput!"

Ultimately America would host over 435,000 POWs, yet only 5,400 of them would be Japanese. When Japan's General Tōjō, released The Field Service Code in early 1941, he wrote, "Do not live in shame as a prisoner. Die, and leave no ignominious crime behind you."

GEN Swing's troopers understood that if the 11th Airborne headed

## Louisiana Maneuvers

to the Pacific, and not Europe, they would face a fanatical enemy for whom victory, or death, were the only options.

Unfortunately, their chance to "Join the Fight" would have to wait so General Swing kept his men busy with their assigned individual field exams provided by Third Army. The 457th PFAB's 1SGT Paul Childers noted, "By this time training was becoming more of a routine nature. Everyone by this time was of the opinion we were heading overseas…"

But overseas to where? The Calcasieu swamps were the perfect training ground for the Pacific Theater which surprised many in the 11th Airborne who, again, believed they were heading to Europe for the invasion. Others in the Division took long looks at their Lousiana environment and told their buddies: "We're going to the Pacific."

As HQ3-511's PFC George Doherty pointed out, "You didn't go to Louisiana with all their swamps and mosquitos, heat and humidity with Europe as your destiny. We knew we were headed for the South Pacific, but where in the South Pacific we didn't know."

Camp Polk was not always *hot* and humid, however. During the first few months of 1944 it was *cold* and humid with chilly rains, sleet and even snow. In these conditions, between February 3-19 the 11th Airborne marched on foot to Hawthorn then spent the next two weeks reviewing tactics in the field for attacking and defending against enemy "flags" and withdrawing, all while cursing the camp's environment. The troopers' miserable foxholes, dug in what they called "gumbo", filled with freezing water and the division's trucks had difficulty staying on slick roads while the heavy rains "killed Jeeps." Needless to say, the 711th Ordnance Battalion kept busy with repairs and the 11th's troopers complained that the chow trucks were always late in Lousiana.

To solve the problem, the 127th Airborne Engineers labored to build corduroy roads even as the artillerymen of the 457th, 674th and 675th frequently had to pull their pack howitzers out of the muck, break them down and hand carry them to new positions.

PFC Clifton Evans of RHQ-187th GIR described their experiences:

"It's really is a tough, aggravating, cold and monotonous grind. We walk with full equipment anytime of the day or night covering from 5 to 20 miles at a time and the land – the best way to explain that is just to say North Carolina sand is heaven compared to this. You sink in up to your shoe tops with every step you take. You can't imagine just how swampy it is. Yesterday alone my outfit spent all day just pulling jeeps out of the mud. They were all covered about the wheels. The weather now is getting cold and of course we have to sleep on the ground. We have plenty of blankets but it's still cold."

"Conditions at Polk were the world's worst," grumbled D-511's CPL Murray Hale. "It was cold and rainy, and living and fighting the elements in addition to fighting the enemy flags were terrible."

There were plenty of warm days, of course, and during a later field exercise the hungry men of H-511 found some relief from their griefs when CPL Melvin L. Mitcher and his squadmates encountered a herd of pigs whose owner arrived just as the Paratroopers were preparing to shoot a few. After successfully talking the Paratroopers down, the man took the soldiers to his smokehouse where they purchased strips of cured bacon and hams.

The pig farmer was lucky; some troopers in the 187th GIR had already held a "bayonet drill" on another herd of pigs in the area and feasted for days, thanks to the know-how of the regiment's resident hunters and farm and mountain boys.

## Swing's Jump School

GEN Swing, well known for his forward-thinking mindset, asked for and received permission to set up a jump school at DeRidder Army Air Field (now Beauregard Regional Airport). Before they were officially committed to combat Swing wanted his entire division both jump and glider certified and since there were no gliders for his division to train with, it was the perfect time to increase his number of parachute qualified troopers.

Swing originally put the 511th PIR's COL Orin Haugen in charge of the school, but the General soon disagreed with the plans Hard Rock submitted. During a spaghetti dinner one early-March evening at the home of the 187th GIR's COL George Pearson, Swing and COL Haugen got into a heated argument over the school. To be fair, everyone had been drinking at the party, so there is that.

As the 187th's MAJ Henry Burgess, who was present for the

disagreement, noted, "Haugen, as you will recall, was a member of the test platoon, had jumped more than probably anyone in the 11th Airborne, and wanted to pattern the school after Benning."

Swing felt that the Benning-way involved too much hazing and simply took too long, and the General knew that time was of the essence as they would soon be shipping out. Everyone, including Haugen, knew the 11th's troopers were in great shape physically anyway. As D-511's 1LT Leo E. Crawford noted, "When we left the sands of North Carolina (Camp Mackall) for the mud of Louisiana (Camp Polk) for final maneuvers, I don't think the United States Army ever had a more physically fit unit with better morale."

Another piece of Haugen's hesitancy to do things Swing's way was the lingering frustration regarding the 511th's attachment to the 11th Airborne itself. Again, Orin had been told that his new regiment would be independent and sent overseas, most likely to fight in Europe. Some of his earliest officers even called their unit the 511th Parachute Regimental Combat Team around Camp Toccoa which makes sense as the 457th PFAB formed there at the same time.

Burying these feelings, Haugen was the consumate professional and disagreed with Swing's Jump School mainly because he felt it shortcut too many necessary aspects of parachute training, including forgoing the 30-foot tower. We must remember that Orin had also been a member of America's first parachute battalion where he had overseen the training of the new non-jumpers at Fort Benning.

As such, Haugen was adamant in his stance, as was GEN Swing. The argument continued until COL Haugen turned abruptly, bumping into the 187th's new arrival MAJ Henry Burgess which caused Orin's plate to fall to the floor. Startled, General Swing turned to Henry and boomed, "Burgess, what kind of shape are you in?" Thinking the General was asking just how drunk he was, Burgess replied, "I'm in Goddamn good shape!"

Henry quickly made his escape, but was awakened at 0530 by the 187th's COL Harry Hildebrand and told to be in Swing's office at 0600. Both Hildebrand and Burgess wondered just what exactly he had done wrong and Hank arrived to hear Swing and Haugen shouting at each other in the General's office. Hard Rock left angry and Burgess went in to find that Swing was putting him, Burgess, in charge of the Division's first jump school.

Henry noted, "He also wanted the school in operation in a week, with ground training for a week and then jump qualification in the second week." This would eliminate two weeks from the Benning-way.

When COL Haugen refused to help Burgess run the "ad-hoc school", Burgess turned to the 457th PFAB's LTC Douglas Quandt, another experienced jumper, who told Burgess that he had quite a problem on his hands. Quandt promised to help however he could, as did the 127th Airborne Engineers' LTC Douglas C. Davis.

Two days after Burgess took over the Jump School, GEN Swing came down to watch his troopers practice in mock fuselages, jump off platforms, and slide down wires. Swing was silent for the first two days of observation. After the third day, LTC Quandt stayed after Swing left, satisfied, and Quandt told MAJ Burgess, "Well, you just made yourself."

When Burgess asked what he meant, Quandt said that that if anybody could do something without having Swing tear his head off, he was doing the assignment properly.

Things never fully smoothed out between COL Haugen and GEN Swing, although the two truly labored to work well together for the good of the Division and their men. Both were both incredibly talented leaders whose men were equally incredibly loyal to them, only Haugen's men put Hard Rock in front of Swing in their "chain of importance", something that Swing was fully aware of and was not afraid to step in to assert authority when he felt he needed to.

B-511's PFC Eli D. Bernheim told of such a occurance:

"I was ordered by Colonel Haugen to build a parking lot in the regimental area.... While laboring away on a very rainy day with a large detail of men, General Swing appeared upon the scene. He asked what I was doing and when I replied he responded in his typically apoplectic manner: 'God damn it, Lieutenant; I'm not interested in leaving any monuments behind. Get these men out of the rain and back to their area.' When I reported back to Colonel

# 7. Camp Polk

Haugen he ordered me to 'build the parking lot when General Swing isn't looking.' The next day while working on the parking lot. General (Albert) Pierson appeared on the scene. He asked me if General Swing hadn't instructed me to cease building the parking lot? I replied 'Yes sir.' Having the long experience of rising to the rank of Brigadier General, he asked me who ordered me to resume building the parking lot. I replied, 'Colonel Haugen, sir!' After dispatching the men to their area I went to Regimental HQ only to arrive as General Pierson was departing. I must admit I was shaken by the blistering ass chewing I received from Colonel Haugen."

## Swing's Angels

Up to this point I have not used the Division's nickname, "The Angels", mainly because according to many in the Division (and other evidences), until Camp Polk the term "Angel" was not used, and even for months afterwards it was done sporadically, even jokingly.

Given their fights with Polk's tankers around the post and in bars around town, plus their additional on- and off-post shennanigans, General Swing's boys were starting to be known as "General Swing's Hells Angels", a well-earned sobrequet that the men seemed to enjoy, and even encourage, to some officers' consternation. This initially seemed to come about due to the 11th Airborne Division's unique shoulder patch which has two decending jump wings that almost look like angel wings. The patch, along with the fact that General Swing's men always feigned complete innnocence when accused of some infraction around North Carolina led to them also being called "General Swing's Angels."

Acting G-2 MAJ Henry Muller noted that "SGT (James "Patrick") Mulcahy, a professional artist, then drew a cartoon of a rough, unshaven paratrooper with an angel's gown. He had a helmet and his oversize jump boots showed below the hem of the gown."

SGT Mulcahy's sketch grew in popularity and the Division's "Hell's Angels" nickname seemed to build on a third outlet regarding the "Angels" moniker. CPT John Conable

*SGT Mulcahey's Angel*

of the 457th PFAB noted that at Camp Mackall during the summer of 1943, the Battery's CO LTC Douglas Quandt had a weekly meeting with his commanders and would ask each one in turn, "Conable (or Utter or Godsman), any of your angels in jail or in any trouble?"

While only an assumption, Swing likely heard Quandt do so, both before and after the Major became his G-3.

These different "origin" sources seem to merge at Camp Polk to at least lay the foundation of the Division's usage of the term "Angels" which would later become common during their time overseas due to two additional anecdotes that I will cover later in this series.

My grandmother Jane Carrico, who spent decades hearing troopers' stories from across the Division, used a different name for General Swing's *Angels*: "They were *hell-raisers!*"

## R&R

While there was little down time at Camp Polk, in addition to exploring the nearby towns (and bars) for entertainment and female companionship, GEN Swing's Angels also continued their penchant for sports. A big reason was that the officers were trying to keep the men busy so unit teams sprang up for basketball, football, bowling, and baseball. Even GEN Swing got into the action and refereed local polo matches in Pinehurst.

Boxing matches were heavily attended, especially boughts between the 11th Airborne and the local armored units and both sides roared whenever their boxer landed a hit on the "much hated other side".

Gambling in the barracks was a favorite pastime and some troopers ended up with hundreds of extra dollars in their pockets. Others made their own "adult beverages" by mixing lemon powder from their rations with water and medicinal alcohol begged, borrowed or stolen from their medics or surgeons.

Swing's Angels' down-time, however, was frequently and annoyingly disrupted by War Department inspectors who checked their immunization cards and dental fillings and painfully corrected any discrepancies (for example, my grandfather 1LT Andrew Carrico of D-511 received nearly two dozen shots for Typhoid, Smallpox, Yellow Fever, Tetanus and Cholera). As one trooper noted, "The medics seemed to be catching up on everything we had ever missed."

## 7. Camp Polk

GEN Swing was all for it; he had heard reports that some divisions had been turned back at the Port of Embarkation and he was not about to have his mighty 11th Airborne endure the same humiliation.

The General motivated his men in a letter, saying, "You are pared down in number and physique until only the steel and whalebone remain. You have every reason to be proud of your training record.... If this same effort is applied in combat, our record there, soon to be written, will be one of which every man of us will be forever proud."

The 187th's PFC Eli Bernheim wrote of this "paring" experience:

"We'd learned to live and work and play together; we'd become proficient with all the infantry weapons and expert with some of them. The leanness of our bodies reflected the succession of long, high-speed marches in full pack demanded of airborne troops. We'd mastered teamwork and fieldcraft in small-unit problems and our training program had featured many night maneuvers and many firing problems."

The 457th PFAB's LTC Douglas Quandt, General Swing's future G-3, exclaimed, "Our men are presently in good enough physical condition for anything they will have to do."

## Moving Day

And then the day the 11th Airborne had been waiting for finally arrived: War Department inspectors cleared the Division for departure. After months of endless training, maneuvers, examinations, inspections, barroom brawls and continuous griping, on March 15, 1944, GEN Swing was told that his division was heading for the Pacific Theater (he did not release the destination beyond select officers just yet).

Assistant Division Commander BG Albert Pierson noted, "General Swing was positively pleased when he learned we were slated for MacArthur's command. I gathered from conversations with General Swing that if he were asked for a choice of theatres, he would have selected the Pacific."

The final assigning of the Division's destination was made by the War Department who was well aware that with both the 82nd and the 101st Airborne Division's in England, the 11th, 13th and 17th Airborne's remained stateside. The 17th was activated two months *after* the 11th at Camp Mackall while the 13th Airborne was barely seven months old. As such, to meet MacArthur's requests the 11th Airborne would head to the Pacific Theater while the 17th was to stay stateside in strategic reserve.

Hoping this was really it, Swing's division packed their A and B bags while G-4 and ordnance made sure their equipment and clothing were ready for deployment. Most wrote vague letters home saying that their loves ones may not hear from them for some time while others helped pack and send off their wives and families.

## Delays & Secret Movements

After all their rushed efforts the 11th Airborne's troopers were surprised to hear they were staying put for another month. The news was generally received with groans and speculations soared since the invasion of Europe was hardly a secret, only the *when* and *where* was. The Angels wondered if they were being delayed because their destination was really the ETO.

Others argued that since the 503rd PIR and the 1st Marine Parachute Regiment were the only airborne units in the Pacific, General Swing's *division* was *definitely* heading west.

"Try as we may, we were unable to get any kind of confirmation," recalled D-511's CPL Murray Hale with a laugh.

Their frustrations only grew when they were restricted to camp and told to remove their patches by April 15. The Division's Paratroopers were doubly annoyed when told to pack their jump boots, wings and uniforms and that they had to wear the much-hated glider leggings. As PFC Steven hegedus of A-511 noted, "A Paratrooper's boots are his pride and joy, right up there with Mom and patriotism. Stomp on his fingers, steal his girlfriend, but don't mess with his boots."

For security reasons, the 11th Airborne was now Unit 1855 and its officers reminded the men to keep their mouths as shut as Camp Polk's gates now were to them. The 11th's troopers, now wearing khakis instead of OD greens, spent four additional weeks training and playing sports, but the truth is the officers were simply trying to keep their restless men busy.

Prior to one of the 511th PIR's many marches, I Company's PVT Vernon Agie stood in formation and whispered, "I gotta piss so bad I can taste it.

I'll give one of you guys twenty bucks if you loan me your helmet."

Only hearing the "twenty bucks" part, Vernon's buddy PFC Eugene Heath quickly took off his helmet and passed it back down the line.

When the helmet came back "full", Gene was pissed (literally?) and Platoon Sergeant SGT Larry "Push Up" Davis, now in on the joke, told him to put his helmet on.

With much profanity, PFC Heath dumped out the contents then used his canteen to wash the helmet before putting it back on his head as they began their twenty mile march. Poor Eugene did so with an empty canteen.

His only consolation came when SGT Davis growled loudly with a smile in a voice the whole platoon could hear, "Agie, pay Heath the twenty dollars!"

To help with the waiting, the announcement was made that the Firing Range was open for anyone who wanted to use it since the Division did not want to have to move all of its ammunition stores.

It helped, but General Swing's men simply swanted to get to it and the longer they stayed stateside, the more edgy they became (which led to more conflicts with Polk's armored units and to some Angels sneaking off post at night).

The 511th regimental dentist CPT Ross Riley expressed everyone's feelings when he said, "To a man we were ready and anxious to go."

D-511's 1LT Carrico noted, "The officers and enlisted men alike were hyped to an extreme degree, anxious to get into battle after all the months of training and preparation."

Uncle Sam was willing to grant the Angels' wishes to face the enemy, albeit after a small seven-month detour.

# 8: Heading West

Camp Stoneman, California – April-June 1944

*"We're in this all together, Folks like you and me
We'll be a United people, And our Country will be free..."*
-PFC Bronnel York, 457th PFAB, 11th AB

Orders to move out came down on April 20, 1944 and at 2400 on April 22, the 11th Airborne's trains left Camp Polk originally heading north (which still left the European Theater option). However, when the trains made large turns to the left, 1LT Andrew Carrico of D-511 noted "we could tell which way the train was heading."

After the Division's band played, "California, Here I Come," General Swing's troopers knew they were bound for the Pacific Theater, at least for embarkation. The United States frequently sent military units to the West Coast only to sail south then east through the Panama Canal in order to head for the Europe, so the Angels weren't quite sure of their final destination just yet.

The matter was much debated during the four-day 2,000-mile trip to Camp Stoneman near Pittsburgh, California, a journey which 1LT Carrico said was on "a troop train and it wasn't much fun. They didn't have bunks and stuff like that."

The train ride was broken up by card games, reading, and discussions about the Division's future. For many of the East Coast Angels, the midwest and west held exciting new vistas as they studied countryside that many had only read about. For the midwest and west coast Angels, the trip brought them feelings of homesickness as they passed through towns, or home states, that they had not seen in a year or longer.

The Angels made daily stops for exercise (they all admitted to sucking air in the high Rockies) and grateful towns often provided sandwiches and snacks as they came through. During some stops, entrepreneurs walked station platforms with beer and other drinks to sell to thirsty young Angels who conducted business out of their car's window. And with no laundry facilities onboard, the men had to wear their same uniforms the entire trip since their bags were safely packed away.

## 8. Heading West

When it rained during their passage through the Mojave Desert, CPT John Conable of the 457th PFAB joked, "Those of us who had never been in California before compared the weather as comparable to that found in Louisiana to the disgust of the native Californians."

The Division finally arrived at Camp Stoneman on April 26 and everyone quickly agreed that Stoneman possessed superior facilities than any of the Division's former posts with its nine PXs, three movie theaters, fourteen recreational halls, bowling alley, athletic fields and large service club for USO shows full of Hollywood stars.

Located near today's Los Medanos College, Camp Stoneman was America's main replacement depot and staging/processing/embarkation base on the West Coast. Three days before Japan officially surrendered in 1945, the one-millionth soldier passed through Stoneman's gates and enjoyed a brief ceremony to celebrate.

The 11th Airborne spent sixteen days there completing wills, filling out GI insurance forms and next-of-kin notification papers, drawing new tropical uniforms, listening to lectures on tropical diseases and shipboard procedures and various other training and preparations. They were also taken out into the water to practice lifeboat drills, climbing up and down cargo nets and jumping off "sinking ships".

Many in the 11th Airborne said that meals at Stoneman's thirteen mess halls were the best they'd had in the service, and given how plentiful the food was, some troopers joked they were being "fattened for the kill."

Paratroopers in I-511 found a way to enjoy their KP duties a little more when they created their own POW uniforms using chalk from a nearby chalkboard. One of their non-coms could imitate a German officer perfectly, so the young Angels spent hours in the kitchen serving their fellow soldiers who thought I Company was a compliment of German POWs housed nearby (and I-511 enjoyed plenty of extra helpings of whatever they wanted).

Every Angel knew that their time Stateside was growing short, so the post's phone booths were inundated with long lines as these last verbal goodbyes would have to last "for the duration" (Stoneman would host the largest telephone center in the world in 1945).

Long letters were written home and the Angels' families (and girlfriends) began receiving copies of the division's yearbook from

Camp Mackall. With so many letters going out, the Division's officers got their first real taste of the philatelic task of postal censorship. Many hated reading other men's personal letters to loved ones, especially their wives and girlfriends, but did their duty "like good soldiers".

RHQ-511's PFC John Kuntz noted, "Sometimes these letters proved embarassing, as in the case of one lad who persisted in telling the folks back home that he was fighting 24 hours a day, and was momentarily expecting the Medal of Honor."

Having spent years reading through the Angels' letters, it always interests me to see what they did *not* write about when I compare their words to what was going on with the Division at the time, especially during later combat operations. As 1SGT Earl Urish of E-187th noted years later, "The thing that impressed me most was how little we wrote about our activities. Censorship, mainly, but also a desire to spare loved ones the worry."

## Knock Their Eyes Out

In addition to all the entertainment, sports, logistics and food, the 11th Airborne's officers tried to keep the men busy with classroom sessions and 10-mile (or more) marches.

The 511th PIR's COL Orin Haugen heard that a Marine Corps unit had set the Camp Stoneman's 12-mile Road March Area record at just under four hours. Knowing his Paratroopers could do better, on a clear morning Haugen ordered the men to assemble with full combat loads, saying, "We will set a record that will knock their eyes out!"

Just as they were about to set out, a unit of African American soldiers arrived, also hoping to beat the Marines' record. The Angels watched the unit smartly march to "Sound Off", a cadence they had never heard before, and the athlete in Haugen practically salivated over the competition. B-511's PFC Bert Marshall noted that Haugen's troopers actually lapped their "competitors" and Hard Rock got a good laugh when one of the soldiers, who was rubbing his sore feet, watched the 511th pass and shouted, "Man, who is that crazy guy leading you all? He must really be crazy!"

When the 511th's column reached Stoneman, they were greeted by the Division band and the post commander. Looking at his watch, COL Haugen realized his regiment had crushed the camp's former record by nearly one hour. It was a standard no other unit would beat during the war.... except, of course, the Angels themselves.

"'We broke the record!' everyone shouted," B-511's CPL James Wilson told me. "Then they said, 'Hold on! A motorcycle brigade just broke the record!' So we marched again. There was no motorcycle brigade at Stoneman! They were just trying to keep us busy. We broke our own record."

## Angels vs. Engineers

Unfortunately, COL Haugen's Paratroopers were frustratingly reminded that they could not announce which outfit had set the new camp record. They, and the rest of the 11th Airborbe Division, were still just plain old Unit 1855.

D-511's 2LT Leo Crawford noted, "Someone overoptimistically tried to *smuggle* 8,000 intensely proud-of-themselves and highly charged young men through Stoneman. Taking off patches and jump boots was ineffective."

Imagine the Division's Paratroopers' outrage when they discovered engineers walking around Stoneman wearing, of all things, jump boots (in reality, boots that *looked* like jump boots)! This was most likely the 4th Engineer Special Brigade and what irked the Angels most was that the engineers' boots were covered in grease and oil and they had the gall to blouse their pants like qualified Paratroopers!

1LT Carrico of D-511 pointed out, "When the two groups met, all hell broke loose."

Fist-fights erupted across camp commons and the Angels' Paratroopers from the 511th PIR, 457th PFAB and 127th Airborne Engineers employed their tried and true tactics of forcefully removing the offending engineers' boots then cutting the footwear to straight-leg regulation height.When a free-for-all melee broke out at the Officers' Club, all but demolishing the facility, the 11th Airborne Division was banned from the club (what was left of it).

"Both sides selected one of their men to settle the score," 1LT Carrico remembered. "A good friend of mine (2LT Leo Crawford) who was the former heavyweight champion of the Army, well we talked him into fighting one of the engineer officers. It turned out to be knock-down fight, ending in a draw, with both sides a little worse for wear."

Neither COL Haugen nor GEN Swing, however, were amused. 2LT

Crawford would write years later:

"The Division accumulated a record number of AW-104's during that period, including myself... I had to report to General Swing after a preliminary chewing by Colonel Haugen. Facing those two in the same day is surpassed only by something on the order of the Bataan Death march. I reported to General Swing bearing a black eye, which I tried ineffectually to conceal with borrowed sunglasses... He bore down. He concluded, 'You are under arrest to quarters until I relieve you.' Some 8 or 9 months later I got a combat promotion to Captain. Since he had never released me from arrest I may be the only one who was ever promoted to Captain while under arrest to quarters."

It was, perhaps, for the best as then-*Captain* Crawford helped lead Headquarters Company of 1/188th GIR in the Soule Task Force during the division's Los Baños Raid on Luzon on February 23, 1945. Their stalling actions gave the raiders and rescued internees time to reach safety. And while he may have been reprimanded by both Haugen and Swing, there was no denying that Leo's fight had done wonders for Division morale.

There was an additional reason for Swing's sending Leo to the 188th at the time. The General knew that while his troopers had tremendous loyalty to their companies and battalions, he needed loyalty to the *Division*, so to "spread the leaven" he instituted interdivisional transfers when circumstances suited while at Stoneman and later in the Pacific.

## The Burma Road

While the 11th Airborne was officially restricted to base (msot units were at Stoneman), countless Angels discovered and made use of what they deemed the "Burma Road", an unguarded path out of Stoneman that led them to going "over or under the fence."

When MAJ Douglas Quandt of the 457th PFAB obtained permission to have dinner with his family in nearby San Francisco, he entered the restaurant only to find some of his Angels already there. Quandt smiled and said, "I suppose I'd have been a little disappointed in you if you hadn't found a way to get out."

Commenting about the penalties to those who got caught or caused trouble at Stoneman, D-511's CPL William Walter replied, "Hell, we were young, brave and thought we could do no wrong. Besides, we knew we were going overseas soon and the Brass was not so likely to set down hard on us."

One poor Division trooper was so homesick he snuck out and made his way to the family home nearby. His father, sympathetic to his plight, let his son stay the weekend and then drove the AWOL Angel back to Camp Stoneman first thing Monday morning.

And just in time, too. GEN Swing was officially given notice that his Division was shipping out. He issued orders for his men to pack their gear, and many filled out their "Notice of Change of Address" cards and mailed them home. Final medical and dental checkups and procedures were completed, as were weapon and equipment checks (Stoneman's armorers were renowned for getting everything working just right). All in all, there was a noticeable excitement in the air around the Angels' area: they were finally heading to The Front (although they still didn't know *which* front).

## Boarding Calls and Departures

The Division was scheduled to sail separately, in most cases by regiment with at least three battalions per ship. Between May 5-18 the Angels marched down Harbor Street to the Pittsburgh water front where they boarded one of three ferries, the *Catalina*, the *Cabrillo* and the *Yerba Buena* (also known as *The Ernie Pyle*) before sailing across Suisun Bay via the Carquinex Straight, then down through San Pablo and San Francisco bays to Fort Mason's wharves.

Encumbered by their heavy bags, the Angels were greeted on the docks by smiling Red Cross girls who served them coffee and donuts (and yes, many Angels attempted to flirt with them).

Munching on his donut, D-511's PVT Billy Pettit told his best friend PFC Chauncey Poole that they were really enjoying first class treatment. Poole gave the seventeen-year-old Paratrooper a long look and replied, "Pettit, we are in this thing now."

"This thing" was the war and Billy later told me, "That woke me up. It went from fun and games to combat."

HQ3-511's PFC George Doherty said, "I remember looking around at all the guys I had just spent a year and a half training with and wondering who wouldn't make the return trip?"

Wearing helmets marked with unit letters in chalk, the Angels' columns had snaked down the docks under the famous sign which read "Through these portals pass the best damn soldiers in the world", something everyone in the 11th Airborne could agree with.

Merchant Marine sailors led the Angels up gangways and through mazes of corridors, storage rooms, ladders and berths to their "quarters". Most of the enlisted men ended up on canvas bunks that were stacked five high in converted cargo holds and whenever a trooper rolled onto his bunk, his nose was ten inches from the bunk above him. Officers, of course, often shared some sort of cabin.

Some of the Division's transports traveled in convoys, but most sailed alone since, as the Angels were frequently told, they were on "fast moving Liberty Ships, too fast for a convoy." While most of the young Angels had never sailed anywhere before, many quickly grew frustrated with their ships "ammenities" and the crews.

RHQ-511's PFC John Kuntz remarked that their transport, the SS *Sea Pike* was "a ship that (so we had been told) was the pride of the Navy. Pride of the fishing fleet she may have been. Beyond that I'd hesitate to make any claims."

HQ-188th GIR's PFC Edward A. Hammrich remembered with equal bitterness, "I sailed on the USAT *CapeCleare* on 17 May 1944. The troops were treated very badly by the merchant marine crew and there was no love lost between them and the troops...."

The 711th Ordnance Company sailed on the USS *Santa Cruz* while the Division HQ and many of the Special Troops went on the USAT *David C. Shanks*. The 187th GIR went on the USS *Mendocino*.

After final roll and mail calls, their transports would cast off and cruise under the Oakland Bay Bridge before heading past Alcatraz. Young Angels crowded the decks as they went under the Golden Gate Bridge, and in accordance with tradition, countless tossed a coin (often a Walking Liberty half dollar) over the side for a safe return.

"The water was loaded with splashes," said D-511's SGT Murray Hale.

HQ3-511's PFC George Doherty noted, "We turned around and looked back at the majesty of the Golden Gate Bridge standing high straight and proud, for she was our Statue of Liberty in the West. As she disappeared into the Pacific fog all of us on the *Sea Pike* stood at the rail knowing we were giving that up for a period of time to preserve those rights.."

# 8. Heading West

It can be easy with our modern perspective of the war to overlook the fact that for many in the 11th Airborne, this was the first time they had ever left the safety of America's shores. Not only had the Army already taken them far beyond their hometowns, even home states, now they were sailing for destinations unknown… and war.

Once they were out of San Francisco Bay, their ships' captains opened their written orders before using the vessel's PA system to announce, "Now hear this, now hear this: our destination is New Guinea." The matter was now settled. General Swing and his 11th Airborne Division were headed to fight Imperial Japan.

Assistant Division Commander BG Albert Pierson described the Angels' general sailing routes, saying, "We were to go fairly well south to avoid Japanese submarines and then travel westward toward Australia before turning north to New Guinea."

A letter from President Roosevelt was distributed which read in part: "You, the soldiers, are a God-fearing, proud and courageous people, who have throughout history, put its freedom under God before all other purposes. The hope, confidence and gratitude and prayers of your families, your fellow-citizens and your President go with you…"

D-511's PFC Alex "Chief" Village Center received a second letter, also with the presidential seal, which generated much curiosity among his platoon. PFCs Chauncy Poole and Russell Hyatt, PVT George Locke and CPL Harry Zertuche gathered as Alex slowly read the letter out loud. The Angels were stunned to hear that The Chief's brothers had been killed fighting in Europe and the letter explained that Alex could go home to his family in South Dakota's Standing Rock Indian Reservation if he wanted.

Everyone stood silently as Village Center quietly folded the letter and looked at his friends' sober faces. "You are my brothers now." Alex chose to stay and fight with the Angels all the way to Tokyo.

## Ocean Crossing

Many of the Angels were delighted, at least at first, with the experience of cruising the open ocean. After morning calisthenics, they spent the day watching flying fish and dolphins in the water, sunbathing when they had time, and watching movies on deck at night. Card and dice games were frequent, as were the offered classes on seamanship, celestial navigation, etc. Paperbacks were devoured and many troopers at least glanced through their new "handbook", the War Department's serviceman's booklet titled, "A Pocket Guide to New Guinea".

Things onboard soon grew monotonous and D-511's 1LT Andrew Carrico said with a laugh that everyone was "Bored as Hell."

As the days wore on and the Angels sailed further south then west, the holds below decks became humid and fetid (many troopers suffered from seasickness) and the heads and washrooms, while cleaned daily, smelled awful. To make matters worse, enemy submarines required a blackout at night which meant closing all portholes and hatches, thus trapping the stifling heat and smells in the ship's holds. Most Angels stripped down to their shorts, but everyone below decks was fairly miserable.

Luckily the 511th PIR was traveling with the Division's band under WO Robert Berglund who often gave "concerts" on deck. Boxing matches were held on most of the transports, and some even enjoyed impromptu plays or other performances. The Red Cross kept most of the Angels' ships well-stocked with books so reading became a popular pastime, as did gambling, of course, though it was rather frowned upon by the higher ranks (someone in the 511th PIR even smuggled a small slot machine onboard the *Sea Pike*).

Both homesickness and seasickness hit many of the barely-out-of-high-school Angels and the later left many confined to their bunks for days until they found their sea legs. Some never did and later joked that they spent more time "feeding the fish" than anything else.

When sparse rainstorms were noticed in the distance, a voice came on the PA declaring, "Rain Coming!" F-511's CPL Ray Brennaman remembered that almost every time, "A lot of guys got out and soaped up and the rain stopped!"

Some troopers volunteered for guard duty and all were told to watch the horizon for submarines. This was the first time the Angels realized they could potentially by fired upon by the enemy.

On most of the Division's transports, the Angels were only allowed two meals a day, one usually at 0800 and another at 1600. The troopers were required to wait in long lines for chow, then eat quickly as the galleys were often too small on the converted ships.

Every trooper I spoke with remembers that the food was awful and one explained that it was so bad that although they were so hungry, no one wanted seconds. Meals consisted of S.O.S., dehydrated potatoes the consistancy of gravel, powdered eggs that were more powder than eggs, some semblance of hot dogs and Spam sandwiches which were so awful that some Angels could never eat Spam for the rest of their lives.

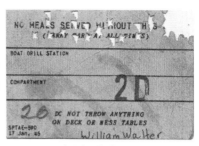

*Meal ticket belonging to CPL William Walter of D-511*

On several of the Division's transports, General Swing's troopers got creative in their efforts to find for more food. Some dug into their stashed supplies of chocolate bars which they had secreted in the hopes of "plying nubile natives" wherever they ended up. Others pilfered life rafts rations whereas others "investigated" galley stores. Some Angels smartly volunteered to cook or bake in those galleys then simply handed their creations out portholes to friends.

CPT John Conable of the 457th PFAB summed up the Angels' Pacific crossing experiences: "The men were packed in them like sardines. No one spent any more time in the holds than necessary. We were fed two meals a day, one at ten in the morning and the other at four in the afternoon. The food was nothing to write home about unless you were in a complaining mood."

Luckily on most ships the troopers were provided with something to listen to. As G-511's 2LT William "Bill" Abernathy wrote home to his fiancee Naomi, "The ship is equipped with a loudspeaker system throughout and plays records most of the day. A lot of them are transcriptions of commercial radio programs, mostly musical. For the most part they are very good. The songs – a lot of them, are the ones that were popular when I was at the Parachute School..."

## Crossing the Lines

B-511's SSGT James Wilson told me that a few weeks into their voyage on the *Sea Pike* someone got on the ship's PA to say, "Now hear this, now here this: we are crossing the International Dateline. Time to set your watches back 24 hours!" Everyone started adjusting their watches until they caught on to the joke.

Shortly afterwards when each of the Angels' transports crossed the Equator, the ship's crew held a "Crossing the Line" ceremony to

*A ship full of Angels crossing the Pacific*

initiate those who had never done so before into the Royal Order of Neptunus Rex, or King Neptune. While many of the "old timers" had served throughout the Pacific before the war, most Angels had not so the enlisted men frequently elected their officers and platoon sergeants to participate in this all-in-good-fun ceremony.

The "volunteers" usually stripped down to just shorts before "The Royal Barber" (from the ship's crew) tried to cut the Angels' already barely-there hair. Next, the "initiates" were smeared with mustard, ketchup, cooking oil and eggs. They then had to follow the orders of "King Neptune" and were paddled by "The Royal Executioner". Some were even told to kiss the sweaty and hairy belly of "The Baby Prince"!

After the ceremony the Angels were officially "Shellbacks", citizens of King Neptune's court with all the rights and privileges therein. Most in the Division received a certificate proving their new citizenship, which many mailed home upon reaching New Guinea.

## A Tokyo Rose Welcome

Nearly every one of the Angels' transports were buzzed at least once, either out of Hawaii or some other island as they sailed closer to New Guinea. This, of course, led to hundreds of sweaty, khaki-clad Angels rushing to the decks as the vessels' captains and crew shouted for them to go below. GEN Swing's stubborn young Angels usually ignored the calls and enjoyed the show.

Only days away from their destination, General Swing's men were surprisingly identified on the radio by the infamous Tokyo Rose who said menacingly, "Welcome to the 11th Airborne Division.... We know where you are. You will never make it to New Guinea."

"That sent chills up my spine!" remembered mortarman D-511's PFC Elmer Charles Hudson of Oakley, Kansas.

Propaganda or not, that Japan knew the Angels were coming was disconcerting to the 11th Airborne's (and Allied) leadership given their attempts at secrecy.

Concerns were temporarily forgotten, however, when shouts of "New Guinea!" were heard across the ships, Angels rushed back on decks for their first glimpse the green speck of land far off on the horizon. After 3-4 weeks of sailing, beginning around June 12, 1944 the 11th Airborne Division finally started to arrive in the Pacific Theater.

# 9: So, This is New Guinea

Dobodura, New Guinea – June-November 1944

*"I still like parachuting and to brag a little, darn proud to be in the greatest branch of any service... Paratroopers have really had a big part in this war and have lived up to everything said about them. For my money they surpass the Marines, in every department – you can quote me on that – yes even to a Marine."*
PFC Clifton Evans, RHQ-187th GIR

The Angels' transports usually stopped for a day or two in beautiful Milne Bay to offload cargo and refill their fuel and fresh water reservoirs. Then, with local pilots onboard, the vessels sailed north and the decks swarmed with troopers eager to study the countless Naval ships in and the jungle-covered mountains around the paradisiacal bay.

2LT Leo Crawford, now assigned to the 188th GIR's A Company, said that during their stop at Milne Bay, "CPT Fred Gamble displayed one of the greatest acts of courage I have ever seen when he went down between two ships to save a man who had fallen overboard at the port in New Guinea where we first made landfall. The water was moving through the space between the two ships like a mountain torrent and I thought Fred had no chance to get out alive let alone get the other man out... He lives in Jackson, Florida now..."

Upon reaching Oro Bay, the Angels were told to police the holds and pack all their gear. Sailors lowered the troopers' duffle bags to floating DUKWs as the Angels made their way down cargo nets "hands on the vertical, feet on the horizontal" as they had practiced back at Camp Stoneman only weeks before.

The DUKWs could carry roughly two-dozen troopers and once loaded, drivers revved their engine and moved towards shore. The sun blazed across the water like fiery glass as the Angels looked towards the beaches. They could see signs of earlier battles in the form of sunken ships, blasted treelines, and even fortifications.

As the DUKWs reached the sand, their gears shifted and the ingenius vehicles began driving inland. Countless Angels took careful note of

## 9. So, This is New Guinea

the vast warehouses they passed full of piles of ordinance and rows of carefully parked vehicles including jeeps, ambulances, bulldozers and even Kenworth 10-ton 6x6 heavy wrecking trucks.

"We moved inland to (what) was to become our home for the next six long, hot, miserable months," D-511's 1LT Andrew Carrico remembered. Their DUKW transports pulled into a large clearing next to an empty planked runway close to where Girua Airport is located today. The 15 steel runways had formerly hosted squadrons of the USAAF V Fighter Command which had moved on to the Markham Valley. When the Angels explored the area, they found the remains of the B-24 "Windy City Kitty" and cut out the panel that held bomber's name (and nose are) and shipped it to the 321st's Bombardment Squadron's commander COL Richard H Smith.

The Grim Reapers were grateful for the Angels' thoughtfulness and seven months later when the 11th Airborne landed on southern Luzon, the Grim Reapers of 3rd Attack Group flew their A-20s all day to protect their new airborne friends.

Careful to avoid the tough, sharp kunai grass which they were told held insects carrying diseases, the Angels plopped down on packs or helmets on the runways and studied the Owen Stanley Range in the distance. The stifling +100° F heat quickly enveloped the troopers like a sauna and it wouldn't take long for the humidity to begin molding everything, including their letters, photos, and Old Gold cigarettes which they started calling "Moldy Goldies."

PFC Clifton Evans of RHQ-187th GIR noted, "The humidity is terrible and the sun hits you just like you're standing by a hot stove."

CPT John Conable of the 457th PFAb remembered, "It took me fully two weeks to adjust to the new climate and the change in body rhythms. I was now getting up when I would have been going to bed back in the United States. I was rather short-tempered for this period of time."

For many of the General Swing's 8,321 men, Papua New Guinea was their first taste of foreign shores and for those expecting a Hawaii-like experience, Dobodura was a disappointment. There were no beach-front bars, no boardwalk shops and worst of all, no nubile girls to ply with their jump boots, chocolate bars, and cigarettes.

The 511th PIR's Regimental Dentist CPT Ross Riley remembered Dobodura dryly, saying, "Our time there was, in a word, uneventful."

*The Angels "hurrying up to wait" at Dobodura*

## The Angels of Dobodura

That is not to say that the Angels lacked things to do, although most duties ended at 1500 until they grew acclimated to the environment. The area around the abandoned airfields provided Swing's crafty troopers with plenty of materials to work with and pyramidal tent cities, gathered by the 408th Quartermasters from Dobodura warehouses, quickly sprang up by companies with enlisted men on one side of roads and officers on the other.

The Angels were issued new mosquito netting, which they came to both appreciate and loath in the hot, steamy months ahead. They were also repeatedly warned about the dangerous diseases the island held, including malaria, elephantitis and scrub typhus.

Fortunately, the division's area had already been cleared by previous units and the surrounding jungle provided the Angels plenty of poles in which to create all sorts of structures including racks to rest their steel helmets on for shaving or washing. Other frames hung over drainage trenches for cleaning dishes and GEN Swing declared that G-511 had the best setup in the entire division.

Unfortunately, of those not setting up on the tarmacs too few heeded the command to dig the drainage ditches and were flooded out the first time it rained which reminded the Angels that the luxuries of their stateside posts were now long gone.

Not ones to sit and sulk, the Angels got to work building areas for recreational use, including "sitting rooms" with planked floors, working radios, and chairs and tables for reading or card games. The Division's engineers also fashioned a central area to view movies at night or watch softball games and boxing matches provided by the division's boxing teams from the 511th PIR, DivArty (Division Artillery), Special Troops, and the 187th and 188th Glider Infantries.

Although frowned upon by the brass, a few entrepreneurial troopers set up large wash basins to make extra money as laundrymen (mechanics in the motor pool later sold homemade washing machines powered by Jeep engines). Other Angels found abandoned P-38 belly tanks and the 127$^{th}$ Airborne Engineer Battalion welded small valves on the 305-gallon containers, turning them into showers which could accommodate a few hundred men at a time.

Wells were easily dug for water and one private from the 457th PFAB decided to "dig" one using a scrounged 500-pound aerial bomb which he set off us blasting caps. Needless to say, he was quickly transferred to the 674th GFAB who months later sent him back.

For the first few days the Angels' food was served from borrowed Australian chuck wagons and the Division's troopers had their first of *many* meals that included dehydrated potatoes and mutton which they grew sick of and many said they would never eat it again.

Wanting to improve their food situation, Angels scrounged materials from abandoned Allied camps to build mess halls and screened in kitchens and bakeries with concrete stoves. As the weeks wore on, the men came to appreciate the wafting smells of baked goods and cooking meals as they learned to perfect the "New Guinea Salute" which involved waving one hand over their mess kit to ward off flies.

While the days of fresh food were mostly over (they did catch and kill a hog later and HQ-11 seemed to enjoy an occasional steak flown in from Australia), the Angels' cooks did their best to make palatable meals from dehydrated and canned goods and everyone learned how to find fresh coconuts and bananas for variety.

Even so, when the leaner 11th Airborne finally left New Guinea several months later, one trooper noted, "There was not a man in the Division who took trousers with a waist over 36 inches."

After dinner, many units pulled out homemade Vegas-style Craps tables for well-attended gambling with some troopers earning hundreds of extra dollars (in pounds) a month from their comrades.

*Typical company street at Dobodura*

## Battle of the Bats

Amidst the initial flurry of construction, on their second afternoon at Dobodura some troopers in the 511th PIR noticed huge bats flying through their encampment. Tales had spread onboard the *Sea Pike* that New Guinea was home to vampire bats big enough to grab onto a man and suck his blood through his neck so the worried Paratroopers shouldered their rifles for "target practice" which sent hundreds of bats swarming out of the trees.

Additional Paratroopers soon arrived and joined in "The Battle of the Bats" and together they expended "easily 10,000 rounds..." one participant recalled, perhaps with a smile.

When it was over, PFC Bert Marshall of B-511 remembers, "They made all the companies line up. Of course, all of the men in our company ran in and cleaned their rifles, but you could still tell who fired. Then, the officers came and started to smell the barrels of everyone's rifle to see who had fired them. The officers smelled everyone's gun, and they never did say which ones fired them. They said they were all O.K. and stated that no one fired. I guess they did not want any of the men that did fire to get into any trouble."

D-511's CPL Murray Hale remembered with some humor, "Colonel (Haugen) gave the order for our weapons to be taken away and returned to a secure area and kept under lock and key."

"I suspect that a number of officers sneaked back to their tents chuckling," noted D-511's SGT Ed Sorenson. "Admonishments were the order of the day for a week or two."

Bats were not the only prey hunted on New Guinea, however. While the main fighting had concluded in the area, some Japanese were still hiding in the jungle so Allied forces set up a bounty system wherein native Papuans received payment for every pair of enemy soldiers' ears they delivered. Over the next few months some Angels joined the locals on these hunts to better learn how to stalk the enemy in the brush and returned with a wealth of helpful knowledge, including how to catch and cook wild pigs, pythons and wallabys, obtain coconuts from high trees and find fresh fruits in the jungle.

## Dobodura Championships

With their camp well established, including a new PX which was greatly appreciated, the 11th Airborne's affinity for sports was renewed and boxing, football, volleyball and baseball games were regularly held, plus nearby Aussies invited them to watch rugby matches.

The Division Football League (tackle without pads to toughen the men after uniforms miraculously arrived) consisted of teams from the 511th, 187th, 188th and Division Artillery (DivArty). To this day, no one really knows who won the first overly competitive match between the 511th and DivArty under the 457th's CPT John Conable and the 711th Ordnance's 1LT Noah "Gus" Dorious.

1LT Foster "Punchy" Arnett, who also oversaw the Division Officers Mess, rewarded his 511th PIR boxing champions with steaks taken from the Division Staff's personal store. Well, until General Swing found out that is and irately had Punchy removed. Swing told Foster, "Keep your damn boxers out of my mess hall."

Given how wide company streets were, many Angels set up volleyball nets and pickup games filled their down time. GEN Swing himself even participated and during one game a new lieutenant arrived at their camp from the states and took one look at the sweaty, unkempt Angels and ordered them get their uniforms on and line up.

*Two Angels sparing: D-511's PFC Joe Juarez and PVT Robert Burnside*

Well, most of the players looked at one older-looking trooper who simply winked at them and said something to the affect of, "Alright, boys. Let's do as he says." Following his lead they moved to comply.

Imagine the new lieutenant's shock when GEN Swing's two stars shone brightly in the sun as he buttoned his shirt and lined up for "inspection." The other Angels struggled to stiffle their laughter as the new lieutenant sputtered out an apology.

New Guinea's humidity did sap their energy, of course, and left their uniforms dripping so the Angels enjoyed refreshing dips in the ocean to cool off. A deep river also flowed down from the Owen Stanley Range, complete with diving board and a twenty-five-foot cliff which the Angels jumped off as if they hadn't a care in the world.

The relative-cool of the evenings was enjoyed with more card games, reading, movies or talking by the light of their Coleman lanters.

## The New Guinea Distilling Company

Such relaxation time was far more refreshing than the Angels' warm drinking water served from lister bags (rubber-lined canvas sacks) which hung on every company street. The warm, halazone treated water tasted like rubber and many troopers took to mixing in lemon powder from their rations just to stand it.

Thirsting for something stronger, and with their stateside access to Beer Gardens, bars and pubs gone, numerous Angels took to the surrounding hills to build stills to ferment their own "Moonshine" or "White Lightening" to supplement their 3.2 rations. It was a Division-wide "problem" and officers struggled to keep up with their mens' creativity and rapid deployment of such engineered operations.

Sugar, potatoes and fruit "mashes" disappeared from Mess Halls and medics had to be told to stop distributing medicinal alcohol to their friends. Officers and NCOs learned to use "The Sniff Method" to find the stills. Some Angels' families had been Moonshiners during Prohibition and it clearly showed that the skills and ingenuity were passed down through the generations. You can't blame the men, however. As one Angel pointed out, the officers had been allowed to bring two boxes of personal alcohol stores with them to New Guinea.

The Whisky Rebellion of Dobodura continued when soldiers from the division's 408th Airborne Quartermaster Company tried to sell

## 9. So, This is New Guinea

*Troopers enjoying a refreshing "drink"*

unauthorized beer rations to the 511th PIR at inflated prices. I don't know who else bought them, but Hard Rock's angry Paratroopers booted the quartermasters out of their bivouac then jumped them "Robin Hood-style" along a jungle road and relieved them of their *questionably* obtained alcohol before sharing the booty amongst the regiment like true heroes. Angels indeed.

One *non*-alcoholic favorite that spread through the Division was a homemade hot chocolate made by heating Eagle Brand Condensed Milk and mixing in chocolate bars. It was a delicious treat that brought a feeling of home which felt very far away as the war raged to their north.

Another pleasantry enjoyed by the Angels was ice cream, courtesy of GEN Swing's foresight. Before the Division left Camp Polk, Swing had ordered that all Battery and Battalion funds be turned over to the Division Special Services which in turn purchased ice cream machines and a supply of ice cream mix.

Swing reasoned that with the average age of his men being so young (19), they would want ice cream in the PTO. He was right and the 11th Airborne, to the Angels' knowledge, was the only unit with ice cream, every ten days or so (a very popular day). There are some discrepancies as to who enjoyed the treat. Some Angels said that only those in Division Headquarters got it while on New Guinea.

One Dobodura unpleasantry that no one ever really got used to was the insect powder that combined with the Angels' sweat to create an uncomfortably messy compound. The 11th Airborne also used insect repellant to fend off the island's mosquitos which some troopers swore were big enough to shoot down with the 152nd's AA-guns.

As an additional preventative health measure, beverages of all sorts were used to swallow their anti-malarial Atabrine pills under the watchful eyes of the medics (some resistant troopers feared the pills would make them sterile). The medicine's main ingredient, quinacrine (quinine was in short supply after Japan conquered Java), was believed to help ward off malaria, a real threat to soldiers in the Pacific. Atabrine had one very noticeable side effect, however.

"We turned yellow in complexion and in the eyes," remembered CPL Murray Hale of D-511. "But it worked!"

Actually, it *didn't* as some in the division discovered in the future months and even years. Atabrine only *suppressed* malaria's symptoms, not prevented it since the drug killed parasites in the bloodstream, but not the liver.

However, as one 187th GIR historian noted, "thanks to the nagging of our medical officers and General Swing, (the Division) was relatively free of malaria, dengue, scrub typhus, and many other tropical diseases."

## (Para)chutes and Gliders

While the Division was crossing the Pacific, GEN Swing flew to Brisbane, Australia to discuss the 11th Airborne's future with USAFFE GEN Douglas MacArthur who explained that Swing's Angels would soon take part in a large campaign they needed to prepare for. Swing took his aide MAJ George Oliver, his driver SSGT Manuel Debacca, and LTC Douglas Quandt of the 457th PFAB whom Swing was trying to maneuver into taking the Division G-3 position.

It was not the first time that Swing and MacArthur had met. In his younger years in the service (and arguably all throughout the war), Joseph Swing was a great athlete, especially when it came to football and polo, a trait that caught the eye of the Army's Chief of Staff, Douglas MacArthur. MacArthur ordered the young Swing to Washington and charged him with raising an American polo team to take on the Mexican team the following year and to win.

The 187th GIR's MAJ Henry Burgess pointed out, "Not only did Swing beat the Mexican polo team, he humiliated them in a number of games. Thereafter Swing was promoted to major, and as a reward sent to Leavenworth and the Command and General Staff School."

Elated with MacArthur's indicated plans for his 11th Airborne in 1944, MG Swing flew to New Guinea and met with each regiment's command staff to review MacArthur's strategies and their current and future objectives. General Joe told his commanders that the Division would spend six months honing their jungle skills before taking part in future operations.

"Think, eat and dream of war," Swing told his men. "We're fighting a desperate enemy."

Technically the Angels already *were* part of combat operations as they were in reserve for the continuing action at Hollandia. While they were not called on to fight, they were required to be on alert and have plane loading plans prepared in case they were. This gave the 11th Airborne Division its first campaign credit and Battle Star and the men were awarded the Awarded the Asiatic Pacific Campaign Medal (thought most of the Angels were unaware they were in reserve).

The Angels' campaign credit was approved by GEN MacArthur himself on February 11, 1945 and in 1988 John B. Wilson, Chief of the Army's Organizational History Branch explained:

"Under the provisions of paragraph 9-4, AR 672-5—1, a unit was given campaign participation credit if it engaged the enemy in combat, was stationed in the combat zone, or performed duties either in the air or on the ground in any part of the combat zone during the time limitation of the campaign. Our records indicate that the 11th Airborne Division served on New Guinea from May 1944 to November 1944, which is included in the time limitation of the New Guinea campaign. Therefore the division is entitled to it."

The Division's BG Albert Pierson pointed out that, "the Biak operation ran into snag and there was some consideration, perhaps very slight, for (our) airborne troops there, but the terrain and enemy defenses positions precluded an airborne drop."

GEN Swing set up his second jump school around Dobodura's vast runways, run again by MAJ Henry Burgess. From June 16 to August the 187th and 188th GIRs' volunteers went through the abbreviated two-week parachute training as did volunteers from across the Division who had yet to earn their jump wings (Swing even nicknamed the 188th a "Para-glider" regiment, the first of its kind).

PFC Clifton Evans of RHQ-187th wrote home after his qualifying jumps, "I like jumping much more than riding gliders. It's almost impossible to explain the thrill in jumping. It's just one of those things you have to do yourself to know what it's like. I sure sweat every jump out, but it's worth it. I really feel I accomplished something in overcoming my better judgment because when you sit in that plane the same question always pops through a guy's mind – 'what the hell am I doing up here?' – but I still like it."

Eventually seventy-five percent of the 11th Airborne's enlisted men and eighty-two percent of its officers were jump qualified, making it perhaps the most parachute-capable division in the U.S. Army in World War II. American Legion Commander Warren Atherton even stopped by during his inspection tour to watch a practice jump on June 16, 1944 and was suitably impressed.

Another motive for GEN Swing's Dobodura jump school was to teach the area's transport pilots, most of whom had only flown cargo, the intricacies of dropping Paratroopers over a DZ. The 503rd PIR's drop on Nadzab had experienced some problems due to the transport pilots' inexperience and Swing wanted to avoid such difficulties for his Angels' potential future drops.

The local troop carrier wings like the 54th out of Nadzab also took part in Swing's *glider* school which "allowed" the Division's new arrivals and freshly-certified Paratroopers to train in glider landings (they all hated it). Many agreed that they would rather jump into combat than "get roped into it."

The glidermen of the 187th and 188th GIRs and the 674th and 675th FFABs, though, were happy to learn in July that they were

*11th Airborne Jump School students on the move*

9. So, This is New Guinea

*Glider training at Soputa, New Guinea*

now (rightfully) authorized to collect the same hazard pay as the Paratroopers: fifty dollars a month for enlisted men and one hundred dollars for officers.

Swing's actions to cross-certify his division were in line with the War Department's post-April 18, 1942 policy which stated that, "Ground units will be trained basically for movement by transport and gliders...."

There was another method to Swing's madness; the forward-thinking general understood that once the 11th entered combat, he may not know what craft were available until the "last minute." If no gliders were available or viable, the Angels could move extra men into the field if more were jump qualified. If few aircraft were accessible, Paratroopers could be shifted to gliders, even if under protest.

And again, the Division was also aware that nearly all of the area's transport pilots had only flown cargo and supply missions, so the Angels labored to teach them over the next few months how airborne operations worked and what would be expected of them in case they were called upon to deliver the 11th Airborne to an objective. As such, the Division's Paratroopers enjoyed countless practice jumps and maneuvers that kept their skills sharp and fresh.

RHQ-511's 2LT William "Bill" Abernathy wrote, "We don't jump in jungles as all the wild places aren't covered with jungle. There are quite a few fields at irregular intervals, which are covered with kunai grass. It grows from four to seven or eight feet high, having a blade about an inch wide. It is very tough and very hard to go through. It makes a good jump field, but isn't pleasant for traveling."

Apart from the obvious fact that the Angels *expected* to be used in a "vertical envelopment" missions, GEN MacArthur himself told MG Swing that he believed the 11th Airborne would soon be used in such a manner during a near-future campaign. As such, Jumping Joe wanted everyone, transport crews included, to be ready.

## The Battle of Camp Sudest

Swing's division also studied how to combat load naval ships in the event they were called on to make an amphibious landing. The Angels also enjoyed a large 4th of July celebration that included special explosives, flares and tracer shells, but the next day it was back to work. Jungle training was emphasized as the Angels ran battalion and company tactical problems in the surrounding hills during which they memorized the settings around the Kokoda Trail, including the Buna and Gona swamps and the Ambogo and Sambogo Rivers.

The 511th's 3rd Battalion became so expert at jungle infiltrations that I believe they were the first in the Division to penetrate the Women's Auxiliary Army Corps housing five miles away on Cape Sudest, despite the vigilant M.P.s, machine gun nests, fences, and a moat on one side. When word of 3rd's "invasions" spread, unauthorized visits to the WAAC compound by Angels exploded. In their defense, the enlisted men argued that the only other way to get a date with a WAAC was with a commission, a jeep and a pistol at your side. After the war, since they were never called upon to fight on New Guinea, the Angels joked that the only action they saw on the island was during "The Battle of Cape Sudest".

To prepare for *future* action, the 511th PIR set up a live-fire field problem, which other division units used, where targets were set up to teach the troopers to return fire when fired upon then move in on Japanese positions instead of falling back after artillery support.

This field problem originally started with MAJ Henry Burgess and the 511th PIR's COL Orin Haugen. Burgess had been sent to help the 503rd PIR plan and execute their jump on Noemfoor and had watched the 503rd's troublesome drops on the under-construction airstrip. Henry then moved forward with the regiment's Paratroopers and observed that during firefights, many in the 503rd fired their rifles aimlessly and without consideration for distance.

MAJ Burgess returned to the 11th Airborne with mental notes about what the 503rd had done and what the Angels could train to do better and discussed them with COL Haugen who convinced GEN Swing to institute a field problem at Sopotua involving one combat team, an artillery battery and an engineer platoon. Some troopers remember

## 9. So, This is New Guinea

the area being so blasted by the time they left New Guinea that there wasn't a branch left on a palm tree and the ground was scorched bare.

Interestingly, Assisant Division Commander BG Albert Pierson noted, "The 503rd was offered to General Swing, but I cannot recall whether this offer was made by GHQ or General Krueger— Sixth Army. General Swing told me that he turned down the offer. The 503rd just wouldn't fit in with his men."

Krueger's U.S. Sixth Army also organized several training programs on the island, including the famous Alamo Scout School at Humboldt Bay created by GEN Walter C. Krueger. The 11th Airborne sent a small group of men to Krueger's school and never some of them again. One such "lost" man, 1LT William E. Nellist of F-511 went on to lead an Alamo Scout team including during the famous Cabanatuan Raid on January 30, 1945.

F-511's SGT Ray Brennaman told me, "Nellist was the best shot I've ever seen. I once watched him drive a nail with a pistol shot!"

Numerous Angels also attended the week-long Jungle Training School run by the Australian New Guinea Administrative Unit (ANGAU) at Higatura. Some instructors were veterans of the New Guinea campaigns and when Swing's troopers came back sporting Aussie caps, they taught their comrades how to eat in the jungle, move quickly and quietly through thick vegetation and many other vital techniques that would keep them alive in the days to come.

*Aussie instructors*

The returning Angels also shared stories from their instructors who warned that the enemy was cunning, sneaky and barbaric. Accounts of Japanese soldiers killing Christian missionaries spread through the 11th Airborne and after listening to tales of the enemy torturing prisoners before grotesquely killing them, General Swing's young men vowed complete destruction upon the soldiers of *dai Nippon* whenever and wherever they found them.

## Ali Swing's Thieves

One of the 11th Airborne's least enjoyable tasks on New Guinea was unloading ships in Oro Bay (they also hated working in the munition dumps and motor pools). With a lack of service troops in the area, even the mighty 11th Airborne Division had to lend a hand.

HQ3-511's PFC George Doherty expressed the feelings of all the Angels: "It certainly wasn't dignified for Paratroopers trained for combat to do this type of menial work, despite what, others may say or think."

The Division's troopers made sure they were paid for their services by appropriating whatever items they deemed "necessary". Everything from jeeps to canned turkeys, M7 grenade launchers to cases of ammunition were fair game and whenever offended supply officers came looking, the Angels claimed innocence and used their jungle training to hide the contraband in the brush or under their tents.

One day the base commander, Colonel Stanley Backman, decided that enough was enough and drove to GEN Swing's HQ to angrily protest the actions of the 11th Airborne's men. GEN Swing grew indignant as Backman railed his troopers and Swing growled, "Backman, God dammit, my men are angels as compared with that bunch of misfits you have in your command".

As for Swing's alleged denial that his "perfect angels" would never steal, my grandfather, 1LT Andrew Carrico of D-511, laughed and said, "It wasn't true. They stole everything they could get their hands on."

This included the Oro Bay generator which kept the docks well-lit compared to the Angels' Coleman lanterns. One night an unnamed "squad" from the 511th PIR (everyone swore secrecy) infiltrated the dock, cut the wires and trucked the generator back to camp. The next evening the 511th's area was lit up "like Times Square."

Unfortunately, about a week later the generator was moved to Division (RHIP), but eventually Oro Bay's livid COL Backman sent men to retrieve the generator from "Ali Swing and his 8,000 Thieves." This theft is quite possibly, and likely, what led to COL Backman's rant.

During the Angels' "moonlight requisition" trips, Swing's troopers used their infiltration skills to sneak into the camps of nearby Australian units and pilfer their stores. While their butter was compared to Motor Oil No. 2 (it was designed to resist melting in the tropical heat), the Angels came to appreciate the Aussies' canned

9. So, This is New Guinea

*A group of "Ali Swing's Thieves"*

goods including turkey, milk and fruit. Loaded down with their procured wares, the young troopers then walked along the road until a pre-arranged truck came by for their bartered ride back to camp.

"Stealing was a way of life," noted D-511's CPL William Walter.

"We buried our booty in our tents under the flooring so instead of a steady diet of field rations, when we were out on field problems, we had a little variety to take along," explained D-511's SGT Murray Hale.

One highly valued item for the enlisted men were .45 pistols which they had been issued until their movement from Camp Polk when the practice stopped, a decision they greatly disagreed with given the close-quarter nature of warfare with the Japanese. Called "the Foxhole Comforter" by General Swing's men, it was not uncommon for entire crates of pistols, and magazines, to go missing.

The 187th GIR's MAJ Henry Burgess noted, "It was may experience and observation that anyone shot with a ..45 caliber pistol was taken out of action at once, either dead or very severely wounded."

Similarly, motorized transportation was a problem the Angels solved their way. Since Air Corps personnel were often issued jeeps, the Angels frequented their areas and returned with their own personal transportation that could be used to visit buddies in nearby units on the island. While MPs in the surrounding units removed distributor caps to prevent theft, many Angels simply carried one in their pocket to make their acquisitions easier. It was said that by the time the 11th Airborne left New Guinea, the jungles around Dobodura resembled a parking lot of stolen Jeeps, trucks and transports, including one DUKW stolen on a lark by D-511's CPL Walter and PFC Clyde T. Johnson.

The 187th's MAJ Henry Burgess made the ultimate "confiscation" while on assignment to GHQ in Hollandia to help plan the 503rd's jump on Nooemfor. Burgess noticed a new refrigerator in a warehouse and managed to sneak it back to the 11th Airborne's area which he presented to General Swing as a gift. Swing never asked where it had come from, but probably would have smiled to know that it had belonged to MacArthur's G-2, MG Charles Willoughby who was waiting for its delivery (it never arrived).

Burgess said, perhaps with a smile, "The propensity to pick up things that were loose was a characteristic of the Division, probably more so with the 11th than any other Army unit."

However, stealing from other units was one thing, but stealing from other Angels was strictly "against the rules" as one trooper from the 457th PFAB found out. It was discovered that he had been pinching others' money so a group of avenging-Angels from the 457th roughed him up until another officer intervened. When the Battalion's CO MAJ Nick Stadtheer, the former DuPont employee, asked what happened, the troopers responded, "He fell down some stairs."

Stadtherr was well aware that there were no stairs for twenty miles, but dropped the matter when it was fully explained.

Perhaps in an attempt to calm the mischief, to the excitement of their chaplains the Division's engineers worked with local Papuans, whom the Angels called "Fuzzy Wuzzies", to build a large chapel without using a single nail. It was a feat of construction that left many troopers amazed. The Papuans then put on a special show for the Americans that included traditional dances, music and singing. Not that the Division's troopers got too close.

The Angels were regularly told to stay away from New Guinea's Two G's: gardens and girls and D-511's CPL William Walter noted, "We soldiers, for the most part, had no trouble obeying that command."

"You couldn't go near them because of the smell," 1LT Andrew Carrico of D-511 grimaced. "I don't think they ever took a bath."

9. So, This is New Guinea

*The famous Division chapel at Dobodura*

The aromas were also, in part, because some Papuans used coconut oil to make their hair strand up nearly straight. The oil itself would grow rancid and led to some of the strong smells the Angels noted.

Another odor problem the Division dealt with came from their battalion latrines which consisted of fifty feet of fuel drums stacked three high with wooden tops, a layout that 3/511's LTC Ed Lahti said "didn't encourage you to 'sit and think'…"

Another trooper disagreed: "The toilet incinerator was a great place to relieve oneself, as the view was fantastic, particularly in the morning when the sun was rising, or when it was setting in the evening… It was incongruous to see hundreds of men sitting on top of the barrels and the (local) women going by with laundry, food and other things, and frequently stopping to visit with the soldiers on the cans."

Companies took turns on "burn duty" and one day D-511's S/SGT Murray Perlman watched South Dakota's PVT Warren E. Milbrandt fill 2/511's latrines with gasoline then toss in a match. The resulting fireball burned off Warren's eyelashes and eyebrows and Murray roared with laughter.

*The Angels watch native Papauans dance*

## Haugen's March

In order to further acclimate their troopers with the nature of the terrain, especially the jungle, swamps and mountains, that they would soon be called to fight in, the Angels' units took to the surrounding hills for numerous "hikes" and maneuvers.

The 511th PIR's COL Orin "Hard Rock" Haugen ordered his 1st Battalion to assemble for a forced march in full field kits, some felt in answer to shenanigans instigated by the 1st including the regiment's famous "Snipe Hunt" known as "The Phantom of New Guinea" which spread across the Division. 1LT Eli Bernheim of HQ1-511 remembered, "We moved out with COL Haugen and LTC LaFlamme leading. lt became apparent that we were going the approximately 14 miles the beach. The road was thick with dust and the kunai grass was high on both sides. lt was like marching in a hot tunnel."

While it was generally felt that troops on New Guinea should not march more than 11 miles, the cocky Paratroopers felt they could march to the beach *and back*. Bernheim continued:

"Since we were taking the march without warning or any indication on a training schedule, no one had extra socks and many had no water in their canteens .When we got to the beach there was hot food, and the order came to take an hour for chow and rest and then march back... The trip back to the camp was the most difficult experience of my life before or since including my football days at Pitt or the marches in Leyte...I recall that I kept thinking that if Hard Rock can make this march I can."

After marching with an open leg wound from an earlier injury,

Bernheim collapsed one mile from camp. Division found out about Hard Rock's march and sent ambulances behind the column and when the exhausted troopers returned to their bivouac, GEN Swing was waiting along with a substantial crowd. Witnesses say he and Haugen swiftly departed for Division HQ; no record exists of their discussion.

## USO

On August 1, the Angels enjoyed a special treat in their 8,000-seat 127th AEB-constructed ampitheater when Jack Benny's USO show came to perform. Unfortunately, the power and microphones went out and while the 127th's engineers rushed to solve the problem, Benny's musical talent and sharp wit had the troopers grinning.

Later performances by singer and actress Martha Tilton, Larry Adler and his famous harmonica and singer LT "Lanny" Patrick Ross brought raucous applause before musician Gerardo Luigi "Jerry" Colonna and his troop of "beautiful girls" got the Angels' attention more than the engineers who had the generators working again.

And just in time, too, as Silver Screen-bombshell Carole Landis brought the men to their feet as she jitterbugged with some of their own and kissed each participant on stage. Everyone was jealous of Division band member PFC Joseph "Joe" Sartori who was selected to carry Mrs. Landis across the stage.

Benny, Adler and Ross went up with a stick of 511th PIR Paratroopers to watch them jump, further cementing their place in

*The Angels with Jack Benny, Martha Tilton, Carole Landis & Co.*

the Division's hearts. Sadly, the USO strictly forbade the entertainers from jumping with the Angels.

The Division spent August and September training for amphibious landings on mockups before heading to Oro Bay for actual landings in 4th Engineer ships. Amphibious landings soon rivaled practice jumps in frequency and the 11th Airborne's troopers wondered which they would see more of in the future.

Some in the Division worried there may not be any future campaigns. After training for nineteen months, morale was dropping as the Angels wondered if The Big Show would end before they could "jump into the fight." They had all listened to radio broadcasts and reports of the D-Day landings in June and things in the Pacific Theater seemed to be moving along as well.

Feeling that time was running out, CPT Stephen Cavanaugh of D-511 noted, "We became like wild horses: over trained and eager to get into the fight."

Through September, the Division's artillery batteries practiced live fire drills while the 11th Airborne's Paratroopers held numerous training jumps near Buna Bay. The 457th PFAB's CPT John Conable noted, "The artillery did more firing than we had done in the States probably because more ammunition was available."

A few weeks later GEN Swing ordered a Division review in September. There was no denying that his Angels looked sharp and it is sad that Swing's feelings at the time are lost to history.

## Heading to War…Maybe

Relief to their anxious waiting finally came in late September when Swing announced that the 11th Airborne would begin preparing for departure, their fourth major divisional move.

After repeatedly being warned that missing embarkation was a court martial offense, the Angels spent October cleaning and storing weapons, packing equipment and stockpiling rations including their "liberated" wares and weapons. This, of course, kept the Division's 711th Ordnance men extra busy.

In early November the 11th Airborne was trucked to Oro Bay where they stacked their footlockers in a Port Command complex. Months later, the footlockers would be delivered to their camp on Leyte

9. So, This is New Guinea

*Division review on Dobodura's steel-plank runway - September 1944*

where the Angels angrily discovered they had been broken into and anything of value (rings, watches, booze, etc.) had been stolen. After such violations, GEN Swing's men were ready to "Open a Second Front" and sail back to New Guinea to battle the Port Command troops (likely from the 491st Port Battalion who perhaps saw it as payback for the Angels stealing their generator and supplies).

On November 6, 1944, the Angels began assembling by the Oro Bay pier to board one of nine APA (troop) and AKA (cargo) attack vessels armed with 5-inch guns and anti-aircraft weapons. Some remembered boarding right from the pier while others had to board DUKWs for short trips out into the bay. HQ-11's CPL James Vignola remembered, "From the shore to the ship the Ducks were in a line and each Duck (DUKW) would approach the big ship and latch on to it somehow and the soldiers would then climb the rope ladder and board the ship. This was with a full pack, helmet and rifle."

While the 511th PIR waited their turn, GEN Swing drove to the dock in his personal Jeep and the Paratroopers grinned when the Navy personnel refused to raise the vehicle onto the deck. To Swing's dismay, the Jeep stayed on the dock when the convoy departed.

The Division enjoyed their twelve-day "cruise" much more than their voyages across the Pacific. For one thing, they had Navy destroyers riding escort, something that had not occured on their voyages from San Fransico to Dobodura.

The Angels also appreciated the Navy's hearty steak, pork chops and frankfurters, sheer delicacies after five months of New Guinea rations. GEN Swing told the Navy personnel that he purposefully shrank his men's stomachs to prepare them for jungle combat, a fact that did little to endear Jumping Joe to some in the ranks, but one can see the wisdom in his efforts given what lay ahead.

Swing wanted the ships' galleys to continue feeding his troopers dehydrated and canned food, but most of the Navy captains said the troops they carried would eat as well as their own crews. I have even heard that one ship's captain who dumped stores of Division-delivered mutton over the side because he believed the Angels should eat better while onboard (plus, the captain disliked mutton).

The 187th GIR's RHQ and the 1st Battalion enjoyed similar treatment onboard the APA *Calabria* while 2/187's troopers sailed on the USS *Calvert* (APA-32). When the *Calvert*'s skipper, CPT John F. Warris looked over the 187th's troopers, he remarked to his officers that the fit glidermen were the leannest troops he had ever seen. "They look downright skinny," he said. "Give, 'em all the chow they want; they'll need it." The 187th's men happily cheered the Navy and enjoyed their food. PFC Clifton Evans of RHQ-187 would soon write home, "It was a pretty nice trip - very good food, fair living quarters, etc.... The trip was pretty nice at least as well as could be expected. The food aboard was excellent. Steaks, pie, cake, ice cream, and all such dishes I haven't tasted in a long time.

The 127th Airboen Engineers said similar things about their own voyage onboard the USS *Monrovia* (APA-31), that their time onboard was spent much as it was on their voyages across the Pacific to New Guinea. By now the Angels had developed close friendships and the card games and discussions went long into the night. Others read while some wrote more letters home.

The tension on this voyage was different, however. This time they were moving to the front itself and one very large step closer to combat.

HQ3-511's PFC George Doherty noted, "I think we all were in a state of shock when we woke up to the real world we found ourselves on an attack transport in a ten ship flotilla headed for Leyte Island…"

## Secret Meeting

We should note, however, that the Angels believed they were sailing north to Leyte, not to fight, but rather to stage there on their way to participate in the invasion of Luzon where they would first see combat.

9. So, This is New Guinea

*A group of Angels in their final days at Dobdoura*

Even so, late one night while sailing to Leyte, the 511th PIR's regimental surgeon MAJ Wallace L. Chambers of Pickens, Mississippi, gathered his medics on deck for a meeting. Knowing what he did about the enemy they would soon face, and how the Japanese tended to fire on those wearing anything with a red cross on it, Doc Chambers quietly issued the medics personal sidearms (likely stolen by other Paratroopers at Dobodura) then collected their red cross armbands and threw them overboard.

## Leyte Harbor

After sailing 2,100 miles, the 11th Airborne's transports entered Leyte Harbor on November 18, 1944. While the views were breathtaking, the Angels were told they needed to unload quickly. Japanese submarines still operated in the area and the anchored convoy made for attractive targets. In addition, as they had been repeatedly told during their voyages to Leyte, enemy aircraft were flying sorties offshore, including the new dreaded kamikazes.

As if to emphasize the danger, the 11th Airborne's troopers heard the distant sounds of incoming planes fill the air.

# New Guinea to Leyte
## November 11-18, 1944

**AIRBORNE 11**

PHILIPPINES
Leyte

NEW GUINEA
Dobodura

# 10: King II Operation

Bito Beach, Dulag & Burauen, Leyte – November 1944

*"Japan 'will defend the Philippines until the last' and will fight on to final victory 'even though Tokyo should be reduced to ashes.'"*
-General Iwano Matsui, February 1945

The young Angels anxiously scanned the skies for danger and HQ2-511's PFC Deanne E. Marks of St. Paul, Minnesota remembered:

> "Six or seven 'Betty' Mitsubishi medium bombers tore into the convoy. The Navy fired its 40mm and other 'Ack Ack.' There was shooting all over the place with nothing getting hit. Soon some P-38s and P-47s came to the rescue, like the cavalry, and shot three down. Our fighters would bore into a bomber and soon you would see a wisp of smoke, then an orange-red blob of flame would envelop the whole plane. Then off towards the horizon, we could see the bomber splash into the sea."

HQ-11's CPL James Vignola recalled the action, saying, "One of the P 38's got behind the Zero and fired at it, then that P-38 peeled off and the other P-38 got behind the Zero and that was all she wrote."

After the aerial battle subsided, the Angels were told to continue disembarking. The Japanese had attacked the rear of their convoy and those in the earlier transports proceeded across Bito Beach's narrow strip (about one hundred yards across) to unit areas that had been marked by the division's G-1 LTC James W. Smyly and G-4 LTC Glen A. Ross only days before the main body arrived.

Located in the Visayan islands' eastern region of the Philippine archipelago, Leyte is roughly 110 miles long and 40 miles wide. Liberating the island was deemed critical, at least by GEN Douglas MacArthur who believed that in the Pacific, "The Philippine theater of operations is the locus of victory or defeat" and wanted to use Leyte as the jumping off point for his invasion of Luzon.

While ADM Chester Nimitz, commander of the Central Pacific forces, disagreed, President Roosevelt sided with MacArthur (some believe the two made a political side deal) who contended that America had a strategic and moral obligation to liberate the Philippines.

After the President dismissed everyone else in the room, MacArthur said that he said, "Mr. President, the country has forgiven you for what took place on Bataan. You hope to be reelected President of the United States--but the nation will never forgive you if you approve a plan which leaves 18 million Christian American citizens to wither in the Philippines under the conqueror's hell, until the peace treaty frees them. You might do it tactically and strategically, but politically it would ruin you and now Mr. President my duties back at my headquarters are calling me and if you will permit me shall withdraw."

According to MacArthur, the President then said, "Come back here Douglas. Douglas, you have nothing to worry about."

MacArthur told GEN Robert Eichelberger during a conversation on October 19, 1945 that he had received a letter from Robert McCormick, Majority Democratic Leader of the House which said:

"I have talked to the President (FDR) often about you (MacArthur) and he always speaks about you with the highest admiration. After he came back from Honolulu he said, 'I had not intended to invade the Phillipines and (MacArthur) is solely responsible for the fact that we went in there and deserves the credit'."

Allied operations for Leyte began in early October of 1944 with air attacks on nearby islands to reduce Japan's air power. Then on October 20, VADM Thomas S. Kinkaid's Seventh Fleet entered Leyte Gulf to support GEN Walter C. Krueger's "Cyclone" Landing Force that would become the Leyte Assault Force.

Krueger's men had been fighting inland ever since and when the 11th Airborne arrived one month later on November 18 (D-Day), the Angels fell under Krueger's Sixth Army command.

## Beachfront Property

With the skies now clear of enemy craft, the Angels continued landing along a 6,000-yard stretch of Bito Beach between Abuyog and Tarragona, forty miles south of Tacloban. Just inland sat a coconut grove about one-hundred and fifty yards deep and behind that an impassable swamp.

Surveying the beach, the 11th Airborne's troopers wondered who selected this terrible location to come ashore. Actually, the decision was made by Assistant Division Commander BG Albert Pierson who noted, "GEN Swing sent me to Leyte ahead of the division to make arrangements for the arrival of the division. My advance party consisted of LTC McGowan (G-1), MAJ (Bill) Crawford (G-4), MAJ John Atwood Signal Officer and my driver CPL John Archbold."

GEN Pierson and his party were shown two potential landing sites by Sixth Army's BG Samuel Sturgis. Pierson wrote, "Both camp sites... were far from ideal. One was on Bito Beach and the other was inland. My selection of Bito Beach proved to be the better choice."

The Division quickly established a perimeter around Bito Beach and began the two-day unloading operation. Forming long lines in the 100° F heat, the work details passed rations, ammunition and supplies from ship to shore. Many of the sweating Angels on the ships took to tossing boxes and cans overboard and letting the tide take them to their comrades standing in the surf.

CPL Edward Hammrich of the HQ-188th GIR remembered, "The weather was fine when we landed, but the next day the monsoon rains began. We thought the island was going to wash away. This weather continued as we moved inland to destroy, as we later found out, all Japanese control of the central mountains."

Those not unloading set up camp and soon pyramidal tents replaced pup tents, followed by thatch-roofed mess halls. Engineers from the 127th AEB also helped the Parachute Maintenance Company's 116 riggers build 15 ad hoc rigging/drying sheds for the Division's rain-

*Leyte's monsoon season drowning tents*

soaked chutes in anticipation of future jumps.

The Angels finished offloading their APAs around 1800 and those on the beach watched the ships steam away in the deepening darkness before the AKAs moved in. The last crate was unloaded on the November 23rd (D+5), but the rapid pace of the whole operation left the Angels with a problem, highlighted by several air raid warnings (three bursts from anti-aircraft guns) that sent men diving into whatever hole they could find. The ever-growing piles of supplies, vehicles, drums and ammunition on the beach were tempting targets for Japanese planes, so the troopers were told to form more lines and move the caches deeper into the coconut grove.

One 187th GIR historian noted, "Some felt uneasy for Bito Beach was one big ammunition dump and no one was working more than a few hundred yards from piles of 155mm projectiles, 81 mortars shells and other explosives."

HQ-11's CPL James Vignola remembered, "After we were ashore, there was a company formation on the beach and I kept thinking a Japanese plane or planes could fly over us and strafe our whole outfit. Fortunately that did not happen and we advanced inland."

Even so, everyone knew the inland grove would not suffice and they got a nightly reminder from "Maytag Charlie" or "Washing Machine Charlie" whose out of sync engines forced anti-aircraft crews to sound the alarm. GEN Swing's frustrated troopers found their sleep constantly disturbed by this annoying irritation as the 127th Engineers under LTC Douglas C. Davis began working on a causeway across the swamps to their front so the division could move inland.

Unfortunately, the quagmire swallowed their work as quickly as they piled it on, evoking colorful responses from the engineers. Things only got worse when a lucky Japanese bomber hit the causeway, destroying the fruits of the engineers' labors. As such, a nearby amphibious tractor battalion sent several of Donald Roebling's LVT-1 "Alligator" tank creations to ferry Angels across the two rivers that boxed the division in on the north and south.

Then, on November 22 (D+4), the 127th Engineers' labors paid off and "US Highway 1", a thin dirt path, allowed the 11th Airborne's 2 ½-ton trucks to begin moving Paratroopers from the 511th PIR out of the area. The timing was fortuitous, as that morning the 11th Airborne received Field Order Number 28 from GEN John R. Hodge, commander of XXIV Corps, which read: *"The 11<sup>th</sup> Airborne Division will relieve the 7<sup>th</sup> Infantry Division along the line Burauen-La Paz-Bugho and destroy all the Japs in that sector."*

The day the Angels had long awaited had arrived: they were headed to "The Front", or at least towards it and they might even meet the enemy along the way. Again, the Angels were originally *not* slotted to participate in the Leyte campaign as the island was to be a simple stopping point on their way to fight on Luzon. As evidence of this, back on October 12 General Swing received orders to move his division to Leyte "administratively", i.e. not combat loaded.

Upon his earlier arrival to the island, the 11th Airborne's BG Albert Pierson went to GEN Krueger's HQ and met with GEN George H. Decker, Krueger's Chief of Staff, and GEN Clyde D. Eddleman, his G–3. Pierson, probably at Swing's urging, was pushing for more, but the news was disappointing. Pierson noted, "There was nothing that they could tell me at that time for any mission (for the 11th Airborne)."

The truth is that GEN Krueger had received a negative report from an inspection team that while on New Guinea the 11th Airborne had focused more on the *airborne* phase during his inspection team's visit than on combat readiness. In an effort to correct their incorrect assumptions, the 11th Airborne's BG Pierson had reported to GEN Krueger at Sixthy Army HQ.

Pierson explained, "I assured (Krueger) that the division *was* an infantry division and was combat ready, also telling him that the division had only seven infantry battalions rather than the nine that the other divisions had and added that we had no armor or the artillery complement that other divisions had. I'm sure the division proved itself to him to be combat ready when we were engaged in the Leyte operation."

Krueger considered Pierson's words, but ultimately the decision was made by GEN MacArthur who asked GEN Swing if the 11th Airborne could handle taking over the 7th Infantry Division's positions since the 7th was twice the size of the 11th and MacArthur wanted to bring the 7th to Leyte's western sectors. Swing replied, "Sure, of course we could." Swing labored to convince MacArthur, and therefore Krueger, that the 11th Airborne was indeed ready to join in the Leyte campaign and with the evolving situation on Leyte at this time, the generals involved decided that the 11th was needed.

As a XXIV Corps operations report notes, "The appearance of substantial hostile reinforcements on the west coast caused a shift in the Sixth Army's weight toward the north to meet the threat against its right flank...

As a result, as one 11th Airborne Division historian wrote, "The Angels were about to make fighting history."

## The Front

There were, of course, thoughts of home and loved ones left behind. No one knew how soon the Division would be committed to combat, but one thing was for certain: some of the faces that were unloading suppplies and setting up tents with would never see home again. Even with these thoughts on their minds, the young Angels were anxious for the chance to unleash Hell on their country's enemies.

On Leyte, those enemies would come in the form of Japan's Field Marshal (*Gensui*) Count (*hakushaku*) Hisaichi Terauchi's 265,000-strong Southern Expeditionary Army Group. On Leyte, Terauchi stationed the 16th Division along the San Juanico Straight, under GEN Shiro Makino, and several service and air units, plus elements of the naval 36th Guard Unit at Ormoc and Tacloban. GEN Makino's *Kaki Heidan*, or "Wall Division", had a reputation as the most proficient fighting unit within Japan's 35th Army. The 16th had fought in China and was implicated in the Rape of Nanking, before returning home then transferring to Manchukuo before invading Luzon in late 1941. In August of 1944 the 16th was ordered to Leyte to shore up the island's defenses which only gave GEN Makino two months to prepare his forces before GEN Krueger's Cyclone Landing Force invaded. It was not enough.

When the Battle of Leyte ended, and the bloodied 11th Airborne came down from Leyte's mountains on December 31, 1944, only an estimated 620 men of GEN Makino's 16th Division remained.

Hindsight reveals that American intelligence underestimated enemy strength on Leyte at 26,000. General Tomoyki Yamashita, commander of Japan's Fourteenth Army, was charged with the defense of the Philippines and while he had planned to make his stand on Luzon, Yamashita's superior GEN Hisaichi Teruchi, commander of Japan's entire Southern Expeditionary Army Group, ordered him to "muster all possible strength to destroy the enemy on Leyte."

## 10. King II Operation - Leyte

Although he disagreed with the strategy, Yamashita obeyed and nearly 50,000 troops were sent towards Ormoc on Leyte, though many of their transports were destroyed en route. The surviving 34,000 would reinforce Japan's 16th Division with elements taken from the 1st, 26th and 112th Divisions, plus other supporting units. Reinforcements from Mindano, Cebu and other islands would bring Japan's strength on Leyte to over 50,0000 troops.

After a hair-raising recon flight in an L-5 Sentinel, GEN Swing's twenty-seven-year-old G-2 LTC Henry "Butch" Muller reported he had observed the reinforcing Japanese transports in Ormoc Bay and with the enemy being pressed on three sides, the 11th Airborne was needed to push them back by securing the Ormoc corridor.

As such, after receiving GEN Hodge's field order on November 22, the Angels took half a day to look over their maps to study terrain and the current positioning of the 7th Infantry units they would be replacing, as well as the air installations they were ordered to protect.

Known as "The Bayonet" or "Hourglass Division", after 7th Infantry's initial Dulag landings on October 20, or "A-Day", the division fought their way inland to capture San Pablo and Dagami. On A-Day itself, 948 days after his ordered departure from Corrigedor, GEN Douglas MacArthur waded to shore where he announced:

"People of the Philippines, I have returned! By the grace of Almighty God, our forces stand again on Philippine soil - soil consecrated in the blood of our two peoples. We have come, dedicated and committed, to the task of destroying every vestige of enemy control over your daily lives, and of restoring, upon a foundation of indestructible, strength, the liberties of your people."

GEN Swing decided that the 11th Airborne's move inland and up into the heights would be spearheaded by the young Paratroopers of COL Orin "Hard Rock" Haugen's 511th PIR. Before leaving Bito Beach, Haugen's Angels stacked their duffel bags on the sand and laid down to watch the Battle of Leyte Gulf still raging offshore. The 511th watched the Navy fend off attacks from Japanese Zeros on the water when suddenly two Japanese bombers roared overhead and the Paratroopers scrambled for cover as bombs exploded nearby. The Angels then cheered an American P-38 who raced in to dispatch the offending enemy who made a fiery crash into the ocean. The victorious pilot then buzzed the beach and gave the Paratroopers a wave before disappearing over the tree line.

The Division would soon head into that same interior, during Leyte's monsoon season no less, and as the 511th's Paratroopers looked towards the dark mountains with their 4,400-foot peaks, they worried about the volcanic outcroppings, ravines, and caves which would provide the enemy plenty of cover and defensive positions. They had trekked through similar terrain during their months on New Guinea and remembered the stories that their Australian neighbors had told them of combat with the Japanese.

RHQ-511's 2LT William Abernathy noted, "The mountains are one ridge after another, heavily wooded, muddy, and with streams in between."

While early propaganda the Angels had read, heard and watched portrayed the average Japanese soldier as near-sighted, weak and cowardly, the Allies had been fighting in the Pacific long enough to prove that reality was a different story. While they had their weaknesses, the enemy repeatedly demonstrated a superb ability to construct fortifications and emplacements in such environments that had already cost tens of thousands of Allied lives to take.

While they cleaned and prepared their personal equipment, ate rations or smoked cigarettes, the 511th's Paratroopers joked at times and tried not to betray the butterflies in their stomachs. They would be the first in the Division to find the enemy and looking over the men around them, countless Angels silently wondered how many of their comrades they would have to bury before the war ended, or if they themselves would be called upon to make the ultimate sacrifice.

## Cold Turkey

At 0700 the following morning (Thursday, November 23, D+5), Hard Rock's Paratroopers ate a Thanksgiving breakfast of cold turkey, fruit salad and powdered potatoes as a dreary rain soaked their mess kits (those who did not eat fast enough ended up with "soup").

The 511th PIR then sailed for Dulag on 120-foot Landing Craft Tanks (LCT) and along the way, the Angels watched a P-38 dogfighting above them with a Japanese Zero which soon trailed smoke. The Paratroopers cheered like it was a boxing match, but their excitement turned to dread when the enemy aimed his damaged craft towards the ship carrying elements of 3/511. They had heard stories of the enemy's new *kamikazes* and this pilot seemed intent on taking one of the Angels' transports down with him.

## 10. King II Operation - Leyte

At the last minute the Zero banked into a cargo ship and the subdued Paratroopers quietly watched flames crawl up the side of the vessel, sobered by how close they had come to burning themselves.

At Dulag the 511th disembarked and loaded onto 6x6 trucks which shuttled them ten miles inland to Burauen. It was slow going since most roads were muddy mires and several trucks got stuck, but by November 28 (D+10), the 11th Airborne had completed its relief of 7th Infantry. GEN Swing's HQ soon took over the 7th's Command Post at San Pablo and the 11th Airborne Division Band was trained to drive DUKWs to ferry their supply caches up from Bito Beach.

The Angels' field artillery set up outside of San Pablo and staged their liaison planes a quarter mile away on the partially-flooooded airstrip while LTC Arthur H. Wilson's 2/187 GIR remained on guard at Bito Beach. The 188th GIR deployed to protect the 511th's southern flank while COL Haugen's Paratroopers passed their time at Burauen doing little more than occupying their new positions along the Daguitan River's mud flats and watching Filipino women wash their laundry.

"At this point it was sort of a phony war," said HQ2-511's PFC Deane Marks. "We sat around all day shooting the breeze, eating our C-Rations and improving our fox holes for better sleeping."

Marks added that there were "Lots of Filipinos wandering around telling tall tales of their fierce resistance during the Jap occupation, most of which was bull shit. Everyone was a guerilla now that the U.S. Army was back. No doubt there *were* many guerillas but I suspect they kept a low profile."

The 511's Regimental S-2 CPT Lyman Faulkner noted, "We had no information on what the guerilla problem was (on Leyte) other than the normal turf battle by those who had (or had not) been effective against the Japanese."

The Filipinos brought the Angels parrots, coconuts and bananas and offered to do odd jobs in exchange for clothing, especially t-shirts.

The Angels' tedium would not last. With the Japanese landing troops at Ormoc on Leyte's west coast the Americans had a decision to make. Would the Angels wait for the Japanese to come over the mountains to them in their newly occupied Burauen positions, or would the 11th Airborne take the fight to the enemy in the mountains and press towards Ormoc? GEN Swing, never one to wait around, asked for permission from XXIV Corps' GEN John R. Hodges to do more than just clear their assigned area. Swing wanted to *attack*.

In reality, Hodges *wanted* the Angels to do what no other Allied unit was in a position or had been able to do. America's 24th and 1st Cavalry Divisions were pushing south from Carigara Bay while the 96th Division was pressing west from Dagami but had become mired down in the mountains. With 7th Infantry moving southwest on the Abuyog-Baybay Road to join the 77th Infantry Division, the enemy had moved up into the hills and someone would have to head west over the mountains to break the enemy's main supply and reinforcement route, the Ormoc-Burauen trail.

LTG Walter Krueger's three-prong press was stalled, and he and Hodges hoped GEN Swing's division could break the stalemate by effecting a "pincer" movement to crush the enemy's 26th Division with the 7th Division attacking north from Damulaan on December 5.

As a November 20, 1944 Time Magazine article explained:

> "The US drive on land slowed down to a walk after it had overrun over 50 percent of the northern half of LEYTE. ORMOC, the key western port where the Japs landed and deployed in a 1-mile semi-circle, could be approached only from the north or south unless US troops attempted to come over the mountains between DAGAMI and JARO, a long difficult pass."

The 11th Airborne would attempt that long difficult pass. The Angels would then have to block all avenues from the mountains into Leyte Valley plus guard the exits into the western coastal corridor, a tall order for GEN Swing's understrength airborne division of just 8,321 men, roughly half the size of a standard infantry division.

GENs Hodge, Krueger and Swing were well aware that the 11th Airborne's streamlined TO&E left the Angels without armor support and seriously lacking in mechanized transports, but this worked in Swing's favor when convincing the leadership to let his Division push west. His men were fresh, he argued, and accustomed to moving on their feet with limited support. Plus, they were physically fit enough to make the trek over the mountains, a journey through terrain that was known to ruin other units in a short amount of time.

As one Angel wrote years later, "Only troops who had been conditioned the airborne way could live and fight over that weird, virtually impassible, terrain."

Given a Zone of Operation over 600 square miles in size, General Joe was also forced to forgo the normal "two up front, one in reserve" battlefield formation because the Angels had no reserves. Adapting to the situation, the 11th Airborne planned their Leyte operations with leap-frog approaches with the 511th PIR's 1st Battalion ordered towards Ananong then Lubi while 3/511 was to head towards Takin, Patog and Manawarat. 2/511, or "Gumbo White", was tasked with clearing and holding the Burauen Heights to the east, which allowed the Division to defend the air installations around Burauen, including LTG Ennis C Whitehead's 5th Air Force HQ.

From their current positions in muddy foxholes outside Burauen, the 511th PIR's 1st and 3rd Battalions studied the mountain pass they would soon have to enter. Waiting for them "up there" was more rain, mud, slippery hillsides, root-tangled paths, sharp cliff sides, jagged rock faces, and deep ravines full of the enemy that the Paratroopers would have to clear, one bloody engagement at a time as they moved towards the Lobi mountains.

And COL Haugen's boys would have to hurry, too, since GEN Walter Kruger wanted all of Sixth Army in position to attack on December 7. This year it would be the Japanese on Leyte who felt the full force of a "surprise" military assault.

## Into the Green Hell

The 511th PIR's companies distributed nine K-Ration boxes to last three days and ball ammunition which reminded the Angels that the next time they fired their rifles it would be at the enemy, who would undoubtedly be firing back. Riflemen carried 160 rounds (eight M1 en bloc clips, plus two bandoliers with six clips each) and two grenades. For machine gun crews who carried their thirty-pound weapon plus four (or more) cans of 250 rounds, and the mortar squads with their heavy baseplates and "stovepipes", Leyte's mountains and valleys would be prove to be an exhausting ordeal. So much so that the heavy mortars were later airdropped onto Manawarat to avoid the nigh-impossible task of hiking them in.

In their musette bags the Angels packed six or seven pairs of socks, a few handkerchiefs, extra shorts and underwear, a spare pair of fatigues and whatever assorted personal items they chose to carry. After throwing out their gas masks, the troopers stuffed the empty cases full, but as many veterans know, you start heavy in your first campaign and end up lightening the load to the essentials.

Before moving out many of the 511th's Paratroopers did just that and took stock of their overweight loads and made final decisions on what to carry. 3rd Platoon's runner PFC Everette M. Hagemeyer of D-511 pulled items from his pack and called them out as he heaved them away with the final item raising several eyebrows.

"Goodbye, Good Book!" he cried before gingerly setting his Bible on the ground. Regimental Chaplain CPT Lee "Chappie" Walker made sure to remind the boys that God would go with them, even if their Bibles did not. Chappie also made sure to take his own Bible as well as a .32, a .38 and a .45, leading him to be, to paraphrase several Paratroopers, "The most heavily armed chaplain in the Pacific".

With monsoon rains and winds dampening their uniforms, NCOs barked orders to "Get on your feet" and the the 511th's 1st and 3rd Battalions formed up to face the cloud-covered mountains. The fight for those heights would be bloody as GEN Tomoyuki Yamashita, who so skillfully defeated Britain's troops on Malaya, had been ordered to stop the Allies at all costs. Again, "The Tiger of Malaya" favored a defensive strategy on *Luzon*, but Imperial General HQ wanted the Allies' halted on *Leyte* so Yamashita obediently did what he could.

Officers watched rain ping off the steel helmets of their men whose nervous but ready eyes looked back into their own. Loads were shifted and weapons checked and rechecked and NCOs hovered like mother hens to square everyone away.

The order to move out was given and the rain-soaked Angels shouldered their rifles and wet packs. The emotions of young, first-time warriors quietly crept into the Paratroopers' thoughts: *Will we succeed? Will I be brave? What if I'm wounded? What if I die?*

It is easy to forget that most of these Angels were barely out of high school and that the war had taken them farther from home than they had ever been before. Some would never travel this far again in their lifetimes. Nearly 500 would never see home again.

# 11: Leyte Mountains

Burauen, Mahonag, Ormoc – November-December 31, 1944

*"The awful, bloody battles fought on Leyte were regarded by the officers and men as the toughest of all the Division's fights. Troopers who later waged bloody battles for Nichols Field and Fort McKinley, and who used bayonets to assault hill positions and rock caves on Luzon, claim that Leyte was the worst."*
—1$^{st}$ Lieutenant Andrew Carrico III, D-511

Not long after the 511th started into Leyte's thick interior one thing became quickly and abundantly clear: the 11th Airborne's "comics" maps of Leyte's interior were worthless.

"After a few miles we ran out of roads, which were reduced to trails," remembered D-511's CPL Murray Hale of 2/511's move to the Burauen Heights. Hale's company commander CPT Stephen Cavanaugh noted, "The area had never been fully mapped, and therefore we simply followed jungle trails leading up into the mountain and nowhere."

A XXIV Corps operations report stated it fairly clearly: "Lack of air reconnaissance and photography during most of the operation reduced available information of this type below the desirable minimum."

The few records the Angels possessed (mostly stolen enemy maps) indicated that while there were no roads as CPL Hale mentions, there *were* three serviceable trails that left Burauen and rejoined again at Lubi, the last stop before the Angels entered the mountains.

"The journey defies description," noted a division history of those initials climbs. "Sucking mud, jungle vines and verticle inclines exhausted the men before they had marched an hour."

RHQ-511's PFC John Kuntz explained, "Leyte is a mountainous, swampy, hot, wet, cold, and dry place, with one peculiar feature that I remember very, very well -- all the mountains go up. There is not a single downslope in the entire place. I am prepared to take an oath to that effect."

D-511's PFC Elmer Hudson remembered with some humor, "We had a Philippine guide with us. We asked him, 'How far to Ormoc?' He always replied. 'Just one more mountain.'" (the Division found limited help in the way of Filipino guides and supply carriers from the local 3rd Battalion, 95th Regiment).

Unfortunately, the 11th Airborne's Paratroopers found that there was "always another mountain" and that seemingly *every* mountain barrio was named "Takin" and towns marked on their Northern Leyte maps were really in the south and vice versa. With rain falling and mud sucking at their jump boots, the "cloaked and soaked" Angels questioned Intelligence's limited intelligence.

It was not the fault of the Angels' G-2 section, and G-2 MAJ Henry Muller himself questioned both the local Filipinos' guidance and the captured enemy maps. *Everyone* soon agreed with the notes on those maps, however, that marked trails as "good for foot troops only - no vehicles". To put the matter to bed, Muller sent out the division's Provisional Reconnaissance Platoon, or "Ghost Unit".

The Recon men discovered that all three trails on their maps converged at the *real* Takin, then separated again before finally meeting at Lubi. It was a time-wasting unknown that came to light after 1/511 set off on the North Trail and 3/511 on the Southern with the goal of meeting "by guess and by God" at Mahonag, codenamed "Pinehurst" (2/511 would later take the Middle Trail).

The Recon Platoon's "Provisional" sobriquet illustrates its "temporary" origin, although it began back at Camp Mackall. MAJ Henry Muller noted that, "The Recon Platoon was not to be a unit. After a good deal of selling General Swing let me form it as a provisional unit with the fillers being taken from TO&E slots in the regiments and battalions... All men were volunteers and carefully selected."

"We were mostly college men," noted recon-man PVT Martin L. Squires. "Outdoorsmen, crazy as hell and intensely devoted to our leaders.... Most of us were westerners and ... (many) of us had handled firearms for years before going to the service. Each one of the Recon was a buddy and the bond between us was such that we all looked out for one another."

General Swing approved the group with the understanding that it could scout terrain and monitor troop movements. The unofficially official unit's members were still listed on their units' rosters but were attached to Division HQ under the command of LT James Polka who reported directly to MAJ Muller. Originally over 300 Angels volunteered for the special platoon from which LT Polka selected the top 35 while at Camp Mackall. The best of the *very* best.

LT Polka wrote, "I had very definite ideas about training and instruction and tried very hard to maintain a high level of interest. Our subjects related to the type of missions of recon unit, stressing communications, survival, etc."

When Swing said "no" to a proposed yellow parachute patch for the platoon's overseas caps, MAJ Muller let his men wear a brass tack in one heel of their boot to identify themselves as Recon.

"This became a source of pride," Butch remembered, "and they shined the tacks as the rest of us shined our parachute wings... The Recon Platoon did a good job and confirmed the fact that the primitive paths were the only routes through the hills."

Unfortunately, LT Polka's time with Recon would only last through Leyte. According to platoon-member PFC Martin Squires, "Polka... made the cardinal mistake of trying to tell GEN Swing that due to the effects of the repeated series of long patrols that the men in the platoon were not in condition to immediately head back up into the mountains, but that we needed a day or so of rest, first. Swing said 'No!' Polka went to the Medics—then back to the 187th."

## Strength From Above

The following morning, November 25 (D+7), a misty fog darkened the sky and the 511th moved with greater caution as their scouts' imaginations ran wild with ears straining for signs of the Japanese. In time, after much blood had been spilt, they would learn to smell the enemy's rotting leather, filthy uniforms and bowel movements long before they could be seen in the jungle's growth, and as many Angels told me, it was hard to see the enemy in the thick undergrowth.

D-511's 1LT Andrew Carrico remembered, "Our westward march across steep hills covered with thick, wet jungle growth was painfully slow. The Japs were everywhere in the bushes."

The 187th GIR's PFC Eli Bernheim noted of their movement across Leyte's "waistline":

"It was a nightmare of climbing, straight up the sides of sheer cliffs, cutting foot-holds as we went, pulling ourselves up by the vines along the trail. Foot by foot we scaled the greasy heights and a slip would have plunged one to his death on the rocks below. Reaching the crests, we'd catch our breath, then slip and slide down the other face of the height only to be met with the necessity of crossing a raging mountain river in the canyon below. Sometimes the trails would wind a few hundred yards along the river beds, then veer sharply upward across another slippery ridge. Then there'd be another rampaging river to cross."

"The trails were slippery from the monsoon rains," D-511's company commander CPT Stephen Cavanaugh added, "and the heavy jungle slowed our movement to a crawl. (Ours) …was a fanatical enemy! It was a dog-eat-dog, no front, no rear battle."

Unlike the European Theater, as the Angels would soon discover, the Pacific's battlefields regularly lacked clearly defined front lines. Over the next few weeks, the Angels would become accustomed to looking for signs of the enemy both in front and behind them, not to mention in the trees above or even the ground beneath their feet.

Slipping along a muddy trail, 2/511's straining ears caught the unexpected whine of a plane coming down and it was *close*. The Angels dove into the brush and tried to get lower to the wet earth as the craft thundered into the ground nearby. Slowly rising to their feet, the astonished Paratroopers of D-511 inspected the impact crater and while the wreck did not burn, it was so mangled they could not tell its model, nor which flag it flew. As there was no body, they assumed the pilot ran out of fuel and had bailed out.

## Sleepless Nights

Moving on, 2/511 reached the Burauen Heights before nightfall on November 25 (D+7) and slept in a deserted village, complete with thatched nipa palm leaf roofs, a luxury the Angels would soon come to appreciate as nighttime in the jungle became one of their worst foes. The darkness came to wear on the Paratroopers' nerves as they strained for any indication that the enemy was "out there."

"At night it was still," D-511's PFC Billy Pettit remembered of the jungle. "You could hear things a half mile away. We all wondered how long the war was going to last so we could go home."

HQ2-511's PFC Deane Marks explained:

## 11. Leyte Mountains

"You couldn't see five feet in front of you and your imagination would run rampant. You would visualize a Nip right out in front of you, getting ready to lob a grenade at you... Sitting in your foxhole at night and waiting to see if they would try to slip through was something else. You just were full of anxieties and had the feeling that a particular Nip was out to get you."

The Angels soon learned to eat before sundown and dig their two- or three-man foxholes after sunset so the enemy could not observe their dispositions. After using targeting stakes and communication wire to hang ponchos overhead, the troopers took two-hour shifts and placed knives, bayonets and grenades with loosened pins nearby due to the enemy's penchant for infiltrations, or *Yugeki* tactics.

G-511's PFC Edward J. Baumgarten recalled, "One night a buddy woke me and whispered, 'T-t-there's a J-J-Jap out there and he's too close to shoot.' I whispered back, 'They're never too close to shoot.' So, he fired. The next morning, sure enough, about twenty feet away was the dead Jap."

Adding in the plagues of Leyte's abundant bugs that crawled into their uniforms all night, it's easy to see why sleep became a lost friend. A-511's PFC Jerry Davis wrote, "The leaves of the trees and bushes were always wet and full of little black leeches that would attach themselves to any body opening or mucous: nostrils, lips, eyes, small cuts, open wounds, rashes, front and rear body function openings." Several Angels made note that the hardest buddies to lose were the ones you were close enough to "check each other for leeches."

F-511's T/SGT Harold Spring joked about Leyte's "leeches and critters (some of which have never been registered either Republican or Democratic)."

While the 511th slew plenty of Leyte's pests, the first official enemy kill for the 11th Airborne was affected by Ghost Platoon member 1LT George Skau of Jackson Heights, Queens, New York. A graduate of the Alamo Scouts School, on November 23 (D+5) Skau was traveling south from Division HQ at San Pablo to the 188th GIR's Regimental CP in his jeep when a Japanese soldier stepped out onto the road. Skau reflexively shot Superior Private Takanaaka in the head then gathered his paybook and insignia for intelligence before returning to HQ to report the incident (Angel lore also says he earned the money pot for the division's first kill).

## Manawarat

Cautiously following the Northern Trail, LTC Ernest LaFLamme's 1/511, minus C Company, reached Lubi without incident. LaFlamme's battalion then followed a river bed towards the 150-foot high plateau at the base of the Mahonag Mountains that locals called *Manarawat*.

Measuring six hundred feet by two hundred feet, Manarawat sits near the Daugitan River and is surrounded on three sides by sheer cliffs with the fourth side consisting of a gradual slope. In the coming days, the Angels would build an airstrip, hospital, supply dumps, cemetery and division CP on its crest. Given its distance inland, and the lack of reliable roads, resupply was mainly by L-4 and L-5 liaison planes.

241 Angels from the 187th GIR, 127th Airborne Engineers and 457th PFAB, plus attached medics, eventually airdropped in and the hilltop's garrison used resupply parachutes as shelters, earning the nicknames, "Rayon City" and "The Million Dollar Village."

It was a dangerous outpost, however, and over a month's time Manarawat's "citizens" endured numerous Banzai attacks intended to destroy the artillery and service units there. The 457th's CPT Luis Burris remembered, "Patrols around our main base were a necessary part of security. Because of the rough terrain, we could never be sure the Japanese had not set up machineguns to sweep our position. Only constant vigilance gave us any degree of security."

*"Rayon City" on top of Manarawat*

## 11. Leyte Mountains

Burris recalled of one of their casualties on Manarawat, saying, "(1LT Charles A.) Jameison of Able Battery was killed (on December 15) while attempting to get vital ammunition which had parachuted into a nearby mine field. Major (Norman) Martin, unwilling to ask any others to do it, went into the slippery mine field and brought out the ammunition and Jameison's body."

While 3/511 was still making its own way to Manarawat, C-511 and a detachment from RHQ-511 left Burauen on the Northern Trail three hours after 1/511 departed. COL "Hard Rock" Haugen, now simply called "Rock", marched with his men through slippery, energy-sucking mud, tangled roots, and never-ending rain, all with wary ears and eyes. Outside of LT Skau's encounter with the now-deceased Japanese Private Takanaaka, no reports had come in of major enemy contact. But Hard Rock's boys knew they were now well within Japanese lines and it was only a matter of time.

## Shooting the Messenger

On November 27 (D+9) a local guide traveling with COL Haugen convinced the colonel to deviate from 1/511's trail near Anonang on what he promised was a shortcut to Lubi. As the rain and fog rolled in, Rock asked the Filipino how far to Ormoc. He replied, "Just one more mountain", a phrase he would repeat several more times as the Paratroopers began to doubt his "shortcut".

Haugen's column questioned the route even more as the ravine tapered and the slopes became steeper and more entrapping. As one trooper pointed out, the young Angels had seen enough westerns to know the dangers of "riding up such a narrow draw."

Moving single file along the cramped bed of the swift Lubi River, C-511's 1st Platoon, minus 2nd Squad, probed ahead. At 0900 S/SGT Mike Olivetti's 1st Squad sighted two Japanese soldiers bathing in the river and washing clothes one mile east of Lubi. S/SGT Olivetti ran back to report to 1LT James E. Wylie who barked "Kill the S.O.B.s!", an order that 1st Squad promptly followed (neither C Company's CPT Tom Mesereau nor COL Haugen were consulted).

Unfortunately, 1st Squad's shots kicked over the hornets' nest and Japanese troops encamped along the river soon opened up. 1LT Miles Gale was hit first in the upper arm and troopers back in the column watched a blood-covered 1st Scout PFC Norman B. Honie, a member of Arizona's Hopi Tribe, walk towards the rear for aid.

Honie's wounding made me think of the words of an A-511 trooper who explained, "The lead scout walked (in front)... with the rest of the platoon strung out behind him in single file. His main function was either to walk up that trail... and signal, 'Y'all come on up. Hain't nobody up here,' or to be shot at--signifying that the welcome mat was not out."

The welcome mat was definitely *not* out and 1LT Wylie ordered 1st Platoon's mortar squad to drop their gear, grab extra ammo and move up the riverbed where they encountered 1st Squad taking cover behind fallen logs. There was no denying the crack of Arisaka rifles and Type 96 light machine guns, one of which soon killed S/SGT Olivetti. The enemy had finally been found and as rain fell at about 1200 and the firing increased, C- and RHQ-511 quickly realized that the Japanese had two advantages. First, they were using smokeless gunpowder deep in the overgrowth across the river which kept their positions concealed. Second, the enemy's "Woodpecker" heavy Nambu and "Canary" machine guns could be traversed to fire *down* on the Angels while the Paratroopers' .30 LMGs struggled to fire *up* the slopes around the river bottom.

Two hours into the engagement, enemy fire began to come in from the Angels' flanks then the rear. Casualties mounted, including PFC Albert H. McMahon of RHQ, one of COL Haugen's bodyguards, who was killed ten minutes after the first shot was fired. Now involved in the battle himself, Hard Rock sent the rest of C-511 to try a lateral envelopment on the left side of the riverbanks, but they were repulsed. Around 1430 an isolated 1st Platoon, who believed the rest of C Company had written them off, attacked down the river and tried to push right up a connecting stream, but after losing eight men and killing twenty enemy said they were forced to withdraw towards Lubi.

1st Platoon's 1LT James Wylie was killed after shouting, "Every man for himself!" and shortly before 1500 Platoon Sergeant SGT Elton Henry, now in command, ordered 1st Platoon's ten remaining desperate troopers to drop into the river and escape downstream. A wounded PVT Francis L. Perez begged his comrades to shoot him rather than leave him for the Japanese and after they moved out, PFC Newton S. Terry refused to go further, saying he could not leave Perez, one of his best friends. Neither were seen alive again.

At about 1600 what was left of C Company, 47 men, and RHQ pushed up the same path 1st Platoon assaulted earlier, and the

## 11. Leyte Mountains

combined force managed to gain higher ground through a bloody hand-to-hand struggle. The Japanese tried to barricade the Angels in the river bottom and in the commotion, about forty RHQ and C-511 men became separated after stumbling down a sharp slope. Cut off, Haugen's S-3 MAJ Fredick S. Wright, the group's highest-ranking officer, decided they would head back to Burauen where they inadvertently started the shocking rumor that COL Haugen and a lot of his Angels were dead.

Those left behind were facing an estimated 200 Japanese and Rock was still very much alive and continued directing the Angels' defenses from behind a tree stump. Columbus, Georgia's PFC George Garrett of RHQ watched a bullet hit the stump and spray Haugen with splinters. Ignoring the disturbance, Haugen continued issuing orders. When another bullet blasted a notch in the log, the irritated colonel scanned the treetops for the sniper. Locating the enemy, Haugen pointed and ordered Garrett to kill the offender. When George failed to spot the sniper himself, Rock barked for his M1 and passed over his own .30 carbine. Haugen then raised the borrowed Garand and shot the enemy who Garrett watched fall to the ground.

Unable to break out of the encirclement, the Angels hunkered down for a cold, sleepless night on the bare, treeless hilltop. The remaining Paratroopers assembled in two defensive groups, one with just thirty-five men in it, to await the reinforcements they prayed would soon arrive. The proud 511th's first engagement with the enemy was a frustrating impasse, though they did count fifty-two enemy dead.

PFC Eugene V. "Scooter" Schoener, another of Haugen's bodyguards, noted, "This was not how our first battle was supposed to be."

The next morning, November 28 (D+10), a Japanese contingent led by the Angels' Filipino guide approached the main body of Paratroopers with surrender terms. Defiantly, the Americans replied with "the word of Cambronne" and like GEN Anthony McAuliffe's response of "Nuts!" at Bastogne one month later, COL Haugen refused to throw in the towel.

Believing he purposefully led them into the ambush, one of the troopers allegedly shot the Filipino guide. Whether it was a trap, or an accidental encounter has been debated

That night, COL Haugen handpicked eight men, consisting of his bodyguards and MAJ Hacksaw Holcombe, and personally led the patrol all night through enemy lines to find help. Before dawn, Rock split his small group, sending five troopers to 1/511 at Manarawat. Haugen and the remaining two Angels made for Burauen, hoping one of the relief units could return before it was too late.

## The Lost Company

By now the 511's C Company and RHQ had been engaged for two days and ammunition and food were running out. While the rest of the Regiment, and Division, knew the column was missing, no one knew *where* since the Filipino guide's shortcut was unexpected and the small group that had escaped the ambush could not point out the location on their maps or photos. In addition, C-511's first radio message gave incorrect coordinates and no one could reach them now.

In response, the 11th Airborne's liaison planes were ordered into the air which was an inteligent, yet difficult solution to pull off. For one, the thick cloud cover left the heights socked in and the island's lush foliage made it even harder to see what was on the ground. Artilleryman PFC Michael Kalamas of HQ-457th PFAB was invited to take such a flight to Dulag with pilot 1LT John Ricks. After flying over the island, Kalamas noted, "(Ricks) circled over Burauen, then over the foothills and past the Leyte mountains on our left. Every thing was lush and green from all the rains... One would never know, at least from the air, that men were shooting at each other down below."

Ricks would be killed after his plane went down in the mountains a few weeks later on December 9 (D+22). While searching for the Lost Company, 1LT Ricks's comrade and fellow pilot 1LT Donald E. Neff of the 675th GFAB noticed a flash from a signaling mirror on the jungle floor spelling "CAMP MACKALL". Swinging around, Neff heard gunfire below and made note of the surroundings. Landing back at Division HQ, Neff met with LTC Norman E. Tipton, COL Haugen's Executive Officer, to show him the location on aerial photographs.

Hearing the report, GEN Swing told "Tip" to jump on 1/511's position near Manarawat in what Angel lore states was the first static line combat jump ever made from a liaison craft. After landing on November 29 (D+11), LTC Tipton took command of the 511th PIR since Haugen was missing (and feared dead) and at 0700 the colonel sent a 60-Paratrooper patrol under RHQ-511's 1LT Merkel Varner, a demolitions man, to find C Company. Now that they had a location, the patrol did find the battle area, but unfortunately the Japanese repulsed their attempts to break through to their comrades. After 1LT Varner was killed at about 1100 (he was awarded the Silver Star for his courageous actions), the patrol returned to Manarawat empty handed, so LTC Tipton sent 1/511 out to find their missing comrades.

One additional dilemma that hampered rescue efforts was that with the area covered by thick clouds, employing large transports to resupply C- and RHQ-511 was declared impractical. As a result, the Division's liaison planes, with their one white stripe on the right wing, were loaded with ammunition and food to be airdropped on the lost column's believed position. Unfortunately, despite the bravery of the pilots and their observers, most of the supplies landed away from the beleaguered Paratroopers and into a killing zone of enemy fire. A box of D Rations did make it to some of the hungry Angels who devoured the concentrated bars which promptly made them sick.

The 511th's S-2 CPT Lyman S. Faulkner remembered, "This was a very confusing time, first combat for most. No one was sure if Tipton or Haugen would be in charge and the regimental staff was shattered. S-3 was evacuated, S-2 seemed out of it. Things cleared up when Haugen appeared and we got the word to move west."

Exhausted after a day and a half trek that should have taken twice that long, COL Haugen's surprising arrival at Division HQ later on November 29 (D+11) caused quite a stir. Along the way, Rock had encountered D-511 outside Burauen and the Angels celebrated their beloved commander's "resurrection" by jumping in the river, with Haugen's blessing (he jumped in with them). It would be their last chance to bathe until Christmas, twenty-six days later.

D-511's SGT Ed Sorenson noted, "My pool-mate was none other than Colonel Haugen who was in the happiest mood one could imagine. He kept saying over and over to me, 'They're fighting sons-of-bitches', showing his pride in what he had instilled in what was to be the army's finest Regiment!"

Of Haugen's trek back to friendly lines, HQ3-511's PFC George Doherty said, "He didn't have any maps that were accurate enough to be worth anymore than toilet paper to guide the three of them back to Burauen and Division Headquarters. Only a man with Colonel Haugen's instincts and resources could have accomplished this feat….his superior West Point training saved their lives."

Standing before GEN Swing's staff, COL Haugen confirmed 1LT Neff's assessment of the lost column's position. Swing later noted perhaps with a smile, "I never reported to higher authority that it was surrounded."

Exhausted, but eager to get back to his encircled men, Haugen said he would lead 2/511 whom he had encountered outside the Burauen Heights. Swing, who awarded Haugen a Silver Star for his courageous night patrol, refused to let the regimental commander head back on such a mission. Instead, CPL Joseph Berg, one of the two troopers who accompanied Haugen to Burauen, offered to jump from a Piper Cub and guide 2/511 in. He just needed new jump boots as his had been worn out by their hard river bottom marching. Finding a pair his size on Swing's G-3 LTC Douglas Quandt (Quandt's first pair, mind you), Berg and his "new" boots jumped on a narrow trail outside D-511's position.

2/511 quickly moved out to find their lost brothers while 2nd Battalion of the 187th GIR took over their defensive positions on the heights. 1LT Eli Bernheim remembered looking out over the surrounding Air Corps units, the 44th General Hospital and 5th Air Force HQ, noting, "The job of the 2nd Battalion (of the 187th) was to protect this whole gigantic, and confused, melange and accordingly, it occupied positions about eight-hundred yards west of the town on a low hill dominating the surrounding flat-land."

Meanwhile, LTC Edward Lahti's 3/511 had left H-511 at Patog just after lunch to serve as a radio relay point and continued to Mawalo just across the gorge from Manarawat, arriving late in the afternoon on D+12. Discovering COL Haugen's predicament via radio, under LTC Tipton's direction at 0800 LTC Lahti sent G-511 with an attached HQ1 machine gun section under 2LT Walter Hettlinger to locate the beleaguered column. G Company's CPT Patrick W. Wheeler had been a West Point classmate of C-511's CPT Tom Mesereau and eagerly accepted the rescue mission with LTC Norman Tipton accompanying to guide them towards C Company's estimated position.

Back at the ambush site, CPT Mesereau, the 6'3" former All-American tackle, urged C-511's remaining troopers to conserve ammunition and "Captain Tom" set the example by hurling Japanese grenades back at the enemy. While football and OCS taught the Missourian to handle pressure, Mesereau admitted that their predicament was looking grim, yet he never lost faith in his Angels, nor their comrades.

Help WAS on the way, but CPT Wheeler's G-511 guessed they would have to search for their lost fellow Paratroopers more by sound than sight. Leaving their heavy packs at Manarawat, Wheeler deployed

## 11. Leyte Mountains

his men carefully to avoid another ambush (there was concern that the Japanese were using C Company and RHQ as bait) and moved down multiple trails. After several hours, G-511 heard gunfire in the distance and late on the third day of C Company's stand (D+12), at 1630 2LT Hettlinger's patrol found their lost comrades. G-511's CPT Wheeler found his exhausted friend, C-511's CPT Mesereau, and moved his fresh troopers into reinforcing positions.

Words fail to explain C Company's and the RHQ men's feelings as they watched G Company take over the perimeter and C Company's worn Angels moved inside to rest. In contrast, CPT Wheeler's men were sobered by the sight of 22 dead troopers and the bloody poncho and pup tent field hospital set up by regimental surgeon MAJ Wallace L. Chambers to treat the wounded. PVT Harry Swan of G Company remembered, "The men were in a deplorable condition, both physically and mentally, having survived numerous banzai attacks."

The Paratroopers of C-511 were tired, numb, hungry and battered. As A-511's PFC Jerry David noted, "You lose track of time in combat. You don't know whether the battle took ten minutes or 3 hours."

For the remaining C Company men, their stand had lasted 3 *days*.

The reinforced Angels passed a cold, restless night as working alone or in twos, the Japanese crept through the wet undergrowth into the Paratroopers' positions to try and knife them in their sleep or ignite a "lunge grenade", a shaped charge on the end of a five-foot piece of bamboo. In the twilight G-511's Paratroopers watched the enemy scurry through the jungle and were amazed when some tripped and fell, igniting their explosives on themselves.

To prevent such infiltrations, the 11th Airborne would string tripwires connected to grenades (or "noisemakers") between trees outside their lines. The problem was remembering where they were in the morning and more than one groggy Angel stumbled through a forgotten tripwire. Upon hearing the "ping" of a grenade's spoon uncoupling, the trooper took off in whatever direction was convenient.

Early on December 1 (D+13), 2/511 arrived and engaged the Japanese near Anannog while B- and G-511 led what was left of C Company and RHQ to Anonang (Manawarat) and into A-511's lines, four days after the ambush began. HQ2-511's PFC Deane Marks remembers moving into the valley to engage the Japanese and seeing C Company's dead, the first combat casualties for the 11th Airborne:

"It was real, real, real. Some how, the mud seemed wetter, the rain colder, the stomach emptier... We saw C Company. They looked pale and tired. I do not know exactly how many casualties. We just kept on tramping up and down on this six or eight foot wide path or trail whatever you want to call it... We pushed on, I don't know to where. Just follow the guy in front of you and hope you don't get ambushed."

The 511th's nineteen wounded were carried on poncho stretchers and although COL Haugen was glad to have his lost men safe, their losses pained him. With 22 men KIA, C Company and RHQ would spend days at Manawarat recovering (Haugen would join them there after parachuting from a Piper Cub, his 38th jump).

## Lonely Outposts

With the 511th PIR's lost column recovered, the rest of the regiment pressed further into the mountains with several patrols. While maintaining contact was paramount after the disasterous Battle of the River Bottom, laying telephone wire from Manawarat became increasingly difficult as the distance and terrain foiled their labors. Additionally, the Japanese frequently cut the wires requiring extensive (and dangerous) efforts to repair. When such wires needed repairing later on December 15 (D+27), HQ3-511's 1LT Evan W. Redmon volunteered to go out. HQ3-511's PFC George Doherty, one of Redmon's men, wrote years later, "Why was he laying wire, you ask? Because, he wouldn't ask any man to do a job that he wouldn't do, and this day it was a particularly hazardous job. He died by the code... Bless you Lieutenant Redmon... most of us will never die by the code, as a man, the way you did."

To solve the problem, in a spark of creativity, COL Jim Farren of the Division's 152nd Airborne Antiaircraft Battalion moved his men in small teams following the 511th's units inland to establish relay posts with their SCR-609 radios. Nicknamed "The Godfrey Relay" the radio positioned closest to a frontline unit could pass a message to the next which would relay to it the next until the reports reached Manarawat or Division HQ at Burauen.

*"Angel Radio" on The Godfrey Relay*

## 11. Leyte Mountains

It was a lonely job for the small AA squads who were more accustomed to shooting the enemy out of the sky with their guns than on the ground with rifles. Several teams of Farren's troopers had to contend with attacks by numerically superior enemy forces. One such outpost outside Burauen, led by St. Louis, Missouri's T/SGT Alexander Ruzycki, noticed a pair of Japanese soldiers crawling towards their position so Ruzycki picked up his carbine and shot both intruders before using his radio to alert Division HQ of the disturbance.

Ten minutes later a trio of Japanese soldiers headed their way and Alex again shot all three. Returning to the radio with a leg wound and a missing finger, Ruzycki asked HQ to send aid. When the friendly patrol from E-187 GIR approached Ruzycki's position they found the sergeant and his three men coolly holding off a much larger enemy force. The patrol jumped into the fray and forty minutes later twenty-two of the enemy were dead. For his spirited actions, Alex received the Silver Star.

On the way back to their positions, E-187's lead-scout PVT Ray Shadden spotted and shot two more enemy soldiers before a third jumped him and tried to grab his rifle. Shadden pulled his knife and stabbed his attacker and was made Private First Class on the spot.

Some men from Dog Battery, 457th PFAB were also sent to help secure the 152nd's radio relay positions on their way to Manawarat.

The other half of the Angels' communications system was airborne and equally innovative. Nicknamed "The Moseley Milk Run", each morning (0730) and evening (1630) division pilots like 1LT Jack Keil and MAJ Arthur L. "Mo" Moseley of Operations (G-3) would fly into the mountains to find each of the 511th PIR's units and the 152nd AAB's stations to receive messages via their own onboard radio. Keil and the Texan Moseley, or "Phone Glider 3", then dropped replies or orders to those below, as well as copies of the Division's newsletter, *The Static Line* (the only source of news). Mosley and Keil also found time to drop copies over the nearby WAC compound, "With compliments of Art Mosley and Jack Keil. Phone Glider 3."

Mosley and Keil would then return to Division HQ and plot unit positions on G-3's Milk Run Map. The Angels' Godfrey Relay/ Moseley Milk Run allowed COL Hard Rock Haugen's 511th PIR to continue advancing through Leyte's mountains with the goal of meeting again at Anas on the range's western slope. There three trails again diverged named the Northern, Middle and Southern

*Pilots briefings were integral parts of the Mosley Milk Run*

and LTC Lahti's 3rd Battalion took the Southern Trail out of Mawalo while 1/511 and RHQ-511 set out on the Middle.

2/511, meanwhile, remained engaged with the enemy force that had so successfully pummeled RHQ and C Company in the river bottom near Anonang. The Angels discovered that the regimental-sized unit from Japan's 26th Infantry was protecting what was believed to be an enemy CP and although heavily outnumbered, the Paratroopers tried twice to destroy the position but were repelled. The decision was made to bypass the enemy pocket for now and GEN Swing sent elements of the 187th GIR to isolate and then mop it up. And with the 188th's southern sector deemed relatively clear Swing later sent them north and west to join the combat actions.

HQ-188's CPL Edward Hammrich would later note, "The weather and the isolation of this part of our campaign, was to my way of thinking, the worse of all our fighting."

On December 2 (D+14) 1/187 took over the defenses of the Burauen heights so that 2/187 could move into the hills towards Anonang and Manawarat. 1/187 set up outside San Pablo near the Division HQ, a position that would be crucial in a few days time.

# Operation Table Top

2/511's difficult engagement with the enemy's reinforced defenses revealed one of the Angels' earliest challenges on Leyte, namely aerial and artillery support. Japanese forces were keenly talented at building fortifications in the most implausible of locations and for the 511th PIR's Paratroopers, calling in fire support would make every difference. However, the ever-present rain clouds prevented aerial coverage and while the Angels' artillery batteries at Burauen supported as far as Lubi, the 511th's Paratroopers were slogging further into the muddy, overgrown hills and lugging pack howitzers inland by hand would be nearly impossible. Even native carabao proved ineffective and several fell off cliffsides in the attempt.

To solve the dilemma, COL Nicholas G. Stadtheer of the 457th Parachute Field Artillery Battalion scoured the area for available C-47s to drop both armaments and men onto forwards positions (the guns would be "spiked" and abandoned once out of range). While most of Leyte's Skytrains were busy shuttling supplies or grounded due to the monsoon weather (or repairs), one 5th Army pilot based out of San Pablo said he would help (some say he was "conned" into it) when not flying search and rescue ops.

On December 4 (D+16), A Battery of the 457th PFAB fixed six parapacks, or paracaissons, (some Angels called them "artillery coffin bombs") to the undercarriage of the willing pilot's plane. With RESCUE painted in large yellow letters on the side of the craft, the artillery men helped the aircrews remove and tape around the plane's door so jumpers could make their exits.

Taking off from Tacloban, the craft flew towards Manawarat with a Drop Zone two miles from the battery's future position. After the first jump's success, COL Stadtheer decided he could hit the small "strip" on Manawarat itself to save his men a back-breaking trek, so there were actually two DZs involved in the Angels' first combat drops.

G-511's PFC George Doherty described the procedure for dropping onto Manawarat's 500 x 150-foot DZ, saying:

"The high mountains surrounding the plateau forced the pilot to follow a moon shaped canyon to the approach run, dive down like a fighter plane and zoom sharply up and to the left when he passed the drop zone, dropping one wing almost perpendicular to the ground which enabled him to slip between to sharp peaks."

After the jumpmaster shouted 'Gooooooo!' the Paratroopers exited the craft, after which the pilot had to pull up sharply to avoid crashing into the surrounding hillside, a feat he completed thirteen times to move A Battery to their new home with Stadtheer acting as jumpmaster every trip. This made Manawarat the 11th Airborne Division's first combat jump made from a C-47.

PFC Deane Marks of HQ2-511 remembered watching the first drops:

"About two or three hours after we set up our LMG (Light Machine Gun), we looked out into this valley and 'holy cow' here came this C-47 barreling at eye level at perhaps a thousand yards to our front. Right in front of us a slew of red and yellow parapacks dropped and troopers started jumping out of the plane. We could actually see their little white faces. They couldn't have been higher than four or maybe five hundred feet...."

With the 457th's A Battery set up on Manawarat, COL Haugen's 511th PIR felt much safer with 360° fire support. Given the difficulty of dropping the artillery men with the C-47, eleven of the division's spotter planes were utilized to jump, one at a time, a platoon from C-187th GIR who provided initial security for Manawarat. This freed up the regular Paratroopers of 1/511 to move into the jungles to face the enemy, though 3/511 remained there for some time.

This also made the 187th's C Company men the first tactical unit to make a parachute jump in a combat zone from liaison craft. The 187th GIR's Joseph B. Giordano noted, "Manawarat was one of the few semi-cleared areas in our entire zone of action, and while it was not well suited for an airstrip, it was well located, and a shade better than nothing."

To create the airstrip, some men from Division HQ and a platoon of engineers from the 127th AEB jumped on Manawarat to clear a larger landing area with explosives which increased the range of the division's L-4s (L-5's couldn't handle landing there) for artillery spotting, unit locating and the evacuation of casualties.

Given the extreme challenges with carrying casualties back to Burauen, medical staff from the 22st Airborne Medical Company airdropped soon after along with equipment for a Portable Surgical Hospital that further enlarged "Rayon City" which allowed the 511th PIR's surgeons and medics to move forward with the regiment.

# 11. Leyte Mountains

*Manawarat's "Surgery Ward"*

Casualties carried to Manawarat were now cared for by three surgeons, ten surgical technicians and other medical staff working out of a thatched and parachute-covered bamboo structure. Once the wounded were stabilized, they either recuperated on Manawarat then went back to their units or 46 were flown to San Pablo then on to larger hospitals at Dulag (or back to the states) for further treatment.

One of the first casualties treated at Manawarat's "Sugery Ward" was A-511's CPT Tom W. Brady of Whitestone, NY, who had been wounded seriously in the head when an enemy bullet hit his helmet and drove a piece of metal into his temple on December 2 (D+13). Other troopers remember that the bullet actually entered Brady's skull and followed the bone around from one side to the other. Either way, when asked who would carry their beloved captain on a stretcher back to Manawarat, every man in A Company volunteered.

After a successful operation on his brain, the twenty-nine-year-old company commander lay recovering for days. When ice cream was dropped on Manawarat from GEN Swing's HQ, those around Brady were astonished to see him smile at the announcement (the surgery had temporarily left him unable to speak or communicate).

CPT Brady was later flown by pilot 1LT Sid Lanier to Dulag for more treatment where he was fully expected to recover. He then flew home to the States where he underwent further surgeries. Sadly, CPT Brady died during one of those later operations.

Three days after Brady's wounding, on December 5 (D+17), 1/511 continued their trek towards Mahonag on the Middle Trail while 2/511 broke off their engagement with the aforementioned enemy forces when relieved by 2/187 GIR which was told to contain and keep the enemy busy. 2/511 was ordered onto the Northern Trail that would make for Mahonag and Anas, so the bloodied Paratroopers shouldered their gear and headed deeper into the jungle.

Meanwhile, 3/511's forward elements became pinned down by machine gun fire on the Southern Trail so LTC Ed Lahti made his way forward to locate the Japanese positions, then returned to direct fire which destroyed the machine gun nest. For his gutsy actions, Lahti earned the Silver Star and the next day, "Big Ed" would display similar courage to earn his first of three Bronze Stars.

During the fighting, I-511's crack shot PFC Eugene P. Heath of Portland, Oregon made eleven notches on his rifle stock. Four days later, the total was thirty-seven, eight of whom were made at over one-hundred yards. In full disclosure, some of Eugene's buddies disputed the total, but never his skill.

## Mud and Ghosts

While the 511th and 187th made their way along slippery trails, whispered curses were frequent as young troopers slipped in the mud or their boots caught in muck-covered roots. Dropped loads had to be picked up again as the offending man was reminded about noise discipline. Leyte's environment was proving to be just as difficult a challenge as fighting the enemy.

PFC Deane Marks of HQ2-511 remembered, "Up and down the mountain trails we went. Wet to the bone. being ambushed just about daily. Bumbling into Japs here and there."

The 187th GIR's Joseph B. Giordano noted of traversing Leyte's difficult terrain, "We were compelled to discontinue using yards or miles as a barometer for distance, and were now using hours or days to measure or designate the distance from one point to another."

Nixson Denton, a news correspondent from Iowa, wrote of Leyte's morasses, saying, "In it, knee deep, our troops are standing, uncomfortable, miserable, sleepless, verging on exhaustion, but attacking with faces always forward, driving on not only against a cunning and fierce enemy, but against mud, and mud, and more mud."

"It rained every day and every night: rain and mud and mud and rain!" lamented D-511's PFC Elmer "Chuck" Hudson.

The 187th GIR's MAJ Henry Burgess described the jungle, saying "You don't have any fields of fire...You see what you can see anywhere from five, no more than fifteen yards. The sky you don't see in most areas. It's like being in a darkened room most of the time."

Some in Leyte's "darkened room" began throwing away their underwear and t-shirts as they were simply rotting away. The Angels in the hills tried unsuccessfully to dry socks against their bodies, but the rain was just too constant and by now, after all the hard marching and fighting some of the Paratroopers' beloved jump boots were starting to lose their soles. The Coracans just could not handle being wet for weeks on end then marched through mud and over sharp volcanic rock. Regrettably, few replacements could be airdropped in (and those were often harder GI boots with buckles) so as a necessity many Angels tied or taped their footwear together while others had to do what no trooper wanted to.

CPT Stephen Cavanaugh of D-511 grimly recalled, "I had to replace my boots with those of a deceased soldier that were two sizes too small and I was forced to cut the toes out in order to wear them."

*511th Paratroopers somewhere in Leyte's "darkened room"*

CPT John Conable of the 408th Quartermasters exclaimed, "The mud was omnivorous. It would eat an infantryman's combat boots in seven days. The tree roots in the rain forest probably served as teeth. Uniforms rotted rapidly. While we were in the tropics some of the rains were cold. It was tough to keep the wounded warm until they could be evacuated."

And then there were the jungle sores. "Most of us had bad skin and stomach ailments," 1LT Andrew Carrico of D-511 noted. "And our legs and feet developed ugly ulcers which, due to being wet all the time, refused to heal."

Records show that Leyte received twenty-three inches of rain during the Angels' campaign. Ironically, the division's afflictions were further affected by a lack of drinking water so the men took to catching rainwater in whatever was available, usually ponchos, to quench their thirst. To make matters worse, due to the dense foliage flank security was difficult which allowed small Japanese raiding parties to frequently strike the frontline units' columns like ghosts in the darkness, leaving the drenched Angels constantly on edge.

"It was a miserable existence," D-511's 1LT Carrico remembered. "We encountered continuous heavy fighting the entire way. We carried our wounded with us as we fought the Japanese further and further back into the jungle."

The 187th GIR's Joseph B. Giordano added:

"The Japanese were active and fought delaying actions, set ambushes and attacked our perimeters nightly. As the situation developed it became apparent that the Japanese would attempt to hold in depth along a line Patog, Ananong, west through Lubi and Mahonag to the head waters of the Talisayan Rivers."

After digging in for the evening on December 6 (D+19), the tired (and hungry) Angels spent the night watching the flashes in the western sky as the Navy fired on Ormoc's beaches to prepare for the $77^{th}$ Infantry Division's shore landings the next day.

"It was like a great Fourth of July exhibition," D-511's CPL Murray Hale noted. "We could see the tracers hanging in the air as they fired. They hung like a red curtain in the sky."

For the young Angels, it was almost a taste of home as they sat in wet, cold, muddy, stinking foxholes half a world away and tried not

## Passwords and Angels' Prayers

After D-511 delivered a load of 81mm mortar shells to HQ2-511 the next day, (December 7, D+20), CPL Murray Hale watched two HQ2 troopers fall by sniper fire, the second as he tried to rescue the first.

Believing the shots were coming from a stolen M1 rifle, D Company's supply sergeant SSGT Paul R. Farnsworth called for his men to take cover. Hale, caught out in the open, tried to inch forward, then elected to remove his pack to provide a smaller profile. As he did so, he said "the loudest explosion I think I ever heard went off, and I was sledgehammered in the right shoulder."

*D-511's CPL Murray Hale*

Stunned, Hale remarked, "I suddenly felt hot and weak. I was bleeding and was probably in a little shock. The fact that I had tried to get my pack off probably saved my life. The enemy hit me just as I moved, which meant he would have hit me in the head or neck rather than the shoulder." It was the first of Murray's three wounds received during the war and his D Company comrades joked, "no one wanted to share a foxhole with Hale."

Several additional D-511 men arrived and from the treeline kept Murray talking as they scanned for the sniper. Medic T/5 Robert L. Lesher carefully crawled through the brush to the wounded Hale who tried to wave him off. Murray recalled, "I cautioned him to stay down, but he was fearless."

Regimental Surgeon MAJ Wallace Chambers wrote years later, "In my opinion every officer and enlisted man in the 511th Regimental Medics has a very personal, deep feeling for all wounded and killed. The medics demonstrated this hundreds of times each day the whole time that I was in the 511th Parachute Regiment."

Lesher gave Murray a shot of morphine and dug the bullet out of his shoulder which he promised to give Hall as a souvenir once they reached safety. The medic then crawled towards the two previously wounded HQ2-511 men which drew additional sniper fire. Murray called out for him to be careful, but it did little good; Lesher was tragically killed by the sniper as he tried to render aid. His remains were never recovered.

After sundown, D-511's T/5 Joseph L. Signor of Philadelphia, Pennsylvania, carefully crawled out and pulled Hale to safety. As the duo made their way to D Company's CP in the dark, they encountered CPT Charles E. "Baldy" Jenkins, CO of HQ2-511, who was leading a squad to pick up his injured men. Obscured by the darkness, the Mansfield, LA native pointed his .45 at Hale and Signor in challenge. Neither could remember the password but managed to convince the determined Jenkins of their identities.

At the Battalion Aid Station surgeon CPT Thomas Nestor checked Murray's shoulder and redressed the wound then gave the weary Paratrooper some rations before laying him down to rest.

"I tried to rest and think straight, which was difficult," the lucky corporal remembered. "But I prayed."

Hale's prayer-filled night resounded with rifle and machine gun fire, shouting in English and Japanese, exploding grenades and the moans of the more seriously wounded around him.

*The "Recuperation Ward" on Manawarat*

Some of the commotion occurred when D-511's PVT Myron D. Pickens of Indianapolis, IN answered the call of nature, only he went *out* of the perimeter instead of *in*. As a result, a shot rang out, hitting Pickens in the chest. Afraid to stand up themselves as no one was sure whether it was friendly fire or the enemy sniper which had been harassing the company, CPT Cavanaugh and two other troopers crawled from their holes to drag Pickens towards the battalion center. Surgeon CPT Matthew Platt of Forest Park, IL, worked on Myron under a poncho, but he died before sunrise.

CPL Hale, who was in the aid station due to his shoulder wound, watched the whole scene. "It griped your heart, as (Myron) constantly called for his mother during the night, before he left us."

Regimental Chaplain "Chappie" CPT Lee Walker would later write, "I wish I had the financial resources to erect a giant tablet in stone where everyone could read the names of our officers and men who gave their lives that others might live in freedom..."

Walker added: "'Angels': that is what people called them. 'Heroes': that will always be their epitaph."

Little did Walker or the rest of the division know they had three more weeks of such hell before their mission would be declared complete.

## The Leyte Air Corps Rescue

Part of that hell came from the 11th's problem with resupply which had existed since they headed into the mountains weeks earlier. One senior officer who desired to remain unnamed laid some of the blame with GEN Swing who was so quick to push for his Division to enter combat on the island without fully understanding just how difficult resupplying the frontline units would be during the campaign.

1LT Miles Gale of H-511 expressed a sentiment shared by frontline troops everywhere, "My humble personal opinion is that our top leadership was far behind the fighting lines and their accommodations were comfortable, so they didn't know what was going on."

This belief was strengthened after the war when troopers heard that GEN Swing and his staff regularly enjoyed steak dinners at their Leyte CP along with drinks at night. While they did so, with no roads to truck in provisions or ammunition, COL Haugen's hungry 511th Paratroopers were in forward positions with no straightforward way to replenish them. Concerned for his boys, Hard Rock radioed

GEN Swing to apprise him of the situation and to propose a brilliant solution. According to H-511's PFC Richard "Dick" Keith, Haugen communicated a plan devised by himself (Keith), PFCs Edward H. Hogan and Lyle D. Henderson, and PVT David H. Renaud in a "foxhole conference." Since they were so far inland, and supplies could not reach them overland, why not look to the sky? While C-47s could not fly in the monsoon weather, the four Paratroopers discussed utilizing the division's artillery spotter planes that were flying the Mosley Milk Run instead. If sixteen planes flew two drops in the morning and two in the afternoon with an average load of 200 pounds for L-4s and 400 pounds for L-5s, the 511th could receive up to 38,400 pounds of supplies every day. Eventually the Angels would fly 176 such sorties a day and drop 19 tons a day.

Although Keith would retire a Major General described as "a true officer and gentleman", the H-511 men were never given full credit for their part in the Leyte Air Corps Rescue. After COL Haugen shared the concept with Swing, "General Joe" sent for his artillery commander COL Francis W. Farrell to discuss the idea. Farrell immediately gathered the division's artillery spotter pilots to explain their new mission then begged additional resources from 8th Army to enact the innovative resupply scheme. Angels of LTC Roy Stout's 408th Airborne Quartermaster Company under CPT David Carnahan began stockpiling supplies on San Pablo Airstrip 2.

The Angels around the strip threw themselves into the work. PFC Michael Kalamas of HQ-457th PFAB remembered, "After the supplies started to arrive, we were very busy. No one told us what to do or how to do it. We all knew that our boys needed food and other vital equipment to survive in those mountains. So everyone pitched in, regardless of the cost and took on the task of moving the supplies as quickly as possible... The hectic work load, turned into a labor of love. It had to be, as the men and pilots, toiled from dawn until dusk."

Fully loaded "Biscuit Bombers of the Leyte Air Corps", the Stinson L-5 Sentinel Piper Cubs piloted by men like MAJ Arthur "Mo" Mosley, then headed into the cloud-covered mountains. It was a courageous endeavor since the planes only had basic instruments.

It was also a life-saving campaign that kept the frontline Angels fighting, and alive, and the troops on the ground were eternally grateful. As F-511s LT Ralph Ermatinger noted, "(Art) Mosley became an instant hero to the troops. His name was known to every man."

## 11. Leyte Mountains

*Sketch by RHQ-511's PFC Frank Lewis of The Leyte Air Corps Rescue*

"What saved us was the piper cubs, the small planes," D-511's 1LT Andrew Carrico remembered. "Those pilots, they'd fly right over us and ask, 'You guys hungry down there?' We'd shout back 'Yes!' and they'd just push the cartons of food out."

HQ3-511's PFC George Doherty said, "Most of the credit for the Leyte campaign is given to the infantry, but without the unsung help of the service troops and liaison pilots flying under impossible conditions no matter how good we were, we couldn't have survived on leaches, snakes and roots of trees like the Japanese did."

During their return trips, the "New Guinea Short Line" men in the back seats would drop grenades or fire bazookas or Thompsons down at any Japanese they saw on the way back to Lubi or Manawarat. While it may not have done much damage, it certainly boosted morale and demonstrated the Angels' willingness to attack.

The 187th GIR's Joseph B. Giordano wrote, "The pleasure and satisfaction of watching the Nips run and the resultant safety from this type at strafing partly repaid the pilots for the splendid, fatiguing and hazardous work they did."

The flyers' gallant efforts came with one adverse side effect, however. The pilots had to fly in circles over a unit's position and wait for a break in the clouds into which they would dive down then almost stall their engines before they or their "riders" in the back would

*The 11th Airborne Division's Leyte Air Corps Rescue*

push out the supplies, sometimes without parachutes attached.

PFC Doherty explained that, "When the cargo chutes opened the boxes of supplies on occasion would slip out of the cargo chute holders at 125 miles per hour, striking trees they would bust apart and scatter in all directions like an exploding artillery shell. A C-ration can would then become a lethal projectile as many of them did…"

K-ration boxes were equally dangerous and would drop like a heavy bomb. Overall it is estimated that between 10-30 Angels were killed on Leyte by such falling "bombardments", and dozens more were injured during the campaign.

Despite the cost, when the weather permitted it the 11th Airborne Division's "Leyte Air Corps Rescue" kept the combat troops fighting and supplied in the heights, albeit with a thin supply route that could be easily disrupted, as we are about to find out.

# 12: Operation *Wa* - The Battle of the Airfields

San Pablo, Buri and Burauen Airstrips, Leyte – December 1944

*"Between five hundred (500) and six hundred (600) Japs were killed in the airfield area during the 'Battle of the Airfields'..."*
-XXIV Corps operations report, February 1945

On December 6 (D+18), 2/511 watched from their positions in the hills as six "C-47s" passed overhead trailing blue smoke. The Paratroopers assumed the planes were coming in to prepare for some future jump and gave the aircraft little thought. Indeed, countless Allied units across Leyte mentioned watching or hearing the transports coming in and giving them no mind. Airplanes were always flying overhead anyway as one trooper noted.

In truth the Allied troops were all watching a *buntai* (squadron) of enemy Mitsubishi Ki-57 Topsys belonging to the Southern Philippines' air group, the Kōkūtai. D-511's S/SGT Wilbur Wilcox noted years later, "Had we known they were enemy planes, we might have been able to shoot them down or at least cripple them."

From a distance, the 95th Sentai's Topsys were hard to distinguish from C-47 Skytrains as they headed to drop enemy Paratroopers on the three airstrips within a three-mile radius around Buraruen: San Pablo Strips Numbers 1 and 2 (Bayug) and Buri.

Stationed outside Burauen, CPL Carl M. Becker of the nearby Headquarters Battery of the 866th Antiaircraft Automatic Weapons Battalion later wrote, "Desperation inspired the plan, and poor coordination doomed it. We knew nothing of the Japanese strategy, only that our lives seemed threatened (once the attack began)."

PFC Michael Kalamas from HQ-457th Parachute Field Artillery had recently arrived at Burauen to help with the Division's aerial resupply efforts. He noted, "The place sure didn't look like much. In fact, it looked so peaceful, you would never know that there was war going on, around us. It was very quiet, and except for two mechanics, working near four or five observation aircraft, you would never know there were anyone here at all." That was about to change.

Following a dinner of "foraged" fried chicken, at around 1830 GEN Swing exited the mess tent near his new San Pablo CP, a beautiful plantation house. Pausing to listen to the incoming aircraft, Swing watched several Japanese Nakajima Ki-49 "Helen" bombers and various fighters circle the airstrips and drop incendiary and HE bombs that set a fuel dump on fire.

PFC Kalamas wrote:

"A friend and I were washing our messkits after having supper. The next moment, the peaceful, warm evening erupted into complete bedlam. Incendiary bombs were exploding all around us. The noise was deafening, and the pieces of white hot magnesium, were flying through the air and covering the ground like so many hailstones."

While the Angels' 152nd Anti-Aircraft Battalion filled the sky with flack, their defense was brief as the division was running low on ammunition. Eighteen enemy craft were downed and some troops on the ground worried since C-47s were being shot down until others nearby pointed out, "Yes, but not *our* C-47s. Look at the red meatballs on the side!"

Ten minutes later some of the Topsys that 2/511 had observed earlier flew over the airstrips at seven hundred feet and between 250-350 Japanese Paratroopers dropped from about forty transports in the twilight. And due to the fierceness of the Angels' antiaircraft fire on the bombers and fighters, the AA crews were out of ammunition and could only stare as the enemy transports flew in to drop their jumpers.

These were not average foot soldiers, but rather the hand-picked *Katori Shimpei* of the 3rd Raiding Regiment, an elite fighting force led by MAJ Tsuneharu Shirai. As a Sixthy Army report notes, "The Paratroops were picked fanatics, all of whom volunteered from various branches of the Japanese army for a suicide mission the nature of which was not specified when they joined."

Concerned about the dangers of the Allies shifting their airpower from New Guinea to Leyte once the monsoon season ended, Japan's 14th Area Army commander GEN Tomoyuki Yamashita had ordered LTG Sosaku Suzuki to retake the Leyte airfields and destroy the Americans' air power on them. The attack was originally set for December 5, but poor weather delayed the Japanese first drop to December 6. The

## 12. Operation Wa

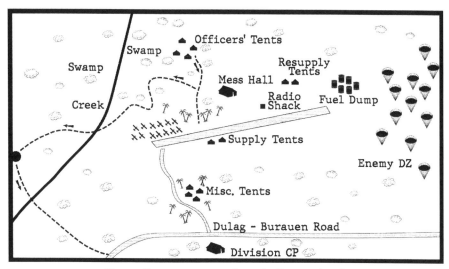

*Enemy Paratrooper attack on the Bayug airstrip*

enemy's "supporting" 26th Infantry units which were to participate in the attack by coming east over the mountains never got the message and attacked Burauen days off from the enemy Paratroopers (the Japanese also never got the message that General Walter Krueger had already stopped work at the Burauen airfields).

And with the 511th PIR doing such an effective job of attacking and blocking Japan's 16th Infantry units in the mountains only a few of those forces were able to join the assault. Even so, at 0630, some of the 16th's soldiers attacked an American bivouac near the 287th Field Artillery Observation Battalion and killed several in their sleep.

During a short lull in the fighting, GEN Swing sent Assistant G-3 MAJ Henry Burgess with a few Angels to check the area. Burgess noted:

"It was a sad sight. The first tent we found was the mess tent. Corn fritters and bacon were done, but no one was around. It was spooky. So we ate and went into the camp. All the white officers and many men had been slain in jungle hammocks with the zippered mosquito netting shut while swinging between two trees off the ground. Being unable to get out of the hammocks quickly, the Japanese Paratroopers had killed them in the first rush, which had also scattered all the remaining 287th's soldiers."

Some of the surviving soldiers had rushed naked from their tents when the firing began and the Angels gave them what rations they could spare. While two squads split off to patrol the area, MAJ Burgess's group counted forty dead that had been killed in their hammocks and on their cots by the enemy. It was a sight that all present remembered for the rest of their lives.

Back at the San Pablo airstrip, the Angels were firing on the descending Japanese with their rifles and machine guns and G-2 LTC Henry J. "Butch" Muller, who followed General Swing out of the mess tent at 1830, emptied two clips from his .45. Being well-armed, Butch filled his pockets with fried chicken while officers around him scambled to find their weapons (and later complained of hunger).

After a notice of the attacks had been found on a downed-Japanese pilot earlier in the campaign (possibly on one of the enemy dead from a crashed enemy transport on November 29), LTC Muller was given a secret "Crystal Ball" report of a possible attack by MacArthur's Chief of Intelligence, MG Charles Willoughby. Believing the enemy lacked the necessary resources to coordinate such an attack, GEN Swing dismissed Muller's warning (per Willoughby's order, Swing was never told the source of the intel).

Muller himself said of his initial report to the General, "I was not myself convinced but had to invent plausible reasons to support my estimate of the coming Jap jump."

In the end, to convince Swing of the reality of the situation, Muller decided to tell the General where his intelligence had come from. Hank was quick to point out that Swing should not be criticized and noted "It was a highly unlikely report with no source given and, in any event, with all the combat elements already in the hills, there was little he could do on such short notice."

MAJ Henry Burgess remembered additional details. With the Division's G-3 LTC Douglas P. Quandt on Manawarat with General Albert Pierson, Hank was the Duty Officer on the evening of either November 26th or 27th (he couldn't remember) when a coded messaged entitled "Alamo Report" was received by the Communications Section. Similar to the "Crystal Ball" report, this message advised that a force of Japanese Paratroopers had left from airfields in Luzon. It was believed that the enemy would soon jump on Leyte to attempt to recapture the three airfields at Burauen.

Burgess took the report to GEN Swing in the Operations tent and with the Crystal Ball report now confirmed the two officers reviewed

maps of the area to determine a course of action should the enemy jump there. Swing then spent the next two days making sure his surrounding units had ammunition and were on alert for an attack.

As one trooper remembered, they were told to stay put at night and "if anything moved it would be assumed to be the enemy and any of our men could shoot at something moving."

Watching the enemy parachutists in the air on December 6, Swing, Muller and Burgess became firm believers in both the Crystal Ball and the Alamo reports. What was harder to believe were the fast-falling Japanese, some of whose quick-release harnesses released with the opening of their parachutes several hundred feet up, sending their former wearers hurtling and screaming to the ground.

The 187th GIR's Joseph B. Giordano noted, "Some had descended without parachute (unless they used a new invisible, non-opening type, not known to the Americans at this time)."

Those who did land safely ditched their parachutes and set out in all directions, setting fire to seven of the division's 35 L-4 liaison planes before moving to destroy adjacent supply dumps. While seizure of the Burauren airfields was the enemy's main objective, destroying the Angels' Piper Cubs would eliminate their use for artillery spotting, resupply and moving troops to forward positions.

MAJ Burgess pointed out that, "If we couldn't supply (our) units in the mountains within several days, they would be doomed or have to withdraw."

But something about the enemy attack was...off. The defending Angels noticed that some of the enemy stumbled around San Pablo as if drunk and bottles of "Liquid Courage" were later found on their dead. One inebriated Japanese paratrooper was shot after seriously angering HQ-11's CPT David Carnahan who reported, "The bastards shot my blue enameled wash pan and my rubber mattress."

GEN Robert Eichelberger wrote home to his wife Emmalina, "(enemy) Paratroopers dropped on one of our airfields, burned up a plane and then danced around it as though they were drunk... We have often thought that their suicide ground attacks in which they attack in mass across the open have been induced to a large extent by liquor."

The Japanese (drunk and sober) on the San Pablo strip faced off against roughly 75 American pilots, support personnel and cooks who dug in on the strip's south side and held throughout the night. Some Angels assumed the enemy planned their attack for the evening so they could quickly hit the airstrip and then fade into and hide in the jungle during the night, though not all moved into the foliage.

English-speaking Japanese shouted to the Angels, "The great Japanese army is descending. All is useless! Surrender! Banzai!" Some of the enemy sang as they moved and others carried notecards with suggested phrases to shout at the American defenders such as, "Hey Joe, where is your machine gun?"

Growing tired of their incessant prattle, CPL Jimmy Smith of CPT Conable's old 457th Parachute Field Artillery calmly dropped three of the "heralds" in their tracks with his rifle.

CPT John Conable who had recently transferred from the 457th to act as Assistant Division Quartermaster noted, "Small arms fire started all around the area. I called for volunteers to assemble and was immediately told by both the officers and enlisted men of the 408th (Airborne Quartermaster Company) that it was not their job to act as infantrymen." Conable, of course, was disgusted by this.

The enemy's plan was to drop most of the first wave on Buri airstrip, with smaller groups assigned to Bayug and San Pablo. However due to the Angels' intense antiaircraft fire, most of the Japanese paratroopers only dropped on or near San Pablo.

And while the enemy's 26th and 16th Infantry units for the most part were unable to meet up with the enemy Paratroopers, Japan's plan to effect a vertical envelopment upon the Leyte airfields was sound. As a Sixth Army report respectfully noted one week after the attack, "The plan was bold and daring, and in ever way worthy of Nippon's (Japan's) glorious tradition... There was probably no avenue of escape for these heroes... (As) was so often the case with other bold and daring attacks, the performance did not quite measure up to the promise."

After sunset, GEN Swing ordered his San Pablo CP into action. The only real immediately available unit for defense was the 127th Airborne Engineers under Battalion XO MAJ G. Eisenberg who were reminded that they were riflemen *first* and engineers second (the 127th would endure 26 casualties in the attack). The engineers had been busy repairing the Dagami-Burauen road and the San Pablo airstrip itself and were joined in their defenses by 1LT Charles L. Hayden and eight enlisted men from the 11th's Parachute Maintenance Company who had arrived on November 29 to prepare chutes for the 457th PFAB's jump on Manawarat.

GEN Swing further strengthened his ad-hoc force by arming HQ's "Typewriter Commandos", but not knowing the full size of the enemy's force, he ordered the 674th Parachute Field Artillery Battalion under COL Lukas E. Hoskas to leave Bito Beach and head towards San Pablo. Hoskas' artillerymen had been stationed there on orders from Sixth Army who wanted their guns set up to repel an enemy amphibious landing which, of course, never occured.

Swing told his gathered troops that he wanted the San Pablo airstrip back in American hands and secured by nightfall (it would take two days to fully achieve this feat). PFC Michael Kalamas from HQ-457 remembered that at the time, "Everything was on fire. The drums of gasoline were burning. Also, the two supply tents on the other side of the runway. The planes farther away from us were also on fire, and couple of Japanese soldiers were tossing hand grenades into the cockpits, as they were heading in our direction."

A group of hidden enemy Paratroopers moving away from the airstrip attacked the platoon leader of B-187's PFC Joe E. Rangel of San Bernardino, CA. Joe leapt in front of the officer, killing all three enemy with his rifle and a grenade. After stabbing another Japanese soldier, Rangel was cut down when an enemy Paratrooper closed in and detonated a grenade against his back. Some of Joe's comrades

When Angels Fall

*Angels gathered around a dead Japanese Paratrooper*

said they found his body under the two dead enemy soldiers, so it is possible that they both assaulted him at once. PFC Rangel was posthumously awarded the Silver Star for his actions.

All efforts to retake, and even cross, the airfield that evening were repulsed. It was a long night for the Angels and the attackers, not to mention the various pilots and service troops spread throughout the area. One P-38 pilot found his way into 1/187's CP to tell how he and the other pilots had tried to hold off the attacking Japanese with their pistols, but that many of his fellow flyers had been killed.

On the morning of December 7 (D+19), three years after Pearl Harbor, the Angels at San Pablo's mixed force of engineers, cooks, clerks and other service troops prepared to assault the dug in Japanese just as the first of the 674th PFAB arrived. After hasty briefings, GEN Swing moved up the center in a jeep to personally command the operation and wheeled the two units into position, engineers on the left, artillery on the right.

The scattered troopers who were dug in or pinned down by enemy fire around the airstrip were surprised to hear a loud voice boom, "We are going across the strip!"

PFC Michael Kalamas remembered, "I turned to look and it was General Swing, our Division CO. There was no mistaking the ramrod figure and the white hair beneath the steel helmet. Seeing him was like shot in the arm... We were in need of help and some motivating force right then, and I'm sure his appearance made all the difference."

Swing would later proudly say of his men, "They were all hard, young, fighting men--the cooks and everyone else."

With GEN Swing shouting, "Go! Go! Go!", the Angels moved forward to sweep the airfield in a straight line much like their forefathers' Civil War tactics. During the ensuing firefights, HQ-11's CPL James Vignola noted with the humor of years gone by, "I remember a G.I. bringing a message to COL (Irwin) Schimmelfineg (Swing's Chief of Staff) and I overheard the Colonel tell the G.I. 'Button your button, soldier.' The shirt pocket button was not buttoned and the Colonel was a disciplinarian. The soldier buttoned the button and then gave the message to the Colonel."

As the battle raged, PVTs Allen W. Osborne and Eustis A. Jolly of the 127th AEB parked their truck under some palm trees to run ammunition out to the troops fighting on the airstrip. After a few runs, the engineers noticed a large Japanese battle flag flying from a nearby tree and being souvenir hunters, Osborne and Jolly tried climbing the tree, but enemy fire halted their efforts. Not to be dissuaded, the duo cut the tree down with an ax and took the flag as a trophy which they later turned over to HQ-127 who passed it on to G-2 LTC Henry Muller who gave it to GEN Swing who in turn gave it to Eighth Army's GEN Robert Eichelberger. The flag now resides in the West Point Museum and superintendent MG Francis B. Wilby once noted that it was the first enemy organizational flag West Point had ever received.

*Photo of Japanese Paratrooper recovered by the 11th Airborne during the Occupation of Japan*

The standard was originally given to the Japanese Paratroopers by LTG Kyoji Tominaga, Chief of Japan's War Department Personnel Bureau and Attendant to the War Minister at Imperial GHQ. He wrote on the flag, "Exert your utmost for your country."

Across the San Pablo strip, the 127th AEB's T/5 William M. Irving was setting up his machine gun when a Japanese sniper "(exerted his) utmost" for his country by firing at William. The bullet ricocheted off an ammunition belt slung over Irving's shoulder which set off a live grenade in his breast pocket. Stunned, the miraculously unscratched Angel, who had once survived a two-streamer jump, looked at the half-dozen men around him who were shocked they were still alive.

HQ-11's CPL James Vignola had a similar close call during the attack, or at least thought he did:

"I hit the ground, beside a fallen coconut palm tree, as a Japanese plane flying just above the tree tops, flew directly overhead. To this day I thank the Lord that the Japanese pilot was not firing a machine gun at the time. I don't know whether I would have hit the ground fast enough to live to tell about it. Since he was not shooting, I assume it was a recon plane taking pictures and I guess I am on a Japanese documentary film somewhere."

By evening, Swing's forces had pushed the remaining Japanese at San Pablo into a coconut grove several hundred yards to the north (other stragglers fled towards Buri). The victorious Angels then pulled the enemy dead off the airstrips and the division's surviving spotter craft were soon back in the air. One pilot flew over a group of B-187's troopers fighting on the ground, pointing and shouting down to them, "Japs, over there!"

The Angels' comments back regarding what was so blatantly obvious to everyone were "profane and derisive."

During the day, numerous Filpinos had fled to the relative safety of the Angels' lines and they recounted how the attacking Japanese coming down from the hills had left behind them a path of destruction including wanton rape and murder. This, of course, only angered the Angels even more and many hoped for more opportunities to avenge those the enemy had so brutally attacked.

The bulk of 1/187 GIR under Sheridan, Wyoming's LTC George N. Pearson arrived at San Pablo from Buri the next day, December 7 (D+19), at around 0900. Many in the muddied 1st Battalion noted that they were down in manpower since C Company had been dropped on Manawarat to protect the forward position. Apparently this was partially in response to the 511th Signal Company's "shutting down at night" since they were drawing fire, an act that angered Swing to no end and he sent his assistant division commander BG Albert Pierson and his G-3 LTC Douglas Quandt to "straighten things out."

The first 24 C-187 men to arrive on Manawarat had been from a platoon under the command of 1LT Chester W. Kozlowski, a Paratrooper from the 503rd PIR who had transferred to the 11th Airborne after the 503rd's Noemfoor operation. Kozlowski and his men had static line-jumped from L-4s onto Manawarat and the rest of C-187 arrived a few days later.

Back at 1/187's positions outside San Pablo, PFC Eli Bernheim recalled their airstrip position, saying, "None of us will ever forget the denseness of the jungle growth to the North and East of our rendezvous. Tall, thick bamboo; sago palm; dense rain forest--in fact all the lush treacherous vegetation of the tropics covered the area and the Japs could have concealed a very large force, indeed, within its depths."

Forming a line of skirmish with two yards between troopers, the Angels headed into the thick jungle and pressed northeast. Bernheim noted, "Most of the time... all of us were groping through that steaming jungle, unable to see the men to the right and left of us and when it was all over we marvelled at the fact that we hadn't shot or grenaded each other. Considering the number of highly personal hand-to-hand fights, a greater miracle was our casualty total: two wounded."

Eli then added with some humor, "SGT MacKenna waxed exceedingly wrath when he felt himself creased across his backside." MacKenna would later find his helmet and head creased by a .50 bullet and was left for dead during a hasty withdraw. His buddies were surprised when he later walked into 1/187's CP and everyone agreed that SGT MacKenna lived a charmed life.

In two hours, the 187th's formerly "green" troopers eliminated 85 of the enemy, much to GEN Swing's delight. Swing then told 1/187th's LTC Pearson to take up positions along the Dagami-Burauen Road and to keep it open. Swing warned Pearson to watch the western approaches as he expected plenty of trouble from that direction.

A patrol from B/187 found that indeed trouble *was* coming. A large group of enemy was massing on a hill to their northwest so LTC Pearson called in artillery fire which Division stopped after a few rounds out of fear that it would hit the nearby 96th Infantry.

Frustrated, and since 1/187's heavy weapons were currently stored

*HQ3-511 PIR mortar platoon - Leyte 1944*

at San Pablo (and therefore under siege), LTC Pearson managed to scrounge up a 81mm mortar from a nearby anti-tank crew. Pearson then climbed to the crest of a hill to direct his men's fire from a position that they knew was less than 100 yards from another group of enemy Paratroopers. CPL Merrill H. Bolner of HQ1-187 spoke of the "incredible feeling of pride and loyalty I still feel for George Pearson, when I remember how he looked, standing on that ridge by Buri Airstrip, over the bubble sights of my 81 mm mortar."

That evening, 2LT Robert A. Jackson's Company A of the 382nd Infantry Regiment, 96th Infantry Division was sent to dig in along the 11th Airborne's left flank (the Angels noted that the 382nd's men fought bravely during the assaults). 2LT Jackson and his radioman were ordered to a nearby Air Corps service unit and Jackson noted, "(We) were not feeling very safe among these rear echelon troops. We felt we might be in more danger from them than from the Japanese.

## 12. Operation Wa

We dug in at the edge of their perimeter and kept our own watch."

The next morning (December 8, D+20), Jackson's A-382 found themselves facing an enemy attack alone as the other Buri defenders already had their hands full. 2LT Jackson wrote:

"In the morning they found themselves facing two machineguns and a company of Japanese firing directly over their heads. Several men were wounded, including the company commander. The mortars brought fire in as close as they dared but could not dislodge the enemy. All of a sudden, one of the company's least effective soldiers got mad and went charging at the enemy, throwing grenades and firing his M-l. It threw the enemy off and the rest of A Company also charged cleaning out the Japanese company. As they moved out in clean-up operations, a sniper shot the soldier who had started the charge. He received the Medal of Honor."

That soldier was thirty-one-year-old PVT Ova Art Kelley of Norwood, Missouri. His official citation for the Medal of Honor states:

"At this critical moment Private Kelley, on his own initiative, left his shallow foxhole with an armload of hand grenades and began a one man assault on the foe. Throwing his missiles with great accuracy, he moved forward, killed or wounded five men, and forced the remainder to flee in a disorganized route. He picked up an M-1 rifle and emptied its clip at the running Japanese, killing three. Discarding this weapon, he took a carbine and killed three more of the enemy. Inspired by his example, his comrades followed him in a charge which destroyed the entire enemy force of 34 enlisted men and two officers and captured two heavy and one light machineguns. Private Kelley continued to press the attack on to an airstrip, where sniper fire wounded him so grievously that he died two days later. His outstanding courage, aggressiveness, and initiative in the face of grave danger was an inspiration to his entire company and led to the success of the attack."

With potentially hundreds of enemy troops now scattered in small groups in the Angels' rear and the surrounding area, GEN Swing received orders to send a unit to help secure the headquarters of the nearby 5th Air Force outside Burauen. With all of his organic units engaged, Swing sent the temporarily attached 138th Infantry Regiment which had just landed at Bito Beach.

A few Angels accompanied the 138th and noted that the 5th Air

Force HQ was "lit up like Times Square". Since the HQ was in charge of planning all air operations in the area, the main buildings were lit twenty-four hours a day and bright floodlights illuminated the surrounding jungle. The 11th Airborne men knew that the skulking Japanese would quickly see the importance of such a building, though they gratefully accepted the flyers' proferred coffee and spam.

The buildings were indeed fired upon by enemy troops and the next day several 5th Air Force generals and one Army general senior to GEN Swing showed up at the 11th Airborne's CP. While the Angels were offended by the visitors' statements that they had failed to secure the 5th's HQ, Swing sent 3 platoons of LTC Douglas C. Davis' 127th Airborne Engineers who brought 7,000 yards of barbed wire from Bito Beach and created a multi-leveled kill zone outside 5th Air Force's camp.

Davis would gather his battalion of engineers on December 9 (D+21) and rightfully congratulate them on their "aggressiveness and daring in the field against the enemy in the recent action on the airstrip."

Late on December 9 the enemy Banzai-attacked the 44th General Hospital just before midnight. Rumors spread around the airstrips that the Japanese had slaughtered countless doctors and nurses, but the rumors were soon put to rest. 1/187's field kitchen crew had set up outside the hospital and when the enemy attacked, the Angels' "Skillete Commandos" stopped them cold.

Cleanup actions filled the next few days as the rest of the 187th gathered under COL Harry D. Hildebrand. HQ1-187's CPL Bolner said with some pride of the day's Buri action:

"At Buri, most of our Battalion watched while Sergeant Eugene Smith of B Company zeroed in on a Japanese soldier crossing a rice paddy, well over a thousand yards away. Eugene hit the man with his second shot, knocking him face down into the mud, where he still lay thirty days later, too far from the road for even the most ambitious souvenir hunter to check out."

In truth, the Angels were lucky as the assaulting enemy forces could have been much larger. A XXIV Corps operations report noted, "Captured orders indicated that three (3) echelons of paratroops, totalling some one thousand (1000) were to be dropped. Apparently, only one (1) echelon of about two hundred and fifty (250) paratroops actually made the attack." This was mainly due to the fact that many of the enemy transports had been shot down or heavily damaged in the attack and poor weather further hindered additional serials.

In addition, the enemy who had come down from the hills appeared to hesitate during periods of the attack on the airstrips which the Angels were both grateful for and curious about. One assumption was that they had seen Allied units moving down the Dagami-Burauen road and held back to wait for additional reinforcements.

With so many Allied troops on Leyte and sailing in the waters nearby, some Angels asked how the Japanese aircraft managed to make it to Burauen without detection to drop the enemy Paratroopers. In the years following the attack, the 11th Airborne's troopers dug into records for the enemy forces they faced and discovered that many of the Allied units on Leyte who did see the enemy transports enroute simply thought they were friendly C-47s.

Plus, as HQ3-511's PFC George Doherty, who would serve as President of the 11th Airborne Association decades later, explained:

"To avoid detection, the planes flew over the Japanese-held central Visayas, passed around the southern tip of Leyte, then continued north over Leyte Gulf, and finally as the sun was setting shortly after six o'clock, turned inland below Dulag to follow the course of a river that led to the Burauen area" after which they turned north and east.

Doherty then noted proudly:

"It has to be pointed out that the 11th Airborne Service personnel, especially the Artillerymen, who were pressed into action as infantrymen did an outstanding job at Bureauen. Not only that, but General (Sosaku) Suzuki the Superior Commander of all Japanese troops as well, as General Tomochika who was in charge of the 'Wa Operation' were nearly captured by the Artillerymen. The Japanese 26th Division was put in total retreat and disarray and ceased to be a major force to reckon with. They were scattered all over in small pockets of resistance and easily annihalated."

Indeed, as one report noted, the 11th Airborne Division destroyed roughly 80% of the enemy Paratroopers. In the days after the attacks, the Angels would search some of the enemy dead for intelligence. They were surprised to find just how well-prepared and well-equipped the Japanese were. The Angels found detailed orders and photographs of the airfields with targeted installations marked. There was also evidence that the Japanese had practiced the assault before effecting it.

And as one Sixth Army reported noted, captured documents explained that "The work of destruction was to proceed in phases, with airplanes naturally being the prime target; after them (antiaircraft) positions, gas dumps, radio installations and bridges were to receive attention. Reassembly areas for use before and after the assault were carefully pinpointed." Because of the Angels' stalwart defenses the rally points, of course, would not be used.

Additionally, documents revealed that Japan's military leadership was aware that most of the troops around the airstrips were rear echelon and service troops, along with the pilots and air crews. The surprise airborne assault was led by crack enemy troops who were highly trained and, at least on paper, would have been more than a match for the American forces on the ground who were neither as well-armed nor well-prepared for such combat.

If not for the Angels' presence around the Leyte airstrips, *Operation Wa* could have had a very different outcome.

In the years following the attack, the airborne troopers of the 11th Airborne came to hold mild respect for the Japanese paratroopers who jumped on their positions on Leyte. While the attack was shortlived, the enemy indeed managed to cause mayhem and disrupt operations around the airfields while also tying-up thousands of American soldiers who had to contend with the sudden "vertical envelopement."

PFC George Doherty summed up their thoughts when he said, "Sacrificed (the enemy Paratroopers) were for Emperor, but it was a brilliant operation for such a small force to have accomplished and should be noted in military annals and studies, what a small but well-trained military force can accomplish without leadership and communication when each individual is trained to continue with his objective if and when senior command cease's to exist."

PFC Eli Bernheim of the 187th GIR expressed the feelings of many of the Angels who had defended the airstrips when he said, "We had killed more than our weight of Jap paratroopers--the best Nippon had to offer... We knew that we were a darned good airborne infantry battalion. We knew we could fight."

While things were returning to normal around the airstrips, for the 11th Airborne troopers in the hills, things were just heating up.

# 13: Pushing West

Mahonag, Anas, Ormoc, Leyte – December 1944

*"As did most career soldiers, I served in literally scores of different combat units, the overwhelming majority of which I considered outstanding. However, I never developed the pride and respect that felt for the 11th..."*
-SSGT James "Bull" Hendry, H-511

## Maloney Hill

Miles from the action at San Pablo, on December 7 (D+19) H-511 had engaged an enemy platoon of 22 Japanese outside Patog. CPT Patrick McGinnis reported their success to 3/511's LTC Edward Lahti. Lahti then told CPT McGinnis that GEN Swing wanted him to regain contact with the enemy unit. Worn out from the fighting and sleepless nights, McGinnis, who had already led another patrol back to the position, scoffed at the general's order.

Pat called back to Lahti, "All twenty-two members of that Jap unit are dead, we just counted them. If General Swing wants me to go back down there and hold a wake for those bastards, I'll be glad to."

Little did McGinnis know that GEN Swing was standing right next to LTC Lahti and heard everything. Luckily Swing had a great sense of humor and roared with laughter at McGinnis' response.

Just to the west, I-511 moved to assault a hill on their way to Mahonag. Hearing firing up ahead, 3rd Platoon's 2LT John Maloney told his men to wait while he went ahead to scout. Platoon Sergeant James "Bull" Hendry noted, "After a few minutes word was passed back for us to come on up the hill and when we reached the top I saw LT Maloney's body lying on the corduroy trail that ran north and south across the small hill. He had been shot once in the forehead..."

Lahti sent H-511 to relieve I Company and the rest of 3/511 moved through their perimeter and continued down the trail before setting up around the heights. 3rd Battalion dug in across the enemy's supply line and at 0800 on December 8 (D+20) a loud voice to their south began shouting followed by numerous others shouting, "Banzai!" The Angels headed for their foxholes and prepared their weapons when another voice started shouting in Japanese to their north.

H-511's 1LT Miles Gale noted, "This was a nerve-wracking time as we knew eventually we would be charged and we had no idea of the number of troops we would be facing."

The Japanese officers' eerie shouts grew louder, as did the countless "Banzais". The enemy then charged and 3/511 opened up with their machine gunes and rifles. Barrels became hot, as did the fighting, and after the Japanese suffered severe losses the jungle grew quiet.

The Angels were surprised to find that they had suffered no casualties in the assault and after waiting for a time they left their foxholes to seach out souvenirs. Then, at 1200, Japanese officers began shouting again, followed by their men's voices bellowing, "Banzai!" Once more, the enemy charged again and once more the Angels forced them back.

A few hours later, 3/511's Paratroopers were suprised to hear the Japanese voices shouting a third time, followed by a third charge during which the Angels bled the enemy dearly.

I-511's S/SGT James "Bull" Hendry added, "No one foresaw that we would occupy those positions for the next 13 nights withstanding numerous banzai attacks... Our wounded were starting to pile up."

## Purple Heart Hill

F-187 under CPT George Ori occupied an old 511th outpost 2,000 yards northwest of Manawarat. Ori's company actually watched the enemy transports fly overhead and thinking they were friendly C-47s grumbled when they failed to drop any rations or supplies.

Eventually F-187's elevated position would come to be called Ori Hill and allowed the Angels to look down on a strong enemy position that 2/511 had assaulted days earlier then were told to leave for the 187th to take care of as the Paratroopers needed to continue their push west and not become bogged down.

CPT Ori's perimeter was hit by Japanese infiltrators who did little damage so the next day Ori probed the enemy's lines and was forced to withdraw under heavy fire. The 187th was discovering what the 511th had already reported: this was a strong enemy position that

## 13. Pushing West

would take significant effort and strength to overcome. The Angels in the 187th would come to call it "Purple Heart Hill."

One trooper remembered, "The precipitous faces of the stronghold were cave-studded and covered the few narrow approaches beautifully while the plateau was thick with coconut-log embrasures, fox-holes and underground galleries."

Ori's men spent the next few days and nights observing the enemy forces while remaining in Division Reserve (they received alerts to prepare to move to support the 511th, but all alerts were cancelled).

Then on December 11 (D+23) the Assistant Division Commander LTG Albert Pierson arrived at 2/187th's position at Anonang along with GEN Swing's G-3 LTC Douglas Quandt (the two had apparently straightened things out on Manawarat and the 511th Signals would no longer shut down at night). Pierson ordered the 187th's troopers to take the plateau and CPT Ori's F Company along with G-187 under CPT James Walters cleared down Ori hill towards Purple Heart Hill. With the 457th PFAB firing from Manawarat, the two companies took separate trails to flank the strong enemy positions, but their forward observers were working with faulty maps and the dense jungle made correcting their artillery support impossible.

At 1600, after little success the attack was called off and F and G Companies returned to the lines at Anonang with their wounded.

Along the way the surgeons halted the column every hours to administer blood plasma to their casualties. SGT Celo J. Harrel, who had been hit in the stomach during the earlier assaults, had walked back up Ori Hill with his intestines in his hands. Harrel's last words to CPT Ori were, "Sir, did we do what you wanted?"

As SGT Domenic Suppa of the 188th's Service Company's noted, "That's when you really start to fear the war. When you first lose a buddy, or somebody, somebody that you know, somebody close."

G-187's CPT Walters would be killed on December 13 (D+25) during another firefight with the enemy and the company would suffer additional casualties around Purple Heart Hill. Later that afternoon 1/187th arrived at Anonang and 2/187 was sent to Mahonag after telling their brothers about their battles for the Buri airstrip. 2nd Battalion troopers wished 1st Battalion good luck, knowing that they had already picked the area clean of edible camotes and wild pigs

(1st Battalion would later bemoan 2nd Battalion's "theft" of their ice cream drop before they moved out).

## Ambushes and Rescuing Easy

Let's move west and back a few days to join 2/511. After another long day of marching and fighting, on December 7 (D+19) the Paratroopers of D-511 were sent through a deep ravine into a small valley where the enemy was reportedly moving supplies. After quickly killing two Japanese soldiers, D Company's CPT Stephen Cavanaugh placed his riflemen and machine gun squads to cover the trail.

As Leyte's unrelenting rain fell, the hidden Paratroopers watched an enemy squad enter the valley carrying sacks over their shoulders. Dispatching all eight, the Angels settled down for the evening with watches set every two hours. They listened to the enemy shouting and moving through the jungle, trying to find and infiltrate their lines and sometime in the night D Company's telephone wire back to Battalion HQ was cut. HQ2-511's 1LT Evan W. Redmon and SGT Eugene Ladd bravely volunteered to go out and repair the line, but sadly both were killed a few hours later.

Later the next day, December 8 (D+20) while GEN Swing was commanding the retaking of the San Pablo airstrip, CPT Cavanaugh was told to rush D/511 back to 2nd Battalion's main position. I wish I had asked Steve how he got word of the order to move before he passed away in 2018, but my assumption is via radio or runner.

The 511th's CO COL Orin "Hard Rock" Haugen was dismayed by the order as he felt D Company should have remained in place to ambush every enemy who passed through the valley. According to CPT Cavanaugh, The Rock chewed out 2nd Battalion's LTC Norman Shipley for pulling D Company, but Shipley had done so for good reason. Easy Company was in trouble.

## Fryar's Stand

As dawn broke that morning (December 8), a stirring 2/511 was startled when the Japanese opened up with machine guns east of Maloney Hill. With bullets zipping through the banana trees over their heads, the Paratroopers smoothly engaged, only to find that once again the enemy held the high ground.

Considering it "a normal morning Banzai attack", one trooper later

## 13. Pushing West

noted, "There was no call for anyone to do anything but sit in his foxhole and shoot along previously planned lanes of fire."

After two attempts to push the Japanese off the hill, 2/511's LTC Shipley ordered a withdrawal to a better position up a nearby ridge (where several Angels argued they should have been in the first place) to reform their lines for another assault. E-511 was ordered to cover the battalion's extraction and when the enemy pressed in, PVT Elmer E. Fryar of Denver, Colorado called in mortar bombardments and directed machine gun fire to break the first Banzai charge. Because Fryar was directing the firing of the Angels' machine guns, some accounts, including from other Angels, mistakenly state that he was firing one himself.

At age eighteen, the 5' 6" Fryar had joined the United States Army and served three years (1932-35) before leaving the service then joining the Marines in 1939 at age 25 for four years. Before World War II broke out, the 147-pound Elmer registered for the draft on October 16, 1940 then worked for the Union Pacific Railroad before volunteering for the parachutes in 1942. In January of 1943 he was assigned to CPT Hobart B. Wade's E-511th at Camp Toccoa.

*PVT Elmer Fryar - E-511 PIR*

During the morning's firefight on December 8, another E Company trooper had his head "creased" by an enemy sniper, and the dazed sergeant stood and began staggering towards the enemy line in confusion. PVT Fryar jumped up from his firing position behind a fallen log and rushed out to haul the stumbling sergeant back to safety as Japanese snipers continued to fire on them both.

Elmer also used his own M1 Garand rifle with devastating accuracy during the fierce assault, but when he noticed an enemy platoon of 40-50 trying to flank their position, Fryar quickly moved to the top of a ridge to reposition himself and opened fire.

E-511's 1LT Norvin L. "Stinky" Davis later testified, "Around the position where Private Fryar had engaged the flanking attack, we found the bodies of 26 Japanese he had killed and evidence that the survivors had carried others away."

As newspapers across the nation later described it, "(Fryar) fired fast and accurately. But he was drawing all the enemy fire on himself. During the fight he was hit in the left arm (above his tattoo) and shoulder, but that didn't stop Fryar."

E-511's T/5 Neal A. Retherford of Wadsworth, Ohio, was near Fryar when the Japanese first attacked. He said, "I had been wounded by a hand grenade and was bleeding quite badly. Private Fryar was on the extreme right and he yelled and pointed out that the Japs were trying a flanking movement. There were between 40 and 50 of them."

Retherford remembered:

"Fryar went forward alone to the top of of a ridge and took up his position there to cover the withdrawal of the rest of the company. He opened up with his M1 rifle. There was a lot of firing and soon he came back and found me. He put a tourniquet on my arm and leg while the lead was flying all around us. He said he got plenty of them. He figured about half of them, anyway. He helped me down the trail and we met the lieutenant leading a wounded man."

The officer was West Point-graduate and regimental transportation officer 1LT Norvin L. "Stinky" Davis of Wells, Nevada who had taken over the platoon when 2LT Robert Norris was killed.

Davis was assisting a wounded PFC Marvin D. Douglas of Oakville, Tennessee. Douglas later pointed out that, "Fryar was wounded, too. I had been nicked by a Japanese .25 caliber bullet and the lieutenant was helping me. As we helped each other down the trail, (a) Jap jumped up from behind some bushes and aimed his rifle at the lieutenant. The other wounded man (T/5 Retherford) and I hit the ground, but Private Fryar moved past us and threw himself in front of the lieutenant."

1LT Norvin L. Davis noted that when the Japanese soldier rose from the bushes with rifle in hand, "I had no chance to move. But Private Fryar came from behind me and threw himself into the line of fire. There were seven bullet holes in his chest and stomach, but he drew a hand grenade as he fell to the ground and pulled the pin. He threw it and the Japanese was blasted all over the trail."

It was the twenty-seventh enemy Elmer killed that day. 1LT Davis added, "He died before aid could be brought to him. But as he lay there with a smile on his face, he asked us to write his to his folks

## 13. Pushing West

and tell them he'd got a mess of Japs before they got him."

A wounded PVT Elmer Fryar, whose valiant stand would posthumously earn him the Angels' first Medal of Honor, died while defending his comrades. At thirty-two years of age, Fryar was the oldest American Paratrooper to receive the Medal of Honor in World War II. Elmer's final words were actually, "Tell my family that I got a mess of Japs before I went out."

For reasons lost to history, Fryar's remains were never recovered, and he is listed with 36,286 of his comrades on the Tablets of the Missing at the Manila American Cemetery on Luzon situated on grounds that his fellow Angels would liberate three months after his death. Today the Fryar Field Drop Zone at Fort Benning is named for the Angel who stood immoveable and made the ultimate sacrifice, as is the Elmer E. Fryar US Army Reserve Center in Denver, Colorado. There is also an Elmer-Fryar-Ring in Stadtbergen, Germany.

Elmer's Medal of Honor was presented to his parents on May 12, 1945, in Denver, CO by MG Willam A. Danielson. Elmer's father Franklin said that Elmer "always loved adventure and he probably was having the time of his life before he was killed on Leyte."

The day after Elmer's stand and sacrifice, December 9 (D+22), while GEN Swing's Angels around the San Pablo airstrip were clearing out the last enemy attackers, 2/511 engaged the enemy in a creek bed and casualties were mounting, especially in E-511. The fighting became hand to hand inside the Angels' perimeter and Leyte's mud turned red with blood as bayonets, knives, entrenching tools and even helmets were employed to hold the line. In the end, seven E Company men would be buried in that stained mud alongside G Company's PFC Clyde Agent.

When my grandfather's D-511 contacted their beleaguered comrades on December 11 (D+23), they passed five seriously wounded Angels from Easy lying under poncho tarps while their comrades (some of whom were also wounded) shivered in wet foxholes. CPT Stephen Cavanaugh told E-511's pipe-smoking CPT Hobert B. Wade of LaFeyette, GA, that D-511 would cover their extraction. Wade was a legend in the regiment (and in the airborne community) as he had been the platoon sergeant in America's original Parachute Test Platoon in 1940.

It had taken a great deal of fighting for D-511 to push through to

Easy's position. D Company's S/SGT Wilbur Wilcox said, "We knew E Company was desperate, and so we pushed on against heavy resistance. The Japs let the 1st and 2nd Platoons pass and then opened up on the 3rd Platoon. Platoon SGT (Albert) Barrerio, PFC (Russell) Hyatt of the mortar squad and SGT (Ernest) Zimmerman, Assistant Squad Leader, were killed that day." (December 11).

At Camp Toccoa, SGT Barreiro was known for shouting during runs, "Come on, keep going you guys. Better men than you are dying in mud like this."

"And the ironic part was he died in mud like that on Leyte," CPL William Walter noted. "A hell of a good soldier. One of the best."

"Barreiro was a great shooter from the very beginning," said PFC Billy Pettit who became friends with the tough Italian at Toccoa and Mackall. "He was a top-notch Platoon sergeant. He was a good one."

*SGT Albert Barreiro's final photo*

D Company suffered six additional casualties but managed to break through the enemy's lines and move into chilly, well-watered foxholes as a relieved (literally and tactically) E Company began withdrawing under fire. S/SGT Wilcox remembered, "The Japs climbed trees around the area and began picking off the E Company men in their foxholes. (They) threw more grenades that day than any other time I can remember. I believe (E Company) would have been annihilated, if we had been unable to reach them."

Wilcox later said that if not for PVT Elmer Fryar's actions on December 8, "I think the whole battalion could have been wiped out. The Japs were on the high ground shooting down our throats."

With the bulk of Easy Company now withdrawn to the safety of 2nd Battalion's position, D-511's 3$^{rd}$ Platoon moved to replace a detached E-511 outpost. During their assault, SGT Ed Sorenson was flipped head over heels by an enemy grenade. Ed said, "(Private Roy) Lipanovich, who was behind me, told me later that as I was falling, I had the strangest expression on my face."

Surprisingly unscathed, Sorenson got to his feet just as PFC Charles

N. Wise shouted for him to look left. The dazed sergeant turned to see an enemy soldier rushing his way from a spider hole and Ed emptied the full thirty-round clip of his grease gun, eliminating (and nearly destroying) the threat.

## Hard Rock/Haugen Hill

As 2/511 attacked and ultimately took the strong enemy position west of Mahonag, the 187th GIR was sent to relieve 3/511 which allowed the Paratroopers to be sent forward to help clear what would become known as Hard Rock Hill, but not after the glidermen told COL Haugen's men all about the enemy's surprise attack on the San Pablo and Buri airstrips.

The 511th's hungry Paratroopers asked the glidermen if they brought any rations. The 187th's troopers said no, then asked the 511th if *they* had any rations to share. "Hell no", came the reply.

Some of the 187th's officers considered sleeping in the clearing's lone nipa shack, but the 511th's Paratroopers pointed out that it was a nice zeroing target for Japanese mortars, and furthermere, its split-bamboo floor made a bayonet attack by enemy infiltrators very possible and even probable. The 187th got the message, though when one of the officers' orderlies shot a parrot to eat, many of the 511th's Angels grew angry, saying the shots would bring unwanted attention.

A rare supply drop occured just before the 511th moved out and although they were given priority since they were moving forward, the Paratroopers left the 187th's troopers a good portion of their rations, for which the glidermen were grateful.

HQ3-511's PFC George Doherty remembered, "We left early the next morning after breakfasting on C- and K-rations, a gourmet delight. We were full of vim and vineger and two days rations, searching for a fight. At this stage of the hide and seek game we were ahead of schedule, the Japanese soldier was still in relatively good physical shape, although he was probably dying for a bowl of currie rice with chicken as we were for a good hamburger."

187th GIR's Joseph B. Giordano remembered:

"The period 11th to 20th of December 1944 was characterized by continued destruction of enemy pockets of resistance in the Anas, Mahonag, Lubi and Anonang areas. By this time it was established that the enemy's main line of defense was now on the ridges east of the Talisayan River, and on the high ground in vicinity of Mahonag. We were not too far form the 7th Division in the Ormoc Corridor in yards or miles, but the enemy's strongholds lay between us, and promised to make a strong bid to keep us from gaining contact."

In their continued effort to clear a path to Ormoc, G- and I-511 had cleared elevated positions outside Mahonag that would leave the Paratroopers positioned squarely in the middle of the main Japanese Ormoc-Buraeun supply line. Aerial reconnaissance and captured maps indicated that the trail entered the mountains at a point south of Ormoc near Anas, and it was decided to cut this trail, thereby cutting off any supply to Japanese positions in the mountains.

During the final push to clear the hill on December 7 (D+19), I-511's 3rd Platoon ambushed a group of enemy soldiers, killling between forty and fifty, while losing 2LT John H. Maloney. The hill 2LT Maloney was killed on would become known as "Maloney Hill" while the higher hill, the Angels' final objective, would be called Hard Rock Hill (others called it Haugen Hill), "Because HE was there," noted D-511's CPT Stephen Cavanaugh of Colonel Haugen's presence.

"In fact," Rusty continued. "Haugen had been personally involved in numerous fights and was gaining a reputation as a true fighter."

HQ3-511's PFC George Doherty described the 511th's new position, saying, "Picture if you will three mountain or hilltops, the highest being in the center 'Hardrock Hill', 'Maloney Hill' on one side and the one to our front and soon to be called 'Cavanaugh Hill'."

2/511 assembled outside Mahonag on Hard Rock Hill in what D-511's 1LT Andrew Carrico called, "a clearing in the jungle where the entire Battalion rested for about a week, sending out patrols and forays for any food we could find."

HQ2-511's PFC Deane Marks further described the position:

"It was a relatively cleared area on a slightly sloped field. I would guess the area was about 150 to 200 yards long and maybe 100 to 125 yards wide in its widest place. It was sort of egg shaped. The center of the area was pretty free of all activity during the day because you could get yourself picked off by snipers in trees outside the perimeter. The battalion was dug in inside the tree line around the entire circumference..."

Next to the clearing was a ridge full of decomposing Japanese

# 13. Pushing West

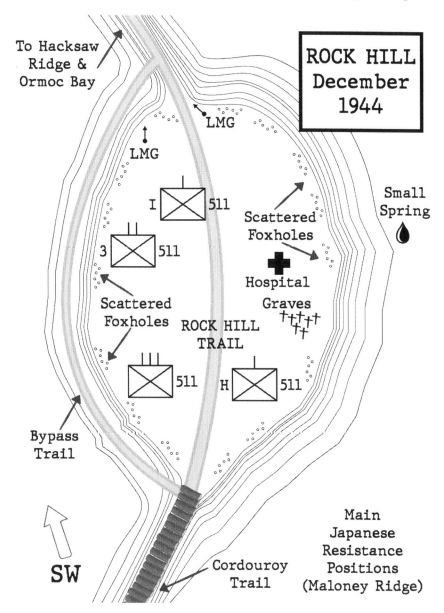

soldiers, tree stumps and potatoes (camotes) which the 511th aptly dubbed The Potato Patch. A hobo camp of poncho and branch covered positions soon emerged and tripwires were strung just outside the perimeter while patrols were organized and sent out. Within a week, the field became pocked with hundreds of slit trenches and littered with discarded ration boxes and cans.

One trooper would later note, "Little did we know that eleven hundred men would share that luxury spot in the beautiful fog, mud and leaches of Leyte for the next two weeks in a rather difficult, but not desperate situation…"

In truth, though some were still relatively fresh from Ormoc, many of the Japanese that Hard Rock's regiment were fighting *were* in desperate shape as illuminated by an intercepted message translated by one of the Division's Nisei interpreters SGT Kazuo "Freddie" Yoshida from the Allied Translator and Interpreter Section (ATIS). Freddie, who had relatives back home in internment camps, rendered the intercept: "There is nothing to eat now, no rations; we have all kinds of sickness. Casualties have been heavy. Our fighting spirit is very low."

PFC Clifton Evans of RHQ-187 wrote, "When (Freddie) was old enough for service he volunteered to prove to the American people he was as loyal or more than the white people. He almost went to Europe because he didn't speak much Japanese, but he said he wouldn't kill a white man – he wanted to kill Japs and he meant it… So, he went to an Army school, learned more about Japanese and came over here."

Even with low morale, the starving enemy on Leyte would likely come looking for those who had cut their mountain supply trail, a mud-covered cordorouy road barely big enough for a jeep to traverse. The 187th GIR's Joseph B. Giordano pointed out that the Angels used this factor to their advantage, saying, "Ambushing along the main Jap supply route was a lucrative business. Dividends ran as high as 80 of the enemy killed in a single action using one understrength rifle platoon plus a section of HMG's to man the ambush."

As such, 2/511's closing on the clearing outside Mahonag was welcomed by 3/511 which had spent three days fending of enemy attacks while ignoring radio calls from Regimental S-2 CPT Lyman Faulkner. Faulkner wanted LTC Ed Lahti to send out pointless patrols (the enemy was obviously nearby and attacking) so 3/511's radios "malfunctioned" for several days until COL Haugen and 1/511 arrived and the problems were miraculously "fixed".

The former CO of D and G Companies, CPT Faulkner's actions never endeared him to the men in either unit. After he left G-511 on New Guinea, CPT Pat Wheeler took over and LT William M. "Buzz" Miley, Jr. noted, "One was a commander and the other was a nuthin'."

Unfortunately, Wheeler would be killed near the "Y" intersection of

## 13. Pushing West

*2/511 dug in on Hard Rock Hill*

Highway 1 on February 10, 1945. As CPL Merrill Bolner of HQ1-187 GIR said, "Being a Battalion, Regimental, or Divisional Commander with the 11th Airborne was risky business. Leading a rifle squad, a platoon, or a company was *really* risky business."

Back on Leyte, given its location deep within enemy territory, Hard Rock Hill and The Potato Patch remained dangerous positions for COL Haugen's Paratroopers. While counting enemy dead on the ridge for an official report, PFC Duane Smith, an 81mm mortarman in HQ2-511, watched in horror as his friend PFC Robert Fleming was killed by a sniper just three feet away before another comrade was wounded in the right wrist. Watertown, South Dakota's SGT Harold Brandt was then hit in the stomach and died a few days later on December 15 (D+28), despite the best efforts of the battalion medical staff.

Brandt's death illuminated a big problem for the regiment which was now deep within Leyte's mountains. While strategically important, the clearing about 2 miles west of Mahonag was made up of uneven ground that would neither serve as a drop zone nor a landing strip. This prevented medical evacuation and since earlier litter-bearers working in teams of 8-12 per wounded man had reported how difficult the several-hour trek back to Manawarat was, the Angels decided that a second field hospital would be air dropped on "Rayon City" then hand-carried to Mahonag, a choice that resulted in countless lives saved. But perhaps the greatest miracle is *how* those lives were saved.

*Angels labor to carry a wounded comrade on Leyte*

## Miracle Medicine

Regimental surgeon MAJ Wallace L. Chambers, CO of the 511th Medical Detachment, wrote: "The medical situation was impossible for anyone not present to conceive... We had two blankets for protection from the rain. The blankets were stretched, and five men were housed under each blanket. It was not uncommon for one or two to be dead the next morning..."

He added, "Suture material ran out. We used sewing thread. Sterilization was bicholride or mercury tablets in a helmet of water from a nearby stream. Dressings were made from equipment parachutes. Many of the men got maggots into the wounds..."

Chambers allowed this because he knew the maggots would keep those wounds clean. In fact, Chambers sent out "maggot patrols" to find more to "treat" some of the wounded with.

2/511's Battalion's surgeon CPT Mathew Platt noted that due to supply shortages he occasionally had to perform "Bulgarian Surgery", meaning no anesthesia was available and therefore none was used. Morphine syrettes and sulfa packets were confiscated from individual first-aid kits and given to medics and surgical staffs who shared in the same frontline dangers. MAJ Chambers himself noted, "I had shells fired on three or four occasions (which) killed everybody around me and tore my clothes to pieces and did not even scratch me."

## 13. Pushing West

When Drs. Chambers and Platt were pinned down by enemy rifle fire and a mortar barrage, a wounded Paratrooper fell fifteen feet away. Chambers quickly rose to rush into the killing zone when Platt pulled him back, saying, "Old Man, you are married and have three children. I am a bachelor. This is my trip."

"Those Medics did a fantastic job under the conditions they encountered," D-511's 1LT Andrew Carrico noted of Mahonag's parachute-covered aid station. H-511's PFC Jarrold T. Davis, who later became a doctor himself, wrote, "These surgeons often worked and did miracles under circumstances which would make the men of 'M.A.S.H.' look like they were performing with the latest hi-tech material and equipment."

Jerry then added, "Many lives were saved, however, because our Regimental Surgeon, Old Doc Chambers, was a country doctor from a small town in Tennessee. During the Depression, he got paid in chickens, berry pies, bushels of corn, and now and then, loin of pork (possibly from a stolen pig.) A fancy New York doctor from the best hospitals would not have known what to do in these circumstances."

A-511's PFC Steve M. Hegedus added, "I have often said that the level of medicine on Leyte was closer to the Civil War 80 years before, than to MASH (sic) in Korea, 8 years later."

When F 511's T/SGT Harold Spring was nearly cut in half by a Japanese machinegun burst to the stomach on December 6 (D+19), he said, "I saw an angel standing on the top of a tree. It looked at me and said, 'Have no fear.'" While Harold felt an immediate calm, the rest of G Company feared they would be overcome so CPT Charles Morgan pulled his men back and Spring's friend PVT Edwin H. Gregory risked the enemy's withering fire to help his bleeding buddy to safety. Spring soon passed out and PVT Ernest Koop and CPL Louis D. Vane joined in carrying the Angel. Harold's entire squad thought the eviscerated sergeant must have died, but medics declared him alive, barely.

As snipers tried to pick them off in their ravine and then along the trail, CPT Charles Morgan ordered a litter made from a poncho and bamboo poles and Harold was carefully carried to the rear where the second-oldest man in the regiment, 1/511's Surgeon CPT Thomas A. Nestor of Providence, RI, went to work (only COL Haugen was older). Although he qualified for a deferral from the draft, Nestor had volunteered for the Army then the parachutes, leaving behind his wife, Mary, and four small children, plus a John Hopkins residency to serve.

"Tom Nestor was one of those individuals who simply was incapable of being anything other than a fine, utterly decent and courageous man," remembered 1LT Foster Arnett of HQ1-511.

After asking that a trench be dug to work in (and to bury Harold if he died), Dr. Nestor told Spring to breath in deeply the ether and Harold joked he was soon "In the twilight zone." Nestor made his incision, scooped out Spring's viscera, placed them in a bucket, then stitched the bleeding black holes, put "everything back in place" and closed the incisions, all under a poncho held up by Sid Solomon of the 221st Airborne Medical Company as Harold's friends held vigil. It was just another example of Nestor's incredible skill which the Angels came to respect deeply (the surgeon even performed several craniotomies in foxholes).

T/SGT Spring was wrapped in a blanket and before Dr. Nestor went to work on his next patient, PVT Koop and CPL Vane anxiously asked what Harold's chances were.

"Not one in a million," the tired doctor replied. Harold's friend PFC Richard B. Lapp stayed by his side all night long to make sure no one buried Spring alive. The next morning a detail came to bury Spring, but to everyone's surprise, Harold was alive. The wounded sergeant was carried by eight comrades to the small jungle "hospital" near the Lubi airstrip and watched over by medic Sam Tassone. Just in case, a wooden cross was laid beside Spring against a tree, but when Harold asked Sam for a razor to shave since his beard was itchy, Sam declared, "This guy ain't gonna die."

To the delight of his buddies, Spring survived his wounds (and the war) and flew in an L-5 to to Tacloban. At Dulag, Spring was loaded onto the hospital ship, USS *Hope* for Hollandia, New Guinea. The Paratrooper was then flown back to the states and ended up in a hospital in Chicago. While recuperating, Harold decided to write British-American starlet Olivia de Havilland who sent the Angel a large signed picture of herself, something that earned the wondrous Paratrooper even more credit among his comrades.

Months later Spring sent surgeon Captain Nestor a Captain Marvel comic book cover as a thank you.

Harold's was just one of many such astonishing stories from the Leyte campaign that Spring's fellow F-511 trooper LT Ralph E. Ermatinger attempted to explain, saying "Many wounded men survived through sheer willpower and courage."

The 511th's MAJ Wallace Chambers agreed: "I feel sure that all medical officers and enlisted men learned the will to live is what kept a lot of our men alive."

"There should be doctors for Paratroopers, and doctors for ordinary people," Dr. Nestor added. As Camp Mackall's armored units testified eight months earlier, the Angels did not know how to quit.

The Angels' "hospital" had its own dangers, of course. One trooper undergoing surgery for a leg wound awoke to find his left arm bandaged and splinted. "Hey Doc!" the confused Angel called out to a nearby medic. "I thought I was hit in the leg."

"You were," said the medic. "But you were in no condition to duck ration boxes. So, now you also have a broken arm."

Realizing that an airdropped ration box had crashed through the roof of the "hospital" and hit his left arm, the trooper grumbled, "This damned war is full of nasty little surprises."

## Mud and Rain

Back at the 511's position outside Mahonag, the Paratroopers participated in several patrols that probed the enemy's corduroy-road supply line then returned to their positions on Hard Rock Hill.

"Our columns were strung out along the trails, although we always knew where nearby platoons were," 1LT Andrew Carrico of D-511 remembered. "Our foxholes were muddy, cold, dark and smelly, but they saved our lives!"

H-511's PFC Richard Keith joked years later that mud was "a byproduct of soil and water, created by the devil to irritate you."

PFC Deane Marks of HQ2-511 noted, "The more time you spent digging the more secure you were when it got dark. I mean black dark. No shadows. no moon, no nothing. We dug in by twos or in some cases threes. With the rain there was always a couple of inches of water at the bottom. The hole was a good four feet deep.... We built little bench-like beds to keep our fannies dry while sitting in the holes behind the gun. Sometimes it worked, other times you would sag into the mud."

As one paratrooper quipped, "there were no lifeguards on duty."

Ironically those rain-filled foxholes became even more important due to other Allied successes. Starting in late November, American Naval vessels had moved into Ormoc Bay to the west, the Angels' final objective, and the Angels had watched them fire into Leyte's hills to support landings by LTG Andrew D. Bruce's 77th Infantry Division. Bruce's "Statue of Liberty" forces pushed inland from Ipil alongside the 7th Infantry Division to seize Ormoc and as they gained ground, the Japanese withdrew into the mountains where they hoped to regroup and meet up with other Imperial units.

Instead, some were rushing right into the 511th PIR's front lines outside Mahonag. The Angels spent two weeks fending off attacks and infiltrations of Japanese forces moving/escaping east while the enemy tried to regain their crucial Ormoc-Buraeun trail lifeline.

HQ2-511's PFC Deane Marks remembered, "Naval gunfire and pressure from the 77th Division landings had forced more Japs than we could handle back into the Mahonag area. There were enough of them around that through just their blundering our supply trails back toward Burauen, Lubi, Anonang and Manarawat were cut. "

GEN Swing's troopers prepared to destroy them all.

With the 77th's successful landings, the Japanese abandoned Ormoc and on December 10, 77th Infantry's GEN Andrew Bruce sent a message to LTG John Hodge of XXIV Corps which noted the 77th's success and invited the 7th ID and 11th Airborne to continue forward: "Have rolled two sevens in Ormoc. Come seven, come eleven."

Indeed, G-511 was on its way to find the 7th Infantry near Albuera, or at least they had been sent out to find them. 3/511's LTC Edward Lahti had not heard from CPT Wheeler since December 9 (D+22) after G Company had moved out to flank the enemy positions on Cavanaugh Hill (2/511 would call it "Hacksaw Hill", but we will get to that later). It was so called because 2LT Joseph Cavanaugh and PFC Mahlon Marshall had volunteered to search for the enemy supply trail and both were killed by a Japanese machine gun bursts to the chest the day before (December 8, D+21).

Mahlon's mother later noted that her Angel's last letter home contained these words: "If I am killed, don't be sad. Be proud. I LOVE YOU." She was, as was G Company who elected to name the hill the two were killed on Cavanaugh Hill.

After their deaths, G-511 would spend nearly two *weeks* practically starving to death while looking for a way to the beaches. When they finally contacted friendly forces above Ormoc Bay, most of G-511's men could barely walk because they were so malnourished.

## Arnett's Charge

On December 12 (D+25), B-511 experienced the regiment's most vicious Banzai attack to date from the eastward-moving Japanese forces. Guarding the northwest perimeter on Hard Rock Hill, the Paratroopers were assaulted at 1730 on three sides. Watching the brutal fighting, 1LT Robert S. Beightler, Jr. of Regimental S-2 turned to his good friend 1LT Foster "Punchy" Arnett of RHQ-511 and said, "God, now I know how those guys felt on Bataan."

HQ1-511's PFC Stanley Young watched with the two lieutenants as the platoon leader for the HQ1 81mm mortar squad out on the perimeter shouted, "Come on! Let's go! They're overrunning us!" Between 15-20 mortar men scrambled out of their foxholes and headed for the "safety" of the CP. Their withdrawal left a huge gap in the lines so 1LT Arnett rushed down the hill, alone, towards the fleeing men with whom he had previously served.

Exposing himself to the enemy machine gun fire, Arnett shouted, "Get your asses back in those holes!" When PFC Harry Labusohr cried that he did not have a weapon to fight with, Arnett tossed him his personal .45, a gift from a friend who had served in World War I.

1LT Arnett's courageous charge turned the mortarmen around and together they held the line. 1LT Beightler said Punchy killed ten of the enemy before his right arm was shattered when a Japanese knee-mortar exploded in his face. While it was feared the 511th's boxing coach would lose the arm, the surgical skills of CPT Thomas Nestor, who was suffering from dengue fever at the time, saved it. Arnett was evacuated back to the States after the Angels came down out of the mountains on December 24 (D+37), twelve days later.

Punchy made sure his trusty .45 went with him, much to PFC Labusohr's disappointment.

## Yankee Devils

The attacks on Hard Rock Hill continued the next day when in the early hours of December 13 (D+21), the Paratroopers in H-511 were surprised to hear a Japanese officer insulting them in perfect

English. "Yankee Devils," he seethed. "Murderers of women and children and being guilty of heinous crimes against humanity. You will be murdered!" The enemy officer's tirade droned on and on so the Angels began hurling back their own invectives which included comments about his dubious parentage, the type of work his mother was in and countless observations about his manhood.

A frustrated CPL Robert DeLane of H-511 shouted, "Come back here you UCLA rascal and I'll shoot your rear off!"

DeLane's H Company comrades roared and began chanting, "UCLA rascal! UCLA rascal!" as grenades were thrown towards The Rascal who grew quiet apart from moans which died out an hour later.

The relative-quiet was then shattered by the distinctive whine of inbound rounds and screams of "Incoming!" The Rascal's friends were walking mortars down H Company's perimeter and while some rounds landed with a dull thud (it was assumed their powder had gotten wet), one round landed in the middle of a foxhole instantly killing a trooper therein. Another cried out to God before dying despite the medic's efforts and the third thrashed around, screaming, "Help me, Mother! It hurts so bad! Oh God, I want to go home."

Moments later there was a gurgle followed by silence; God had taken him home.

The Rascal's friends then attacked like ghosts out of the fog and a vicious firefight ensued. H Company held firm and as morning broke, the fog lifted, and the Paratroopers surveyed the mass of enemy dead at the bottom of the hill. Slamming fresh clips and magazines into their rifles, the surviving Angels listened to the groans of the enemy and their own wounded and thanked God for seeing them through another engagement.

As PFC Deane Marks of HQ2-511 expressed, "There was always that feeling of, 'Glad it wasn't me.' We all felt bad, for a short time, when a buddy was killed, but deep inside, you were thankful to God that the shrapnel or bullet didn't take you. I never saw anyone who was willing to trade places with a corpse. We were so tired and burned out that all we wanted was to be left alone."

When a buddy was killed, Marks noted, "You didn't get any 'madder' at the Japs, just hated them more."

A few hours later a Piper Cub flew over a hungry and worn H

Company and only dropped batteries and crosses.

## Kill 'Em

After repulsing the enemy's multiple attacks, it was time fot the 511th to go on the offensive. According to my grandfather, 1LT Carrico of D-511, the Angels "engaged in destroying enemy strong points and securing dominating terrain" around Mahonag. During one of their many engagements around Rock Hill, COL Haugen shouted over the radio to GEN Swing, "Hell, General! We are surrounded. We don't have to look for the Nips to kill 'em."

Looking for the enemy at night was another matter and nearly everyone in the 511th PIR experienced the eerie sound of Japanese officers shouting speeches in the dark before their men yelled "Banzai!" and attacked en masse. 1LT Miles Gale of H-511 noted, "This was a nerve-racking time as we knew eventually we would be charged and we had no idea of the number of troops we would be facing.

The Angels could not understand why the Japanese, who were so adept at camouflage, would attack in such a brash manner. By the time they left Leyte, GEN SWING's troopers all agreed that the enemy's assaults would be much more effective if they simply kept their mouths shut before attacking. As G-511's PFC Edward J. Baumgarten noted, "I must have seen hundreds of Japs die—they wouldn't surrender. They'd come out like in a turkey shoot."

The 187th GIR's 1LT Eli Bernheim observed, "Their night attacks enabled us to kill them in large numbers with less cost than attack operations."

188th GIR Gabe Allen said, "the Japanese as a soldier, they were very good, but regimented to the extent that the individual was a non-thinker and simply blindly followed orders..."

PFC Deane Marks of HQ2-511 added, "Had the Japs attacted in force at one particular place they may have been able to break in. We were only one foxhole thick. The Japs lost a lot of men at Mahonag. From what I saw laying around, between Mahonag, Lubi, Manarawat and later Rock Hill. I'd say three or three hundred fifty people."

After enduring several banzai attacks between patrols, Grandpa/1LT Carrico of D-511 said, "I decided after a couple days not to put myself in the Platoon middle, which was standard procedure (for Platoon

Leaders). It was difficult for me to shoot at the enemy without hurting one of my own men."

His decision followed COL Haugen's creed: put your men first. Rock required platoon leaders like Grandpa to learn the names and squad positions of every man so they could be identified in the dark.

Making the move out of the platoon center with Grandpa was his runner, PFC Marion A. "Bud" Crowl of Canton, Ohio. Jane Carrico added that Marion was also Andy's "bodyguard" and when I asked what she meant the answer made sense: taking out an officer could disrupt unit cohesion. The Angels' SOP on Leyte and later Luzon declared that "Commanders should habitually be protected by regularly assigned body guards." Crowl was there to keep Andy alive, as was PFC David Vaughn who shared the duty. The trio became close during their tribulations and would remain friends long after the war.

## Squitters

My grandfather noted that after weeks in Leyte's jungle, the Angels were "Always hungry, always wet, always miserable. They were the worst conditions one could imagine."

When the 187th GIR's 2nd Battalion arrived at Mahonag along the 511th's flank on December 15 (D+23), they took one look at the clearing and declared, "It looks like a carnival site for damned souls."

One trooper remembered that "permeating its atmosphere was the horrible sickening odor of unburied, decomposing bodies. At once we were assaulted by the largest, most prosperous swarm of flies we'd ever seen."

To make matters worse, nights at Hard Rock Hill/Mahonag were so cold at the higher elevations that Angels took to biting on handkerchiefs to keep their teeth from chattering too loudly. Most of the 511th's and 187th's troopers had thrown away their wool blankets as they were unbearably heavy when wet and while ponchos were valued, they did not breath and the men sweated in them during the day which led to chills at night (they performed better as canopies).

Others used their last cigarettes to keep their hands warm and the chain-smoking COL Haugen used a small stick to hold the butt of a final cigarette to keep from burning his fingertips.

On top of all that, even before the 187th caught up with them in mid-

December, many of Hard Rock's Paratroopers were suffering from dysentery, or "the squitters", which left them weak and miserable. Grandpa noted that many in D-511 chose to wear one-piece coveralls, not the common two-piece GI uniforms, since the coveralls allowed them to crawl through Leyte's mud without sludge slipping into their trousers. It was a nice solution, yet for those who had dysentery it meant completely removing their webbing *and* coveralls to answer the frequent calls of nature.

Some made it in time, some did not. Finding himself in the "did not" category, an ill CPL William Walter of D-511 was razzed by his comrades, one of which exclaimed loudly, "Hey Willie, your pucker string broke."

As if those privations were not enough, Leyte's mosquitos carried dengue fever which the Angels called "breakbone fever" as it left their bodies achy and enervated. When a trooper suffering the ultimate misery, dysentery *and* dengue fever, stood to go to the bathroom, his bones would "break" or give out and he would collapse to the ground. In his weakened state, after the call of nature was done calling, the miserable trooper had to be helped to a nearby stream to clean up.

One 187th trooper noted, "Dysentry--or diarrhea, we didn't know which—-was shared by all, regardless of rank. We could console ourselves, slightly, in this affliction because we knew the Japs were similarly distressed. In fact, we'd shot several who'd cut away the entire seats of their breeches to facilitate speed in emergencies. It seemed a logical solution for this type of problem."

Although the Angels were using halazone tablets to purify their water, one small group from the 511th PIR became deathly ill when they filled their canteens in a nearby brook. Investigating medics later discovered a rotting Japanese corpse in the water upstream.

Several platoons away, D-511's PFC Charlie Jones was ordered to take as many canteens as he could to another stream. Charlie went weaponless but two comrades went along for protection and he filled several canteens before sensing another presence. Slowly looking upstream, Charlie was surprised to see a Japanese soldier doing the exact same thing several yards away.

After staring at each other, the two charged and a fistfight broke out, Jones used his helmet as a weapon while shouting for his "protectors" to do something, much to the enjoyment of the two Paratroopers watching from the hillside. After cheering like spectators watching a boxing match, they shot the enemy soldier and Jones cursed them all the way back to D Company.

## Hunger Week

Now three weeks into their jungle campaign, the Angels, whose meals had already been sporadic, began to fully face the curse of forward operators: hunger. LTC Norman Shipley, CO of 2/511, radioed COL Haugen to say, "We have been dropped no rations today. We are eating our last meal tonight."

"We rationed our food," remembered SGT Ed Sorenson of D-511. "First day, one meal divided between two men. The next day, one meal for five men. The last day for our platoon, I remember dividing two meals (between) thirteen men."

2/187th's PFC Eli Bernheim remembered, "We averaged one third of a K ration per day for 30 days and went one period of 5 days with nothing but stewed camotes... Our diet was one step above starvation and men died needlessly as a result."

Bernheim added, "(We) halted for several days and dug in on both sides of a river to wait in vain for resupply of food and clothing—mainly boots and fatigues which were in shreds."

While Bernheim and the Angels were enduring the hells of Leyte, Eli's friends in the 507th PIR, his former unit, were recuperating in England after their own trials by fire in Normandy during the D-Day landings. A few weeks later they would find themselves back in Europe to fight in equally harsh conditions during the Battle of the Bulge.

While the enemy's airborne attack on the Buri, Bayug and San Pablo airstrips had disrupted the Division's aerial resupply via liaison planes, another problem arose when a ship carrying fuel for their planes was destroyed and *then* the monsoon weather strengthened which made flying even more dangerous.

The result was that some of the Angels in the hills went anywhere from five to fourteen days with rations being dropped.

"We were a long time without things to eat," D-511's 1LT Andrew Carrico recalled of Leyte. "We only carried a three-day supply of K-Rations as we started up into the mountains. We went a whole week and nothing, nothing to eat..."

## 13. Pushing West

"One of my greatest tests was when I was offered to swap three (D-Rations) for my jungle sweater," D-511's CPT Stephen Cavanaugh recalled of his cold, hungry Hard Rock Hill ordeal.

D-Rations, which "taste a little better than a boiled potato" according to Hershey's chief chemist Sam Hinkle, were a combination of dark chocolate, sugar, cocoa butter, skim milk powder and oat flour. The later-developed Tropical bar for the Pacific Theater tasted about the same (bitter) and the mixture was so thick that Hershey's employees had to pack it into molds by hand.

When D-511's PVT Billy Pettit and PFC LeRoy Richardson were issued their last D-Ration bars on December 12 (D+25), Pettit cautioned his friend to save half for the next day. Sitting in their muddy outpost, Richardson thought about their platoon sergeant T/SGT Albert Barreiro who had been killed and replied, "Hell, Billy, I may be dead tomorrow." They both shrugged and ate the bars in one shot.

"A couple of days later, even a bite would have been most welcome," Billy remembered. He told me later, "When you're hungry, things taste good. Doesn't matter what it is."

The Angels' problem came down to resupply which as we have discussed was a ongoing issue for the 11th Airborne on Leyte. While there were three C-47s in the Angels' operational area, the Skytrains could not fly without fighter support. Plus, flying such large craft between Leyte's steep ridges and deep valleys where the 511th was located was extremely dangerous due to the thick monsoon cloud cover. And when the C-47s *did* fly, their air-dropped crates and boxes frequently drifted into enemy-controlled areas which led the Angels to call them "10-in-1s: ten for the Japanese, one for us."

A-511's PFCs George P. Nicklau and Frank S. Feussner volunteered to search for some supplies that had missed the Manawarat hospital and fallen into the nearby the ravine. They duo found a box of hand grenades and some blood plasma, which they carried back to the hospital. Some of the plasma bottles were broken, but they were packed inside sealed packages, so the liquid was still there. When medics expressed disappointment over the loss, Doc Chambers ordered them to strain the liquid thru some mosquito netting and to administer it to the wounded. "I'd rather have them die next week of glass in their blood than from lack of body fluids today," he said.

The first C-47 to try for a Mahonag/Rock Hill drop was heard circling overhead, and through a break in the clouds, my grandpa's D-511 saw the air crew standing by the jump door next to a huge stack of rations boxes. When the pilot banked to turn the craft around, the boxes shifted which caused the plane to crash. Deflated, D Company was ordered to search for the wreckage and any survivors. Miraculously the plane's crew chief had been thrown from the open door and was found dazed by the crash site after falling through the trees. Grandpa's 1st Platoon buried the flyers remains after removing their boots (so the Angels could use them and the enemy could not) then gathered what meager supplies they could salvage and carry.

A second patrol was sent to the crash site led by A-511's 1LT Albert A. Giddings which also happened to find the first evidences of the enemy's main supply trail on the island for the division.

The downed C-47's crew chief's survival was not the only miraculous story involving the crash. PFC Michael Kalamas from HQ-457th Parachute Field Artillery was temporarily transferred to the Tacloban airstrip to assist with Division's aerial resupply efforts. One morning Kalamas went to help load two C-47s, but before he could board, the ground crews said they would handle the drop. When he later heard of the crash, Michael inquired which plane went down. "543", was the reply, the craft he was supposed to be on.

When asked about what they did to survive at Mahonag after the crash, Grandpa/1LT Carrico said, "We ate anything we could find: dogs, roots, potatoes. When you're hungry you'll eat anything. Hunger was a constant gnaw in our stomachs."

Their "menu" included poinsettia roots, heart of palm salads and occasionally lemons. Some rice and canned was found earlier in the campaign on enemy corpses stuffed in socks, but that source of food became sparse as the Japanese were also running out of food after the Angels cut their supply lines. PFC Deane Marks recalled, "After about two days of nothing to eat the pangs of hunger disappear. We would sit around and fantasize on what we were going to eat when we got home. Malted milk ice cream, T-bone steaks and thousands of those greasy 'White Castle' hamburgers. Our morale was not at its highest."

Other items and recipes discussed included apple pie, Mom's fried chicken, etc. Several Angels had dreams at night of eating meals back home and the starved 511th and 2/187th troopers at Mahonag paraphrased Corregidor's 1941 defenders, saying, "(N)o papa, no mama, no Uncle Sam, no ammo, no oil, no can of Spam."

## 13. Pushing West

After vainly trying to boil water buffalo in their helmets (some Angels cooked tough "buffalo steaks" over small fires when possible), the famished Paratroopers tried to find wild deer and boar in the surrounding hills. The *one* boar they caught in a hunter's pit was split between 500 hungry mouths and some Angels used the fat to grease their weapons.

In 1999, my eighty-two-year-old grandfather wrote, "Being hungry is the worst feeling I have ever experienced, and I hope that none of you ever have to go through that."

With a laugh, he told us a few years later, "I remember sharing a foxhole with my platoon sergeant one time and I looked over at him, thinking, 'I wonder how he tastes.'"

Although they were "starving to death!" as one trooper put it, the 511th's officers noted that the men never failed to adhere to the highest principles of good soldiery. D-511's CPT Stephen Cavanaugh remarked, "morale remained exceptional and the men accepted the conditions with few complaints. I expect that all of us…felt that these conditions were what we had been trained to endure."

PFC Clifton Evans of RHQ-187 wrote home, "At present folks I'm high in the mountains on a little job. It's a little rough, but I'm doing fine. Of course I can't tell too much about what I'm doing but above all I want to point out the fact I'm safe and happy and proud to be up here with a great army and outfit, helping out."

"Morale was quite good," D-511's PFC Billy Pettit declared of the Angels. "We were hungry, of course, but not ones to feel sorry for ourselves. We were all in the same boat."

HQ3-511's PFC Robert LeRoy wrote, "We were anxious for battle," for we thought it better to die fighting than from starvation."

F-511's 1LT Ralph Ermatinger explained:

"Hunger subtly alters moral values instilled from childhood as the mind concentrates upon food for survival… Yet, in the deepest trough of mental depression on 'Hungry Hill' when ill and hungry men would say, 'the enemy would do me a favor if he put a bullet through my head,' the mere appearance of a Japanese soldier galvanized them into instant action. In the adrenaline of the fire fight, lethargy vanished, and hunger and bodily ailments were forgotten as the troops set about accomplishing the missions for

*Angels dug in around Hungry Hill*

which they were so well trained—destroying the enemy."

Unfortunately, ammunition, especially grenades, was also running low so the Angels of the 511th PIR and 2/187 were warned to be careful in firing their weapons, and to eliminate test firing. When H-511's PVT John Coats flipped the safety off his M1 and fired off three quick shots, SGT Willie L. Valentine boomed, "Coats, stop wasting ammo!"

John plopped back down in his foxhole and declared, "I'm not wasting ammo, I just shot three Japs."

As Coats' famished comrades lay in their cold (it was between 45-50 degrees at night), wet foxholes, thoughts of home helped them endure. Their mostly empty musette bags contained the last of their Leyte treasures: letters (from New Guinea) and photographs from loved ones (those not ruined by the rain).

Many Angels would pull out those photos or read the few letters they had carried into the hills and for a few precious moments the horrors of war, and the hunger pains, melted away.

# 14: Breaking Out

Mahonag to Ormoc, Leyte – December 1944

*"I'm in the Parachute Infantry and it's the toughest, best damn outfit in the world."*
-PVT Sidney Smithson, B-511, January 1943

## War Trophies

Although suffering from such deprivations, the 511th PIR and 2/187 GIR maintained regular patrols that reported frequent contact with the enemy along the razor ridge west of Mahonag.

D-511's CPL Murray Hale, who was recovering from his shoulder wound, remembered: "The walking wounded did our best to lend encouragement to our buddies as they went out on patrols every day, feeling badly that we couldn't join in. It was not a good feeling, but there was little else we could do."

Occasionally the Angels' "patrols" were little more than payback missions undertaken by small squads who had lost a buddy or officer to a lone sniper or infiltrator. The enemy dead and captured booty made some recompense, at least.

Their captured Leyte "souvenirs" included Japanese battle flags (*hinomaru yosegaki*) which, according to Shinto beliefs, embodied the spirits of deceased ancestors and kept their owners safe.

*Senninbari*, or "belts of a thousand stitches" were given to Japanese soldiers by women to promote good luck in combat, evoke courage and provide protection from injury. Many soldiers rejected the latter belief and instead believed their *senninbari* would allow them to bring great destruction upon the enemy before their own life was taken in service to the Emperor.

Despite being warned that souvenir-worthy items could be booby-trapped, D-511's 1LT Andrew Carrico noted that these objects were prized possessions for many young Angels (when they did not end up in some higher-ranking officer's footlocker, that is). Carrico said with a laugh, "After all, there was little else of value in those jungles of

*A group of Angels with captured Japanese battle flags (hinomaru yosegaki) "l*

Leyte." A small handful of Angels initially sought out the gold in the teeth of enemy dead so they could melt it down later to make gold jump wings, but that habit was highly frowned upon.

The Angels were doing far more than just souvenir hunting, of course. On December 15 (D+28), GEN Swing wrote to his father-in-law, Peyton C. March, "the Father of the U.S. Army" who General Joe knew he would appreciate the Angels' Leyte undertakings. He wrote, "It appears that we are a 'secret' weapon although we have been in the line since 20 November. You notice that no mention has been made of our activities in the daily communique. Nevertheless, we've killed over 2000 Japs…" in what Swing called "a process of extermination…Casualties on our side are not light…"

The next day, December 16 (D+29), some of those very men fighting westward, including the casualties, gathered for Mass as chaplains stood in a Mahonag foxhole. It was not a complete Mass as there was no "fruit of the vine" for the Sacrament. Instead, the dirty, unshaven 511th PIR Paratroopers humbly used water sprinkled with lemon powder and a few crumbs from a K-Ration biscuit to take Communion.

Feeling strengthened in body and spirit, the faithful Angels listened to "Chappie" talk about God and his power over mortal and eternal life as their dead lay buried just meters away.

## Chappie Walker's Miracle

It was towards God that many in the 11th Airborne frequently looked on Leyte for succor (if not to Him at least in His direction). D-511's 1LT Andrew Carrico testified that many of his fellow Paratroopers told him, "If I learned nothing else from the war, I learned to pray."

Many of GEN Swing's "Hell's Angels" quietly relied on faith to see them through as they studied their Bibles, found ways to serve their buddies and shared meager rations in muddy foxholes.

Such was the case with PFC Robert LeRoy. After surviving two days and nights of vicious banzai attacks, the Paratroopers of Robert's HQ3-511 were growing weak from a lack of food and sleep. When LeRoy, the former cowboy, tried to climb out of his foxhole on December 18 (D+31), he felt an invisible hand push him back down and he fainted. When Robert came to, it occurred to him that he had only eaten a small handful of rice in the past seven days. Crawling under his raincoat, LeRoy prayed: "Please Dear God, give us all more strength to help us win this war for thee, and for our country, that someday we may once again worship you in peace and happiness."

*Chaplain CPT Lee Walker*

Stength was on the way, but when GEN Swing heard that the 511th PIR's regimental chaplain CPT Lee E. Walker was going to jump out of a Piper Cub to visit the weary 511th on the frontlines and conduct funerals around Mahonag, Swing said, "The Chaplain doesn't have to go there."

CPT Walker replied, "That's where the Chaplain is needed." On the ground, on December 18 (D+31) "Chappie" invited PFC LeRoy and those in the 511th not on perimeter duty to join him for a special service at noon.

After reading from the Bible, CPT Walker declared, "Now men, we are ready to ask for supernatural help from God. Let us all pray."

*Hungry Angels looking skyward for relief*

The Paratroopers of the 511th PIR meekly knelt in the same mud they had slept, fought, bled, and buried friends in as Chappie prayed. After the "foxhole church service", PFC LeRoy returned to his place on the line, feeling renewed and fortified. As he looked up at the overcast sky, Robert watched the never-ending rain clouds finally part for a few minutes to reveal a beautiful blue tropical horizon. The hungry men of HQ3-511 then cheered when a single C-47 flew overhead to drop badly needed supplies and rations.

In the eyes of the 511th PIR, God had heard the Angels' prayers and many in the 511th agreed that "Chappie Walker's Miracle" met all the requirements for sainthood (although there were some 3rd Battalion troopers who had just soaped up to bathe only to watch the rain stop due to the clouds clearing).

When some HQ-511 troopers were tasked with digging a grave for a fallen comrade a few days later, Chappie Walker noticed that the men were struggling due to the physical energy required and the emotional loss. Chappie took turns with their shovels so they could rest and its easy to see why Walker was so loved by the Angels.

Over five thousand miles away, Germany readied its last major offensive of the war. As the hungry Angels' endured Leyte's brutal trials, their brothers and friends in the 82nd and 101st Airborne Divisions were about to face the equally brutal Battle of the Bulge.

# 14. Breaking Out

## Patrols

On December 17 (D+30), the day before Chappie Walker's Miracle, a ragged D-511 moved out on a trail-clearing mission where they encountered a small enemy force. CPT Cavanaugh's men pushed the Japanese back into the forest then were recalled to 2nd Battalion after several additional firefights with LTG Kurishu's 26th Division troops.

During another D Company patrol, Grandpa/1LT Andrew Carrico led 1st Platoon down a trail to their southwest where they found themselves cautiously entering a long, narrow canyon. Scouts reported that a large Japanese force, perhaps an entire regiment, was in the process of breaking camp so 1st Platoon swiftly spread out along the canyon's ridges and dispatched over sixty of the enemy, nearly twice their own number. The Angels were shocked to find that the Japanese had cruelly left their wounded behind in a primitive field hospital, bound and gagged, to die.

D-511's successful engagements only confirmed what RHQ-511 and GEN Swing's staff already knew: the enemy's forces in Leyte's mountains were being systematically eliminated by the Angels. COL Orin Haugen's staff estimated that the 511th PIR had completely destroyed Japan's 12th Independent Infantry Regiment. Intelligence also believed the Paratroopers were now engaged with the Japan's 4th Company of the 11th Independent Field Artillery and the Izumi 5319 11 Company of the 26th Engineering Regiment.

## The Shelling

After their eventful day, an exhausted D-511 rejoined 2/511's perimeter where at 1900 LTC Norman Shipley and another officer foolishly started a very visible fire to heat water for coffee. Astounded, PFC James Wentink of HQ2-511 screamed for the officers to put the fire out before he shot it (and them) out.

Wentik wrote years later, "Getting started on the trail the next A.M., Shipley gave me a very dark look, and meanwhile an artillery spotter plane, L-4 or L-5, was cruising around right overhead. I don't think the Japs had small artillery spotter planes in this area..."

As 2/511 moved north towards Maloney Hill at about 0900 on December 18 (D+31) the column was violently shelled. D-511, who was just ahead of Fox Company on the trail and had just eliminated six Japanese, heard the shells roar in followed by explosions then screams (had the barrage happened minutes earlier, D Company and potentially my grandfather would have been hit). HQ2-511 lost several men, including CPT Charles Jenkins, and F-511's CPT Charles Morgan reported that 10% of his company had been hit. LTC Shipley himself was seriously wounded in the leg and many in 2/511 Battalion angrily blamed him for the whole incident as a spotter probably saw his fire the night before.

PFC Wentink said, "I have learned in later years that Shipley would probably have been brought up on charges had he not lost his leg."

HQ2-511's PFC Deane Marks said, "We had at least a dozen dead and close to forty wounded, some very badly wounded. (Drs.) Platt and Chambers saved a lot of them. Some they couldn't."

As a regimental journal notes, "Today's casualties 14, burials 13..."

Regimental Surgeon MAJ Wallace E. Chambers, 2/511's Battalion Surgeon CPT Matthew Platt and the medics indeed saved many lives that day. They operated on the injured, including boxer and original Toccoa-man SGT Peter E. "Kuts" of HQ2-511 who had what was left of his leg amputated by Dr. Platt on the spot with a trench knife as he cried out for his wife Margie. A few minutes later, the wounded LTC Shipley was brought to Platt's position, shouting and whining loud enough to draw attention from every Japanese in the area as he demanded the doctor's attention. SGT Kut, who lay panting on a stretcher, opened his eyes and said, "Aw, go ahead. Forget about me and take care of that big cry-baby."

*SGT Peter Kut*

The surgeons did so then Kut weakly called out to the men around him, "Say, let's everybody bow our heads and have a moment of prayer." Division chaplain CPT James O. Morman reported that the former prize fighter from Pennsylvania led the prayer as bloodied medics, troopers and surgeons bowed their heads. Kut then told them he was ready for the hospital as Drs. Nestor and Platt organized poncho stretcher bearers from what was left of F-511 to take the twenty-five wounded to Mahonag two hours away while D-511 continued towards Haugen Hill, attacking several Japanese groups along the way until they entered 1/511's perimeter at 1800.

At the regiment's Mahonag field hospital, SGT Kut asked "Chappie" Morman to pray for his wounded captain, HQ2's CPT Charles E. "Baldy" Jenkins, who unbeknownst to Peter died in the shelling. Chaplain Morman remembered, "In all his agony he was interested in something else, thinking of how his captain was coming through."

RHQ-187th GIR's PFC Clifton Evans said of Morman, "A Chaplin doesn't have to do anything in the service except practice his religion or for that matter he has the right to get out of the army at any time, but Chaplin Morman says, 'If the rest of my boys jump, I jump too' and he did. He took the hard two weeks training with us - exercises, tumbling and all the rest. That just goes to prove what a fine man he is."

Despite laboring all night, the surgeons were unable to stop the bleeding and SGT Peter Kut, another fine man, passed away at 0400 the next morning (D+32). Words of his valor were sent to his wife, Margaretta Pale who was caring for their nineteen-month-old son.

"We laid him to rest temporarily in our little cemetery up on the side of the mountain," recalled Kut's friend, D-511's CPL Murray Hale. Some in 2/511 angrily argued that the young boxer could have been saved had the surgeons not been so busy tending to the bawling LTC Shipley, a fact that only enflamed their animosity towards the officer.

2/511's regimental surgeon CPT Mathew Platt later reported that he was treating 25 wounded and that five others had died at the hospital. The sudden influx of casualties used up the hospital's remaining supplies and regimental surgeon MAJ Wallace E. Chambers's request for resupply went straight to GEN Swing who

*The 511 PIR's cemetery on Rock Hil, "the saddest place on earth"*

made sure the Doc's needs were met that day.

H-511's PFC Gerold "Jerry" Davis noted, "At the 'hospital', foxholes were dug double-width, so that (wounded) men could lie side by side--one not in pain to warm and comfort and hold and quiet his partner, in pain, and maybe cold and afraid, too."

The source of the six-round barrage has been debated with many Angels believing they were from a Marine battery of 155s back on the Dulag beaches to the east. Arguments could also be made for Army guns on Ormoc Bay to the west and if either case is true, the carnage-causing shells may have ironically been unloaded by the Angels themselves during their time as stevedores on Bito Beach.

Perhaps the most likely culprit would be a nearby enemy 75mm gun that was visually sighted on 2/511's column. Another possibility were the enemy's two 105's found located at Lonoy five miles from the Mahonag area which could have been used to support the enemy's drive towards Burauen. Either way, given the accuracy of the first three round burst and that the second was fifty yards ahead of the column, the Japanese probably had eyes on the Angels, though again, the Angels themselves debated whether it was friendly or enemy fire that had caused so much damage to 2/511.

Leyte's dark campaign was wearing on the 11th Airborne.

## Chappie Morman's Miracle

Nearly a week into their Hungry Hill "fast", on December 19 (D+31) COL Haugen's hungry men heard the engines of a half-dozen "Biscuit Bombers". It was a timely appearance as "Flying Parson" Chaplain CPT James O. Morman, the Texan Baptist with a Clark Gable mustache, had only moments before asked the Paratroopers to pray. Morman's Miracle was equal to Chappie Walker's the day before.

RHQ-511's PVT Melvin B. Levy jumped to his feet when he heard the planes, exuberantly yelling, "Chow call!" The famished men of RHQ laughed as the Kings County, NY native listed off the food items he believed would soon float their way. Cheers erupted as red and green parachutes started dropping from treetop level, but the excitement turned to alarm when some boxes and crates came in much faster than others. The L-5s made another pass and this time their crewmen pushed out parachute-less fifty-pound boxes of K-Rations which crashed to the earth, sending troopers diving into their foxholes.

Oblivious to the danger, PVT Levy continued his joyous tirade. "It's raining chow, boys!" Shockingly, one of the large boxes landed squarely on Melvin's shoulders, decapitating him instantly as his good friend T/4 Rodman "Rod" Serling looked on. Levy's death was difficult for Rod and was one of the many combat experiences that left a lasting impact on the future creator of the famous "Twilight Zone" television series.

*T/4 Rodman "Rod" Serling*

Rod marked Melvin's grave with a Star of David in honor of his friend's Jewish heritage and a subdued RHQ-511 quietly gathered the dropped supplies. Unfortunately, some troopers found themselves becoming miserably ill as their deprived stomachs struggled to digest the processed K-Rations, though plenty of veterans argue that *always* happens with K-Rats. One Angel proclaimed the packaged meals "unfit to eat, but you had nothing else."

D-511's PVT Bill Dubes explained the general attitude of many of the Angels at this time: "That's a soldier's lot, an infantryman's anyway; he's always hungry and never gets enough sleep."

With the miraculous yet limited drops of rations, COL Haugen sent out a stern order, saying that "Any unit found with any rations not belonging to them does not get the next issued meal. Any man found with another's equipment or in a food line illegally will be court-martialed."

## Maloney/McGinnis and Maggot Hills

With F-511 and HQ2-511's return to Mahonag due to the disasterous December 18 barrage, on December 19 (D+31) the rest of the 511th PIR around Haugen Hill watched Battery A of the 457th PFAB bombard the slopes of nearby Maggot Hill (so named because of the abundance of maggots eating the Japanese dead). Pleased with the results, COL Haugen radioed Manawarat at 1130, saying, "457 are doing a magnificent job." He would tell GEN Swing a day later that the 457th's fire on McGinnis Hill was "near perfect."

At 1430 H-511 with three attached flame thrower teams began their climb up Maggot Hill, struggling in the slippery mud as they went. The

*One approach to Maloney / McGinnis / Purple Heart Hill*

Paratroopers made it 25 yards of the enemy lines when the Japanese opened up from their MLR. The Angels could see the enemy dug in on the hilltop and hours later, after utilizing the attached flame throwers and demolitions, a portion of the hilltop was theirs.

The Paratroopers would later count 432 of the enemy dead from Japan's 12th Independent Infantry Regiment on the hilltop, mainly due to the Angels' artillery barrages, and H-511 named the crest McGinnis Hill in honor of CPT Patrick McGinnis who led the charge. This was the same hill that I-511 had earlier named Maloney Hill after 2LT John H. Maloney who was killed there on December 7.

For reasons much debated, H-511 had been ordered west and after 1/511 elements were pulled off the hill, no security was set which allowed the Japanese to quickly reoccupy and reinforce their positions, and those H-511 had abandoned, which they fiercely defended against I and H Companies' subsequent attempts to retake it. The resulting casualties frustrated many in 3/511 who lost friends because of the poor decision to abandon the high ground. A regimental journal later explained the "loss of McGinnis Hill and recapture because of extended regimental perimeters."

"It is safe to say that efforts to retake it resulted in over 50% of the Regiment's casualties on Leyte," wrote Triple CIB recipient, I-511's SSGT James "Bull" Hendry.

No wonder the 511th called the bloody height "Purple Heart Hill."

H-511 moved back into A-511's position (A Company pulled back into the perimeter) to watch the 457th PFAB's test rounds land on the enemy positions. The artillery battery was then told, "Harassing fire 90 or 100 rounds tonight. Save 300 for tomorrow because we are really taking the hill. Be on call at 0700 tomorrow."

The troopers in RHQ-511 then grumbled at COL Haugen's directive to shave in preparation for GEN Swing's arrival the next day. There was no lack of expletives as the Paratroopers scraped off a month's worth of growth and regarding Haugen's order to "check on latrines, police-up perimeter", I-511's SSGT "Bull" Hendry later tersely commented, "Somebody was dreaming."

Knowing that his Division was close to their breakthrough to Ormoc Bay, MG Swing had flown to Manawarat in an L-4 and then started out on the trail at 0805 on December 20 (D+33) to meet up with COL Haugen and the 511th at Anas. He was accompanied by LTC Douglas Quandt who wanted four bodyguards to accompany the General in the form of four G-511 Paratroopers who had sufficiently recovered from their wounds to rejoin their outfits. As the group prepared to leave Manawarat, one of Swing's bodyguards PVT Clifford W. Servias suggested the general remove his stars which reflected in the limited sunlight.

G-3 LTC Douglas Quandt noted, "(Swing was) always going where he shouldn't to see what is going on."

"Nothing doing," Swing responded to PVT Servias's request, saying that he'd be "damned if he'd remove his damn stars for any damned Jap." After a sniper fired a shot between him and PVT Servias standing nearby, Servias declared, "General, I don't care if YOU get hit or not, but you're drawing fire in MY direction." Swing removed his stars. One unknown trooper who was there wrote, "It didn't take stars for everyone in the Division to recognize Swing."

Another division historian wrote, "We simply couldn't see how the enemy could miss a tall, gray-haired gentleman, wearing Major General's stars. Looking like a composite of all the great warriors of history--except those whiskered Civil-War characters, of course."

Given the size of the ridge and the strength of the enemy's defenses that the 511th was facing, 3/511's LTC Edward Lahti told COL Haugen that he wanted to use H and I Companies to retake the heights. Haugen said he would ask Swing for permission (Swing did not want the companies moving across open ground down the trails without his consent). Following his three hour hike from Manawarat on December 20, Swing arrived at Haugen's CP and permission was given. Although they faced stiff resistance H- and I-511 pushed 250 yards west up a nearby crest with steep sides which Operations called The West Ridge, but 3/511 called Lahti Hill after LTC Edward Lahti. I-511's assault led them to within 20 yards of the hill's crest at which point they fixed bayonets and took the crest one bloody foxhole and trench at a time.

Keen to push to the coast, COL Haugen then ordered 2/511 to "get off your ass and get going" to take the north side of the ridge. 2nd Battalion pushed through 3rd Battalion's perimeter and gained 400 yards on what *they* called "Hacksaw Ridge" after 2nd Battation's MAJ Frank S. "Hacksaw" Holcombe of Westminster, SC who had replaced the wounded LTC Shipley as battalion CO.

Holcombe was not the first in line for the promotion, however. After Shipley was injured in the shelling, 2/511's three company commanders had unified before COL Haugen to object to the assumed command of the "not too highly regarded executive officer," as one put it. Instead of punishing them for their mutiny, Haugen promoted his respected S-2 MAJ Holcombe to the position with CPT John Norwalk taking over HQ2-511 (a few weeks later 3/511's LTC Ed Lahti would become Haugen's new XO).

As the Paratroopers continued their fight for Hacksaw Ridge/Lahti Hill, the 127th Airborne Engineers Company A were pushing east from Ormoc Bacy as they labored to complete their preparations for the division's arrival on the coast. The engineers had been ordered to find and improve the enemy's supply line trailhead near the 7th Infantry Division's CP on Ormoc Bay then widen it enough for trucks and ambulances to await their descending comrades who were carrying out their wounded.

Having completed their task on December 19 (D+32), A-127's CPT Kenneth H. Keim sent the coordinates for the road to COL Haugen who ordered the 511th to head for Ormoc where the 408th Airborne

Quartermaster Company had spent over a week creating an immense supply dump to replenish the Angels. Having successfully destroyed the enemy's mountain supply line at a cost of 92 KIA and 13 MIA, Hard Rock was eager for his battle-worn men to complete their rendezvous with 7th Infantry. He told his staff, "We want our turkey intact and ready for the stove when we arrive at coast."

Unfortunately, a strong line of enemy forces stood between the Angels and their holiday dinners and as D-511's CPT Stephen Cavanaugh noted grimly, "(The) enemy showed every sign of continuing his defense at all cost."

## Hacksaw Ridge

On December 21 (D+34) COL Haugen again sent Companies H (on the left) and I (on the right) to engage the enemy on Hacksaw Ridge. Given his regiment's acccomplishments, and losses, Haugen then told GEN Swing that he wished his T/O strength was like that of the 503rd PIR (of future Corregidor fame). Hard Rock then explained that he had several 1st Lieutenants that were acting as company commanders and that his enlisted men were to be commended for their willingness to fight.

While 3/511 cleared Hacksaw Ridge's north side, including several reinforced log bunkers, there was still a strong body of Japanese on the southern end, some of whom cannibalized the bodies of a 3/511 machine gun crew killed in the fighting. Enemy dead were later found carrying cooked pieces of human flesh in their pouches which could explain why a Japanese prisoner captured that day had his throat slit by an unknown trooper before the Japanese Language Detachment team could interview him.

It is of note that the 11th Airborne only captured twelve prisoners on Leyte (some documents list 10). D-511's PFC Bill Dubes declared, "We never took prisoners and I know they never did either."

Eighth Army's GEN Robert Eichelberger noted, "I have never heard of live infantryman captured by the Japanese from Milne Bay and Buna to the Philippines who came out of it alive... Our men knowing this had a tendency to fight to the death like rat when cornered."

Although they were not cornered, COL Hard Rock Haugen's 511th PIR was fighting fiercely themselves. Haugen knew that GEN Swing had ordered 2/187 GIR to move out along the trail towards Ormoc on

December 23 (D+36) to help finalize the break through to the coast. Trusting his men, COL Haugen radioed 2/187's LTC Arthur H. Wilson, saying, "We will not need your help to take the southwest hill."

Wanting to complete their mission before the "Glider Riders" arrived, Haugen sent the 511th's E and F Companies up the steep southern flanks of Hacksaw Ridge. The young Paratroopers could smell the sea breeze in the air but found themselves facing a well-entrenched foe. The young Paratroopers inflicted heavy losses on the enemy and at 1550 Hacksaw Holcombe's 2/511 reported, "We have assaulted hill and taken it." COL Haugen then told him to push as far as possible before setting up their perimeter.

Although they had gained 900 yards, 1LT Andrew Carrico of D-511 noted, "After repeated unsuccessful attacks against a tenaciously defended enemy strongpoint, 2nd Battalion was forced to disengage and establish a perimeter for the night."

After the exhausted Angels dug in, the Japanese shouted down to F-511 while shining flashlights from the hilltop. They should have known better, but a handful of irritated Paratroopers fired on the enemy's lights. The Japanese, in turn, used the muzzle flashes to drop 81mm mortar shells on the Americans' revealed positions.

## The Rat's Ass Charge

COL Haugen, fresh from another meeting with GEN Swing on December 21 (D+34), decided an early attack would be the most effective means of eliminating Hacksaw Ridge's last defenders who had repelled E and F Companies' assaults earlier in the day. As 1LT Andrew Carrico of D-511 explained, the 511th had learned that "The Japanese were famous for sleeping late."

There was, perhaps, another reason for Hard Rock's orders. GEN Swing had given him permission to send 2/511 up the hill for another attempt to take the heights, but *only* if LTC Arthur H. Wilson's 2/187 did not overtake them first. And I doubt Hard Rock wanted to wait.

At 1900, CPT Stephen Cavanaugh was notified that D-511 would affect the frontal attack the following morning at 0630, December 22 (D+35). Rusty was also informed that the trail leading up to the enemy positions was narrow and densely forested and with night's darkness upon them, no reconnaissance could be made. With far too little information for his taste, Cavanaugh left Battalion HQ.

## 14. Breaking Out

*D-511's initial narrow approach up Hacksaw Ridge*

"We are going to hit them just before daylight and take the ridge," he told his assembled officers. Gambling on stealth and surprise, Dog Company would pass through Fox Company's positions (the ones trading shots with the Japanese) and cross the Line of Departure in a column of platoons. 1st Platoon would take the lead and affect the main assault and Rusty elected to march directly behind 1st Squad which would allow better operational control.

"We were issued three K-Rations…and I ate all three that night," said PFC Charlie Jones. "E and F Companies had the hell knocked out of them; I thought 'Why save them?'"

A few hours later as a morning rain fell scout PFC David Vaughn led 1st Platoon across the LOD at 0400 while the rest of D Company hung back. At first, the "trail" led up a ridge so narrow that CPT Cavanaugh said theirs was an "attack with a two-man front."

Breaking into squads, the Angels quietly scaled the trail to roughly two hundred yards from the enemy's suspected positions. Pausing to fix bayonets and recheck their rifles, machine guns and ammo, under orders for silence the Angels shared nods of good luck before 1st Squad wheeled left off the trail while 2nd Squad headed to the right.

1st Platoon consisted of:

*Platoon HQ* included Platoon Leader 1LT Andrew Carrico, T/SGTs William Corley and George Cushwa, CPL Eldon Norton and PFCs

Marion Crowl, Joseph Signor and Al Haar.

*1st Squad*'s thirteen members consisted of S/SGT George Taylor with SGT Archer Copley as assistant, ammo carrier PFC George Schlobohm, T-5 George Locke and riflemen PFCs Sam Sheffield, Arthur Chlebove, Elmer Eutsler, Charlie Jones and John Tkaczyk with and PVTs Cass Wotusiak, W. E. Milbrant and George Hammond.

*2nd Squad*'s roster consisted of PFCs William L. Dubes, John H. Bittorie, Russell C. Kilcollins, Thomas W. Talbot, Earl Richardson, James W. Tuten, Charles N. Wise, Augustus F. Wilder, Harvalee L. Watson, Henry A. Olbrych, David V. Vaughn and PVTs Stewart D. Stevenson, Gilberto C. "Slick" Sepulveda, Myron W. Pickens and William R. Pugh.

As dawn crept weakly through the heavy clouds, the advancing Paratroopers discovered and silently eliminated two enemy outposts. By 0530, 1st Platoon's 2nd squad was well within the main enemy position. PFC Billy Pettit said the quiet Angels watched "Japanese soldiers… milling about the area, some half-dressed and others preparing meals."

Noticing a sentry at the edge of the bivouac's field fifteen yards away, everyone watched scout PVT Sepulveda of El Paso, TX sneak forward, bayonet at the ready, but when the enemy turned and noticed Gilberto, "Slick" shot him which drew the attention of the sentry's comrades lounging close by (some remember this was PFC Charles "Red" Iles who initiated the action).

An enemy machine gunner opened fire and sprayed the area which alerted his buddies who also opened fire, erratically, which stopped 2nd Squad in their tracks.

Hearing shots off to his right, Grandpa/1LT Carrico bellowed D Company's catchphrase, "Rat's ass!", which signaled 1st Squad to throw grenades at the enemy positions to their front and hit the dirt (PFC Vaughn declared once back during stateside training, "I don't give a rat's ass!"). Explosions shattered the morning air as 1st Squad engaged the startled Japanese positions on the left. 1st Squad's SGT George Taylor then led six of his men into a strong enemy position which they destroyed with more grenades which allowed the rest of 1st Platoon to move forward into the fight.

There were some in D Company who said 1st Squad's SGT George

## 14. Breaking Out

Taylor was the one who shouted "Rat's Ass!" when the attack stalled at the enemy position, while others said it was 1LT Carrico. Just one of the many clarifying questions I wished I had asked Grandpa before his passing in 2016.

During these initial movements, CPT Stephen Cavanaugh stayed just behind my grandfather, 1LT Carrico. With radios ineffective, Rusty said this position allowed him to command the operation verbally.

Off to their right, 2nd Squad's PFC John Bittorie of Brooklyn, NY began hurling phosphorous grenades on the run to burn enemy positions and in all the excitement, the 6' 2" machine gunner ran into a tree branch which smashed his nose and sent his helmet tumbling (John had already lost his front teeth in a North Carolina bar fight). Eyes blurry from the pain, Bittorie failed to notice the Japanese soldier six feet away drawing a bead on his head. Luckily PVT Augustus Wilder did and promptly dropped the enemy.

Bittorie's ammo carrier PFC Russell Kilcollins and Assistant Gunner PVT Stewart Stevenson ran to the dazed machine gunner, still on his back, who muttered, "Sunnuvabitch, right between the eyes." Realizing that the Brooklynite believed he had been hit, Kilcollins pointed to Bittorie's "enemy" and yelled, "You're the dumb sunnuvabitch! Get up, you ran into that tree limb!"

The firefight grew in intensity and after pushing up the hill, D-511 realized that besides the expected Main Line of Resistance (MLR) 1st Platoon's thirty-five Angels found themselves almost face-to-face with a withdrawing Japanese column of around 150 Japanese on a trail 10-15 feet wide.

"It was a machine gunner's dream," Grandpa/1LT Carrico recalled.

Japanese in the column opened fire and heavily outnumbered 1st Platoon found themselves taking cover. PFC Deanne Marks remembered, "The Jap fire in small arms and heavy machine guns was heavy, but not accurate. We were pinned down. We were in a hell of fire fight. Out of the blue someone hollers 'RATS ASS! Who's with me?' It was guy by the name of John Bittorie..."

Full of adrenaline, PFC Bittorie had shaken off the stinging pain from his damaged nose and asked for a full belt for his .30 machine gun which PVT Stevenson helped load as bullets zipped overhead. John then slung his 30-pound 1919A4 Browning light machine gun on webbing over his shoulder. Grabbing the barrel with an asbestos mitt, Bittorie charged the enemy column, shouting, "Banzai! Rat's ass! Who's with me?!"

1st Platoon watched the exposed "Bad Soldier" fire a burst from the hip at 400-550 rounds per minute. With decaying jump boots and rotting uniform exposing jungle ulcers on his legs and body, John's charge galvanized the platoon into performing a Banzai bayonet charge of their own. PFC Marks noted of the extreme danger John put himself in, "Most important, if you did fire from the hip you had to stand and anyone who stood up in any kind of fire fight was dead — right then."

Marks continued:

"As (Bittorie) hollered he began shooting. He was defying the Japs and certainly inspiring us as we were hugging the ground. He cut loose with two long bursts. Spontaneously the whole line jumped up and started laying down fire and hollering, 'RATS ASS.' A couple of woodpeckers opened up, but our fire power overwhelmed them. When we got into the Nip area past their M.L.R. (Main Line of Resistance) you could see them laying all over the place in grotesque positions. Half in and half out of their holes. Some were dead, some convulsing, some moaning. All were shot. A lot of them ran away... The whole fire fight lasted three or four minutes. We did not lose one person dead, but Bittorie took a .25 slug in the shoulder..."

"Bittorie was a soldier that was a great soldier in combat, but he wasn't worth a damn in the every day," John's platoon leader 1LT Andrew Carrico chuckled. "He was always in trouble, stuff like that."

"He was an excellent soldier," remembered PFC Billy Pettit. "But he was a brawler. He was always fighting someone."

Inspired by Bittorie's charge, 1st Squad on the left led by 1LT Carrico and SGT Taylor and 2nd Squad on the right led by SSGT George "Reb" Cushwa and PFC William Dubes began a trotting marching fire line up the hill that decimated the Japanese column and defensive positions on the ridge. Cushwa had helped evacuate the wounded to the rear then hurried back to lead 2nd Squad and for his daring leadership, Carrico recommended the Staff Sergeant from Roxboro, NC for the Bronze Star, saying, "he was a helluva nice guy."

Many in 1st Platoon also felt John Bittorie deserved the Medal of

Honor for his actions that day. The "screw-up" from Brooklyn, who would retire a Command Master Sergeant with over 30 years of jump status, said decades later, "There are two kinds of military reputations. One is official and on paper in Washington, DC. The other is the one that goes from bar to bar from the mouths of those who served with you there. That is the only reputation I ever really cared about." A modest John also said that because of the leadership of CPT Cavanaugh and my grandfather 1LT Carrico, D-511 was able "to get so close to the Jap position undetected and the fast reaction of the assault while catching the Japs withdrawing was the key to success."

Inspired by John's charge, the Angels rushed forward with shouts of "Rat's Ass!", "Banzai!", "Habba, habba!" and their old chant of "48, 49, 50!". PFC Charlie Jones of 1st Squad remembered watching panicked Japanese soldiers diving off the ridge, saying it was like shooting rabbits in heavy brush.

CPT Cavanaugh noted, "The suddenness of the attack panicked the Japanese. With D Company at it's heels the enemy sought to reestablish a defensive position against the attack but were hit before they could establish any resistance... This forward surge by the company continued for two to three hours with the enemy running in desperation, but losing the race."

"I think the frustration and pent up anger of many days of hardships and siege set off this charge on the enemy position. (We) shot everything in sight," PFC Bill Dubes added.

A note in the regimental journal at 0850 simply says, "1st Platoon of D Co pulled a 'rats ass' charge on the Japs at dawn... The Japs haven't stopped running."

And lest we picture a group of fresh, healthy Paratroopers making the assault, the truth is that most of 1st Platoon was sick with one debilitating jungle malady or another (or several) and all were suffering from malnourishment. SGT Royalle Streck, for example, was so feverish that he had to be guided down the hill after the fight as he could not even walk straight. No, D-511's assault was affected by a small band of brothers who refused to quit or let each other down. As Marine aviator, astronaut and U.S. Senator John Glenn explained, "You train people to have more loyalty to their unit than they have to themselves, to the point where people will go out and do things that defy all instincts of self-preservation."

Like make a Rat's Ass Charge against ten-to-one odds.

"Jungle foliage was thick, making it difficult to get through," Grandpa/1LT Carrico noted of their push up and across the ridge. "We somehow kept together, fighting until about noon when Captain Cavanaugh passed another platoon through us and we were able to stop for a much-needed rest."

With rain falling, 1st Platoon moved into the retreating enemy's former positions. Enemy dead lay everywhere, and some were still twitching as the Paratroopers kicked dirt over the corpses at the bottom of the trenches. When one moved towards PFC Alex Village Center, The Chief reflexively beheaded him with his machete.

The young Angels of D-511 breathed sighs of relief that they had survived another engagement as the success of their assault settled in.

"I estimated we killed over 300 that day," 1LT Carrico recalled.

Listening to reports of the D Company's effective rout on the ridge, COL Haugen turned to his staff and said, "Tell (General) Swing we will have the trail (to Ormoc Bay) open for him today."

"With more bravado than sense," CPT Cavanaugh recalled, "I sent a runner to the rear to inform the Battalion Commander (Major Holcombe) that we had overcome the enemy with a bayonet charge and that he was on the run and that we were in hot pursuit." Rusty wanted to press the attack with the rest of D Company, but his runner surprisingly returned later with orders to halt.

"Needless to say," Rusty said dryly, "I disregarded the order, feeling that if we paused the enemy would have a chance to regroup and establish defensive positions."

D Company pushed forward a short distance when another runner arrived and emphatically repeated Holcombe's order to stop. Four hours and 2,500 yards after the attack began, Rusty reluctantly had his sweat-drenched company move off the trail to rest in a grove of palm, mango and papaya trees overlooking Ormoc Bay where they could see 7th Infantry positions at the base of the mountains.

At about 1000, G- and E Companies of the 187th GIR passed through their lines and continued pressing towards the coast. The 187th GIR's Joseph B. Giordano noted that his fellow glidermen were impressed by D-511's Rats Ass Charge-work. He wrote:

## 14. Breaking Out

*Some of D-511's 1st Platoon after their "Rat's Ass Charge"*

"(2/187) went forward to overtake the lead elements of the 511th who were pushing forward at a breakneck speed along the Japanese supply trail which ran along the razor back ridge in the direction of Ormoc. It was difficult to understand how a unit engaged in bitter fighting could keep up the terrific rate of march forward. The trails everywhere were littered with enemy dead, as was the slopes of the ridge."

We will follow G- and E-187's hike to the coast in a moment, but the next day, December 23 (D+36), the rest of 2/187, led by GEN Swing himself, passed D-511's perimeter to contact the 7th ID near Albuera (and receive the accolades, though there was some very minor enemy contact along the way). Jumping Joe only paused long enough to tell D Company's CPT Cavanaugh, "Nice job, Cavanaugh," before moving on.

"My thoughts regarding that gentleman were at that (moment) anything but complimentary," Rusty recalled. With steel in their eyes, D Company watched the clean-uniformed and apparently much better fed glider-riders march past their grove towards the beach. With most of the fighting finished, the exhausted Paratroopers believed the march to Ormoc Bay should have belonged to the 511th PIR. It was rumored that COL Haugen's men had been halted, in part, because of their haggard appearance. While they had inflicted destruction upon the enemy, the Brass felt the Paratroopers looked like death warmed over and wanted a fresher, cleaner-looking unit to arrive on the beaches for publicity.

This treatment was a source of resentment for the 511th for years since Swing later boasted that on December 22 alone "his Angels" killed 750 enemy and captured 2 mountain howitzers and 16 light and 7 heavy machine guns.

"D Company never received the acknowledgement deserved for affecting the breakout from the mountains of Leyte," CPT Cavanaugh objected, "except for our Regimental Commander (Colonel Haugen) who recognized what we had done."

A regimental journal notes, "Haugen is pleased with Holcombe's early morning attack. It stressed the value of assault and pursuit, and late-morning breakfasts."

There is, perhaps, a simple explanation to Swing's actions. After speaking with Paratroopers from the 511th PIR and Angels across the division, I think Swing knew the truth: Hard Rock's 511th PIR had led the 11th Airborne's push into and over the mountains and after a month of heavy fighting, the mighty Paratroopers were down to roughly 60% strength. CPT Cavanaugh noted, "We came out on the other side of the island a pretty well decimated regiment."

PFC Eli Bernheim, now of 2/187 and formerly of B-511, said, "I can recall that the 511th troopers were really pissed off when we passed through them, but they looked extremely beat."

One 187th historian noted, "For weeks (the 511th) had been fighting desperately, repulsing banzai attacks at night, attacking the Nips by day and using all available men for carrying patrols. Hence neither side got much rest. Its men were emaciated from lack of food, many fell prey to jungle fevers, all were taut with strain. Their feet were in horrible condition for most of their boots were worn out. So, now they hobbled about with their feet wrapped in banana leaves."

Though tired and worn down, 3/511's LTC Edward Lahti proudly noted, "the 511th had all but wiped out the Japanese 26th Division and much of the 16th Division. For all practical purposes, the fight for Leyte was over." At least for the 511th.

## Friendly Contact

On December 22 after D Company's successfully pulled of their famous Rat's Ass Charge, G-187 GIR's 2nd Platoon passed through

## 14. Breaking Out

their lines and continued towards the coast. Although I'm sure he was frustrated that his men were told to halt and not continue to the beach, the 511th PIR's COL Haugen told G-187's lead elements, "You must keep going as fast as possible. Run if you have to, but don't give the Nips a chance to set up their weapons; we've got them with their pants down, you can't even stop to kill them all, just push through, we are behind you and will take care of them as we come to them. Just keep going, fast, any questions?" There were none.

G-187 eliminated several tiny defensive positions with handfuls of defenders and after climbing up the side of a gorge, 2nd Platoon fired a purple smoke grenade into the air then watched as another was fired from a ridge four hundred yards away by soldiers from the 32nd Infantry Division which the 187th eventually made contact with after rough hiking along the "trail".

One 187th GIR historian noted:

"While it was the 511th Parachute Infantry that spearheaded the entire move across the mountains and made the junction possible, it was the 2nd Battalion 187th Glider Infantry, lead by Company G, that actually made physical contact. Major General Joseph M. Swing, Commmanding General of the 11th Airborne Division, was present at the time this contact was made, and was the first man to walk into the lines held by the 7th Division."

Another gliderman wrote:

"We cheered again at our first glimpse of the sea and the western slopes of the mountains. That night we were securely snugged in at ALBUERA, camped on clean grass beside a stream. Aside from the parties detailed to carry out the litter cases, the war on LEYTE was over for the Second Battalion. On Christmas Day our kitchen trains arrived, bringing with them-plenty of turkey and trimmings."

Because of the Angels' successes in the hills, the road was finally open between Burauen and Anas and the area west of Mahonag was cleared of the enemy, including the breaking of the Japanese supply line on the island.

As 2/187 camped near the beach and interacted with the 7th Infantry units, 2/511's exhausted and worn, but *not* beat, Paratroopers sat overlooking Ormoc Bay. Over six-thousand miles away CPT Richard "Dick" Winter's Easy Company, 506th PIR huddled in their own foxholes in Bastogne's frozen soil.

Feeling slighted by division brass, 2/511 dug in for the night on December 22 (D+35), grateful that they were within a grove of fruit trees which provided a dinner of papayas and mangos while some sang, "I'm dreaming of an Ormoc Christmas" to the tune of Irving Berlin's 1942 hit "White Christmas".

While the stench of 200-300 Japanese dead made slumber difficult, the men of D-511 which had punched through the enemy's last line of resistence rested easier, knowing that after a month of heavy fighting they could see (and thankfully smell) the ocean just a few miles away.

Let GEN Swing and his darlings in 2/187th "clear" the last stretch; D Company knew that they had paved the way with their blood, sweat, toil and tears. While the Paratroopers later accepted that the 187th and 188th had fought well on Leyte, it was the 511th who suffered 75% of the Division's casualties while destroying Japan's 26th and 16th Infantry Divisions.

For trooper PFC Deane Marks of HQ2-511 there was some satisfaction in their order to halt. From his position on the hill he could see a half-buried Japanese corpse that lay submerged on the trail. The dead soldier's uniform had become the color of the mud and his body was buried under a few inches of that mud. Thinking it was a stone that would carry them over the muddy low spot, on their leisurely walk to the beach many of the 187th's "Glider-Riders" inadvertently stepped on the dead soldier's back with a sickening crunch and a small plunge into the filthy water.

Marks remembered:

"We would sit there and watch the look on the faces of people that, thinking it was a stone, would step on it, sink in and thus cause the most sickening noise you ever heard. This was especially gratifying when we were told to sit tight and let the 187th pass through the 511th and be the first 11th Airborne troops to get to Ormoc and the sea. Every other person stepped on our 'rock'."

Deane gleefully never warned the 187th about the "landmine."

# 15: Down From Heaven & Healing Waters

San Pablo, Buri and Burauen Airstrips, Leyte – December 1944

*"The 11th Airborne Division encountered extremely bitter resistance in the MAHONAG-ANAS (29-27) area but after much hard fighting at close quarters broke up organized Jap resistance in the passes and eventually succeeded in reaching the west coast and making contact with the 7th Division."*
-XXIV Corps operations report, February 1945

## It's Christmas

On December 23 (D+36), the battle-worn Angels began shuttling their wounded from Manawarat to Mahonag and from there to the 511th PIR's position's on the slopes overlooking Ormoc Bay. At 1745 a message was sent stating that "The main mission of this unit now is to get all of the wounded out before Christmas."

During December 24 (D+37), the 511th's Paratroopers kept busy carrying rations from Mahonag to the different battalion positions as well as continuing to bring their casualties forward to Hacksaw Ridge where COL Haugen's CP lay just two hours from the bay. B-511 and a platoon from the 127th Airborne Engineers's B Company cleared the CP and continued on to the coast, as did a group from the 221st Medics who were assisting the wounded from Mahonag.

After the battle for the Burauen airstrips, B-127 had followed the 511th and 187th into the mountains to improve the trail between Burauen and Albuera. C-127, in the meantime, had been busy improving the Angels' trail west to Mahonag while A-127 had widened the trail from Ormoc east towards Mahonag.

At 1747, COL Haugen received orders that his men had been waiting two days for: the exhausted 511th PIR was to march down to the coast the next day. The good news was then added upon when RHQ-511's CPT Ben Petrie radioed, "Turkey at base camp 26 December."

Hard Rock told all his battalion commanders, "All units will move at

0730. Carry out all possible supplies. Merry Christmas. Gumbo 6."
The 511th PIR's bloody campaign on Leyte was officially over.

On December 25 (D+38), at 0730 the 511th PIR's platoon leaders and NCOs got their men on their tired, muddy feet for the march down to Ormoc Bay. With shin-gunto swords and Japanese rifles jutting out of their packs, their last cigarettes safely tucked in cartridge belts, and hunching over from the weight of their equipment, the emaciated Angels trudged toward the beach with faces muted by the hells of war.

CPL Murray Hale of D-511, one of the walking wounded, recalled, "The march to the beach was literally a dream. Dreaming of a hospital, a shower, a meal and a bed – and not necessarily in that order."

2/511's column stretched over half a mile, followed by 3/511, RHQ and 1/511 who brought up the rear with COL Haugen. Nearly 250 men had to carry their wounded, including those from Manawarat and Mahonag who could be moved, on what RHQ-511's T/4 Rod Serling called "a gray morning carved out of gray clay and shadowed by fog."

Hobbling on a wounded knee that would pain him for the rest of his life, the future creator of the "Twilight Zone" did not feel like celebrating his twentieth birthday on "a God-forsaken mountaintop". Rod noted, "(I)t was not the weather, it was the mood, I remember— the kind of mood that is the province of combat and is never fully understood by those who have not lived with the anguish of war."

I-511's S/SGT James "Bull" Hendry described carrying their wounded, saying, "Carrying those litters was pure hell, not only for us, but even worse for the wounded, many of whom had been wounded for up to two weeks. Most of us still walking were 30- to 40-pounds lighter than we had been a month earlier, many had minor wounds and we all had the GIs and jungle rot."

The men in the Angels' winding column had physically survived, yet words fail to fully describe the emotions of that survival, the odd blend of relief to be leaving a combat zone and the numbness that came from time in it. Their once-vigorous bodies were worn and atrophied by weeks of hunger, illness and exhaustion. Their formerly bright faces now had "tired inward-looking eyes reflecting nothing." Their jungle ulcer-covered hands had inflicted death on the enemy and buried friends. Their revered jump boots were falling apart, their uniforms rotted, and their spirits raw. Even for Angels, war was Hell.

## 15. Down From Heaven & Healing Waters

Or as one paratrooper put it, "After Leyte, Hell was a vacation."

RHQ-187th's PFC Clifton Evans noted, "It was just a miserable way to have to live. I was in the mountains all the time. It hardly ever let up raining and the mud and slop was terrible. I never had a dry feet and I was always having trouble with them. They will start cleaning up now though. It seems to me like I walked a thousand miles all told and in those mountains it's pretty rough."

2/187th's PFC Erni Bernheim wrote years later, "Actual combat was much fiercer on Luzon, but in my entire military experience, nothing could top Leyte for sheer human misery and endless mud, insects, rain and truly horrendous conditions."

Of their island ordeals, D-511's PFC Bill Dubes simply declared, "It was a nightmare."

The 511th PIR's Regimental Surgeon Doc Chambers, who had done so much for the Paratroopers in the hills, would later write, "I am emotionally depressed at our high casuality rate."

HQ2-511's PFC Deanne Marks noted, "The division lost 168 killed, 12 missing and 352 wounded. This was the fourth highest casualties and third highest in dead in the XXIVth Corps. When you consider the understrength of the 511 and the rest of the division, this was a high average."

D-511, for example, left Bito Beach on November 23 with 117 men; twenty-one of their comrades now lay dead in the mountains or were being carried out on poncho stretchers. The 511th itself was down to 60% strength and Doc Chambers estimated that after they came down from the hills, the regiment's remaining men (many of whom were exceedingly ill) needed six weeks to recover.

G-511's David Webb remembered, "Battles across Leyte produced a truly pitiful looking bunch of Paratroopers by the day we finally trudged into the Ormac Bay area. An ordeal we all wanted to forget. Exhausted, sick and wounded, we had done ourselves proud, but were too tired to realize it - or to give a damn might be more fitting."

As the 511th PIR continued their slog down the hills, someone at the front of the column stopped and whispered, "It's Christmas…" Troopers around him grew quiet, which alerted those further back in the column that something was going on. Normally whispers meant the enemy had been sighted, yet as simple Christmas greetings drifted down the line, the Paratroopers were touched by the emotions of the moment and became lost in their own thoughts of home, loved ones and the buddies who would see neither again.

Their quiet revere was broken as one 2/511 trooper began to sing.

*"O come, all ye faithful*
*Joyful and triumphant*
*O come ye, o come ye to Bethlehem*
*Come and behold Him*
*Born the King of Angels!"*

Other broken voices soon joined in.

*"Yea, Lord, we greet thee,*
*Born this happy morning;*
*Jesus, to thee be all glory giv'n.*
*Son of the Father,*
*Now in flesh appearing;"*

Sing choirs of Angels, indeed.

T/4 Rod Serling wrote:

> "I continued to lift my feet one after another, and suddenly I wasn't aware of the cold rain or the mud. I gave no thought to the sickening ache deep inside the gut that had been with me for so many days. Someone had transformed the world... We sang as we led the wounded by the hand and carried the litters and looked back on the row of homemade crosses we left behind... It had come indeed—the Holy Day. The day of all days. It was Christmas."

Reading Rod's words of that holiday miracle on Christmas over sixty years later, my grandfather 1LT Andrew Carrico of D-511 softly noted to us with tears in his eyes, "I remember."

The only disruption to the Christmas spirit that Leyte morning came from LTC Norman Shipley who had been wounded in the leg during the December 19 shelling. From his stretcher, Shipley repeatedly called out to surgeon CPT Matthew Platt, "Platt! I'm giving you a direct order to *stop the pain*." Regimental lore states that a guard had to escort Shipley to Ormoc to prevent the complaining officer from being thrown over a cliff (plus, he was still blamed for the barrage and the resulting casualties).

About 250 Filipinos, Army brass and 32nd Infantry Regiment troops turned out to watch the singing Paratroopers, marching in broken jump boots and rotting fatigues with oozing jungle sores covering their bodies. In spite of their ragged appearance, and the Brass' earlier concerns, the 511th PIR entered the encampment with power.

H-511's PFC Richard "Dick" Keith later wrote, "The glue that held (the regiment) together was the strength of character of the men; their cohesiveness, discipline, and their love and respect for each other. Add to this the word courage; the ability to go out day after day, attacking the enemy, fatigued but strengthened in their resolve to defeat the enemy, and eventually get on with their lives."

RHQ-511's 2LT William "Bill" Abernathy who had helped with the division's aerial resupply efforts between San Pablo and Manawarat and the 511th's units in the mountains (and courageously led patrols to the forward units to deliver updated area maps) described what he and his fellow Paratroopers endured on Leyte:

"Recently I've made a couple of trips over the roughest trail one ever saw. It's like climbing Mt. Everest for hours and is a rugged trip for anyone. However, the regiment made it and then fought when they got there.... It (was) still resupplied entirely by air as nothing else can get in. It rains here more than on could think possible and when it rains – no resupply. Once the outfit wasn't resupplied for several days due to the weather, but kept on with the mission just the same."

As Regimental Sergeant MAJ Fredrick Thomas declared with pride, "(The) 511th withstood combat experiences in the mountains that would have ruined an ordinary army unit."

A-511's PFC Steven Hegedus wrote, "All the fun we had, all the pranks we pulled, all the camaraderie we developed during Basic Training, Jump School, and more training was the bond that the agony of Leyte only served to make stronger."

MG Joseph Swing's men had indeed come out of the mountains steel and D-511's young PFC Billy Pettit later declared, "I feel privileged to have had the opportunity to serve with them."

## An Irate Rock

While 2/511 was singing as they came down from the hills, COL Orin "Hard Rock" Haugen was at the rear of his regiment's column where at 0900 he and his bodyguards and staff came across a lone Angel sitting along the trail. PVT Lee told Hard Rock that he had been left there, alone, by 3/511 and RHQ's attached medics.

Hard Rock, who was suffering from Breakbone fever at the time, exploded. That one of his wounded men would be abanded on the trail with enemy still prowling around by more of his troopers was unfathomable.

## Healing Waters

The Angels' wounded were passed to the Medical Corps who loaded the men onto landing craft for a short trip down the coast to Baybay where an old church had been converted into a hospital (most were later loaded onto a hospital ship bound for Hollandia).

There are some discrepancies as to what the 511th PIR did next. While most of the 11th Airborne's units were trucked back to Bito Beach on the east coast, some of the Paratroopers agreed that they were trucked back. Others said they sailed back and even the regimental journal mentions "2nd Battalion and 3rd Battalion and part of Regimental HQ are ready to load on boats" on Christmas Day, yet Paratroopers from all battalions remember differently, even from what the regimental journal indicates.

Either way, after returning to their initial landing area on Bito Beach, the Angels were issued new fatigues and mosquito-proof jungle hammocks. GEN Swing's smelly, dirty and tired Angels moved to the beach for a warm-water swim. Splashing into the surf, the naked young men scrubbed their mud-, sweat-, blood- and insect repellent-covered bodies and felt skin slough off their feet.

HQ3-511's PFC Robert LeRoy described the overall feelings of the day, saying, "We were happy... What a thrill it was to drop my packs and weapons, take off my boots and worn out socks, then slide my aching feet into the warm ocean sand."

A division after action report stated that, "By 25 December 1944 all organized resistance except in the ANONANG area had been broken in the division sector. The remaining Japanese were scattered into small, isolated groups, incapable of any further coordinated action."

GEN MacArthur's Christmas Eve message was distributed throughout the theater and the Angels were pleased to find themselves finally mentioned: "Operating in the central mountain regions southeast of Ormoc, the 11th Airborne has been waging aggressive warfare along a wide sector. The Division has annihilated all resistance within the area."

MAJ Edward Flannigan of the 457th PFAB proudly noted, "Other units had maintained, after actual attempts, that the central (mountain) ranges were impassible and military operations could not be conducted in the area. We proved otherwise."

The 457th's PFC William Skinner wrote proudly that he was "part of the greatest military group there ever was - the 11th Airborne Division. How proud I am yet to belong to this ELITE group..."

When the 457th's Battery D left Manawarat on New Years (after firing all their remaining ammunition) and hiked back down to Bito Beach, they found themselves looking at a strange sight. CPT Luis Burris noted, "Down in the mud flat there were two strange looking individuals with a jeep. As we came closer we saw they were Red Cross Girls with hot coffee and donuts. The usual wise guys had nothing to say."

"Reports say we killed 5,760 Japanese on Leyte," D-511's 1LT Andrew Carrico added to GEN MacArthur's use of annihilated. "Altogether our platoon (of thirty-five men) probably killed 500 between November 22, when we went into the mountains, and December 25, when we came out."

Doing the math, D-511's 1st Platoon had an 83-to-1 kill ratio with the Division's being 45-to-1. The 457th PFAB's CPT John Conable noted, however, that "The count of (enemy) dead is probably low because of the nature of the terrain."

For their actions on Leyte, the 11th Airborne received 69 Silver Stars, 6 Soldier's Medals, 90 Air Medals, 138 Purple Hearts, 240 Bronze Stars and 1 Medal of Honor.

HQ3-511's PFC George Doherty proudly exclaimed, "The 11th Airborne Division proved that a small airborne division strategically placed could contain and defeat a whole army."

Tokyo Rose, of course, told a different story. HQ-11's CPL James Vignola wrote, "I remember a radio broadcast from Tokyo Rose when she said the 11th Airborne Division had been wiped out."

## First And Second Christmases

To help the 11th Airborne celebrate Christmas, the division's 408th Airborne Quartermaster Company acquired ten thousand turkey rations. The Angels also distributed Red Cross packages and the division's chaplains held holiday services before the highly anticipated chow call was sounded.

"General Swing promised us the best Christmas dinner we had ever eaten if we ran the Japs off Leyte," D-511's 1LT Andrew Carrico remembered with a laugh of their December 26 meal. "He kept his word. We had turkey with all the trimmings and pineapple ice cream."

D-511's CPL William Walter added, "We had only been supplied, 11 days out of 30 and were so hungry we gobbled up everything."

It was the first true hot meal most had eaten in seven months and twenty minutes later, Paratroopers rushed for the beaches or slit trenches. Grandpa noted, "Everybody got sick. Our stomachs couldn't handle it because we'd gone so long without good food."

The good food also helped make up for another tropical problem the Angels endured. Upon arrival back at Bito Beach, GEN Swing's troopers discovered that the gear bags they stacked under palm trees over a month before were rotted through. After throwing away ruined uniforms, books, letters and other decaying items, the Paratroopers took to sun tanning, swimming in the ocean, and playing ball in the sand or cards in their tents. They perused newspapers, watched movies and generally allowed their tired bodies and minds to rest. For now, their nights were free from enemy infiltrations and the nightmares that would come later.

Mail Call was christened "Second Christmas" as the "mailmen" made their rounds and the Angels' biouvac filled with the sounds of cheers, shouts and "YIPPEEs" with news of births, hometown victories and other positive developments (or curses with the occasional "Dear John" or notice of a friend's death in the service).

"We didn't even get mail in those 30-plus days (in the mountains)." D-511's 1LT Andrew Carrico remembered. It should be noted that the frontline units did not, but Division HQ, the rear echelon units and those at the hospitals at Manawarat and Mahonag did recieve the occasional mail drop.

Church services were held to renew their spirits and RHQ-511's

2LT William Abernathy remembered, "Here the church is open air, and the pews are containers with mortar and artillery ammunition inside. The service was good and well attended."

## Meeting General MacArthur

As their bodies healed, the 511th's Paratroopers spent more time on the beach and in the ocean. Some took to exploring the surrounding areas and units, including two young Angels who did something most Privates would never dream of: They called upon a five-star general.

The 511th PIR's PFC Ralph Merisicki (H-511) and PVT Charles Feuerisen (HQ3-511) had been tasked with delivering a captured enemy map of California with invasion sites clearly marked on it to General Swing's HQ near Buareun. The map had been found in a dead enemy officer's satchel. After visiting GEN Swing's CP, the two Angels were told to deliver the map to GEN Douglas MacArthur's headquarters at Tacloban.

PVT Feuerisen, the former Fort Benning Jump School instructor, turned to his comrade and noted, "Ralph, we'll never get this close to General MacArthur again. Why don't we visit him?"

A duty sergeant outside MacArthur's office was less enthusiastic about their plan and turned them down. Undeterred, the two Paratroopers found LTC Roger O. Egeberg, MacArthur's physician, who told them to come back in an hour. They did so and MacArthur greeted them with outstretched hand, saying he had visited both of their hometowns (the Bronx and Cleveland).

MacArthur and the two Angels spent ten minutes discussing the 11th Airborne's actions in Leyte's mountains while overlooking operational maps. The privates were surprised with just how aware the General was of their beloved division's undertakings and they boldly asked why the newspapers back home were not reporting on their victories and advances.

MacArthur explained that he was leaving the 11th Airborne out of official communiques to keep their presence a secret from the enemy as they were a "secret weapon." That satisfied the two Paratroopers, but GEN Swing later said with a laugh, "He had blarney all right."

Before leaving, PVT Feuerisen asked another question his comrades had been wondering about: why were the Angels being used as ground infantry and not jumping behind the enemy lines as they had been trained to do? MacArthur assured him that they would be jumping soon as he had something special planned for them.

The 11th Airborne's Assistant Division Commander BG Albert Pierson noted, "MacArthur throughout our time with him showed he had soft spot in his heart for airborne troops..."

Perhaps to further assuage the Angels' pride, as Feuerseisen and Merisiecki made their way out, MacArthur declared in front of all the generals and other Brass who were waiting to meet with him (and who were annoyed that two lowly privates had taken so much time), "Tell your boys that I'm real proud of the 11th Airborne."

Back on Bito Beach, the 11th Airborne's troopers were doing their best to rest and recuperate after their mountain ordeals. On December 30 with hands covered in jungle rot, D-511's 1LT Andrew Carrico wrote home to his wife Lois (on borrowed stationary since his letters and photographs had almost all been ruined by the jungle):

> *"War is a terrible thing, honey. I never realized how much until I got into actual fighting...*
>
> *"That saying that 'there are no atheists in foxholes,' certainly is true. I heard more than one man say, 'If I didn't learn anything else, I learned how to pray.' I don't want you to let me forget God when I come back, honey because He certainly hasn't forgotten me.*
>
> *"The American Army, honey is the best in the world and I'm proud and honored to be a member of it. There is no doubt in my mind that we shall win."*

Some letters were more difficult to write. Company commanders did their best to compose messages to the families of those killed in action. Each battalion also assigned one officer and each company one man for a recovery detail which headed back into the mountains to retrieve their comrades' remains.

"I said to myself, 'Good God, I hope I don't get that,'" 1LT Andrew Carrico recalled with a grimace.

HQ2-511's PFC Deanne Marks explained, "The guys that died, when we could get to them were buried. The wounded we carried. Some of the dead we never did get back. The buddies that we *did* bury were exhumed after the campaign and sent to various military burial sites."

A-511's PFC Steve M. Hegedus noted, "It must have been a gruesome and stinking task to carry those body bags out of there."

It was a duty no one wanted, and one that would prove extremely difficult, but the Angels assigned tried to complete it with respect.

## The Battle for Ormoc - 1/187th 188th

While the 511th PIR had come down from the hills and enjoyed a day-late Christmas dinner, there were still an estimated 27,000 Japanese on Leyte. GEN Swing decided to send 1/187 and the entire 188th GIR to clear out the stubborn pocket of enemy troops which were dug in 1,400 yards north of Anonag. This same pocket had been bypassed by the 511th PIR after the enemy had repulsed both patrols and assaults by the 1st and 2nd Battalions.

The 511th called the main ridge "Purple Heart Hill" (the 187th would second the nickname) and Swing wanted it destroyed. However, the general realized that the position was a gathering point for enemy troops in the area, and that it could only be taken with a multi-battalion well-coordinated assault. With the 511th busy pushing west to comply with their Sixth Army orders, Swing had left one battalion at a time in place to contain the Japanese which S-2 estimated was numbered around 1,000.

But the 511th PIR had moved on and the task was now given to the divisin's two glider regiments.

Earlier patrols, including those made by the division's Recon Platoon, or Ghost Platoon, said that the enemy was dug in along two parallel ridges full of spider holes, caves and machine gun emplacements cut out of the middle of bamboo thickets which skillfully covered the approach trails. The enemy's bivouac area was stockpiled with enough ammunition and supplies for a regiment and the area's trees would likely be full of camoflauged snipers when the Angels attacked.

Even so, on December 26 (D+39), the 188th GIR's COL Shorty Soule ordered his men to begin their assault. LTC Thomas Mann's 2/188 moved out from their position to the enemy's southwest to deceive the Japanese into thinking that once more the Angels had moved on.

In truth, 2/188 was moving into a narrow river bottom which hid them from the enemy, after which LTC Mann led his men east and up the southern side of Purple Heart Hill. The glidermen made it to within visual range of the Japanese when, as one trooper declared, "All hell broke loose."

The enemy opened up with their machine guns and rifles and rolled grenades down the hill towards the climbing Angels, laughing as they did so. GEN Swing's troopers gave as good as they got, but the enemy's reinforced positions were just too difficult to take with manpower alone so 2/188 was pulled back off the ridge.

PFC John Chiesa of E-188 told of a close call he had:

"I was opening up the can (from my K-ration), when 20 feet from me this Jap jumped out of the bushes. He looked at me and I looked at him. I think he was as surprised as I was. I had an M-1 rifle laying across my lap. Everything was done automatic (our training came in handy). I grabbed the rifle, turned to pull the trigger, he was doing the same thing, but I was luckier."

Later that evening COL Robert "Shorty" Soule asked what they should do to push the enemy off the hill. Surprised that a colonel was asking a private's opinion, a tired PFC Chiesa replied, "Bomb the hell out of them. Blow the hill up."

And that's what they did (Soule asked Chiesa his opinion because the trooper had assaulted the hill earlier and knew what was up there). After a heavy bombardment, courtesy of the 457th PFAB's Battery A on Manawarat, E-188th took the hill the following morning.

*COL Robert "Shorty" Soule*

The hill had also been blasted at 1400 by 105mm and 155mm guns outside Burauen which, as PFC John Chiesa suggested, "(Bombed) the hell out of them." COL Robert "Shorty" Soule himself went forward, crawling to within 200 yards of Japanese positions, to direct their artillery fire until the opposition ended.

Liaison pilot MAJ Arthur Mosley, the "Savior of Leyte" flew over the CP of the 511th PIR's COL Hard Rock Haugen near the coast and radioed a brief description of the glidermen's Purple Heart Hill operation, saying, "Accounted for approximately 100 Japs... Gimlet is still in contact with the enemy. It has been a very strong position and difficult to attack."

The artillery barrages were destructive and intense and the enemy's few survivors flew north and west in an attempt to escape. Those who fled north were met on the ridge by 1/187th under COL George Pearson which had been seasoned by their defense of the San Pablo airstrip. The climbing glidermen found the enemy demoralized by their losses and shocked by the power of the Long Tom's shelling. Pushing forward, COL Pearson's men opened fire and said it was like shooting fish in a barrel. The 188th GIR pressed from the opposite side of the field and cried, "Feed the bastards, they're hungry!" as they poured intense fire into the enemy.

The Japanese who tried escaping west off Purple Heart Hill ran straight into an ambush set by F-187 and were destroyed.

The troopers of 1/187 counted nearly 240 enemy dead on Purple Heart Hill and described the area as being littered with body parts from the artillery strikes' power. No one had any idea how many Japanese had been killed and were buried in destroyed foxholes and caves, but the Angels estimated it was in the hundreds.

They also discovered that the enemy's main supply line on Leyte, the very one they had been sent into the mountains to find, ended near Purple Heart Hill at Anonang. GEN Swing's G-2 Henry "Butch" Muller looked at the evidence and gathered intelligence and said that it was likely that Purple Heart Hill had been the headquarters of Japan's 26th Infantry Division which the 11th Airborne had destroyed.

A division after action report on the King II Operation noted, "Engaged by the strongest Japanese forces encountered by the division, seven days of fierce fighting supported by the fires of three artillery battalions were required to neutralize the enemy forces."

With Purple Heart Hill secured and the enemy destroyed, GEN Swing's 11th Airborne Division was completely reassembled by January 9, 1945. Tallies were made and delivered to GEN Swing. The 11th Airborne Division had suffered 507 casualties during the entire Leyte campaign: 40 officers and 467 enlisted men.

For now, the Angels' war with Japan was over.

# 16: On to Tokyo...via Luzon

Bito Beach, Leyte – December 1944 - January 1945

*"I'm in the Parachute Infantry and it's the toughest, best damn outfit in the world."*
-PVT Sidney Smithson, B-511, January 1943

After the reduction of the enemy forces around Purple Heart Hill, the Angels of 1/187th and 188th GIRs moved down from the mountains to join the division's gathering forces on Bito Beach.

LT Leo Crawford of the 188th GIR noted that similar to the 511th PIR's Paratroopers, the glidermen came down from the hills and "almost everyone in the outfit was covered with sores on their legs from being constantly wet. Swimming in the salt water and a couple of weeks in the dry climate of Luzon at that time of year caused the sores to disappear."

GEN Swing made sure the glidermen received their promised turkey dinner and the general sent his liaison pilots back up into the hills to drop Red Cross packages, candy, books and even ice cream on those still on the trail, especially those few still at Manawarat or Mahonag.

The division's 674th and 675th Glider Field Artillery Battalions remained stationed in the heights around Burauen for patrolling while the 457th Parachute Field Artillery Battalion sat outside Burauen itself to support those in the hills, including Battery A which eventually fired all of its remaining ammunition and returned to the beach.

D-511's PFC Elmer "Chuck" Hudson joked of the Angels' journey across the island, "Leyte was 30 miles wide and it took us 30 days to take it. We made about a mile a day - one half mile down and one half mile up to the high ground where we stopped at night."

On January 2, GEN Swing lunched with GEN Robert L. Eichelberger, commander of the new U.S. Eighth Army, to discuss what role the 11th Airborne could/would play in the future invasion of southern Luzon. Despite their losses, Eichelberger wanted the Angels for

## 16. On to Tokyo... via Luzon

*Christmas turkey (canned) arrives for those still on Manawarat*

his fight to liberate Manila, perhaps because as Swing noted to his father-in-law GEN Peyton March in a Christmas Eve letter, "We've killed about twice as many Japs in proportion to our own casualties as has any other division."

Yet even as the generals dined, many of Swing's men lay on their cots, too sick to move. The streets and beaches were lined with "evidence" of those who were too weak to make it to the latrines and the medical staff kept busy day and night with their care. By every right, the Angels were in no shape to go another round, yet that is exactly what they would be asked to do.

To help with their recovery, many regimental commanders made sure their troopers enjoyed fresh meat and vegetables along with their coveted beer rations. Many tents even had a Filipino youth to run errands, an indulgence beyond words for Angels who were often too ill to stand in line for chow.

On January 9, the 152nd Anti-Aircraft troopers who had so bravely manned their radio relay stations in the hills as part of the division's Godfrey Relay (and resisted countless attacks on their positions) finally made their own way down to Bito Beach and GEN Swing could report on January 15 that all his men who had not been medically evacuated were gathered in one place.

While his men were recovering and participating in limited training, on January 10 Swing met again with Eighth Army's GEN

Eichelberger. Eichelberger wrote home to his wife Emmalina, "He certainly is a fine looking chap and full of pep. He is a good type for me to have under my command... Joe Swing is grand to deal with."

A week later on January 17, Swing and his Assistant Division Commander BG Albert Pierson attended a briefing with the Navy's Admiral Frank Fechteler and 5th Air Force's Chief of Staff MG Donald Hutchinson at GEN Eichelberger's headquarters. Plans were discussed for the invasion of Luzon and Eichelberger let Swing know that 11th Airborne would indeed play a part in the island's liberation.

The plan angered GEN Swing and a few staff members who were the only ones to know about it at the time. To prevent the enemy's forces in southern Luzon from moving north to reinforce Manila against Sixth Army's assault, the 11th Airborne was planned to drop 200-man reinforced companies from the 511th PIR piece-meal across the southern parts of the island to engage pockets of Japanese forces.

Given what he knew of the enemy's strength in southern Luzon (and the lessons he had learned while acting as airborne advisor to GEN Dwight Eisenhower during Operation Husky), GEN Swing believed his men would suffer severe and unnecessary losses.

According to the 457th PFAB's CPT John Conable, "General Swing was livid at the suggestion that we be scattered all over. He was reported to have said to higher headquarters, 'If you want to take my Division from me, relieve me of command. But give my men a fighting chance.'"

Swing later wrote to his father-in-law GEN Payton March, "In my estimation, the Battle of Luzon is going to take everything we've got out here and maybe a little bit more."

The concept of dropping the 11th Airborne in pieces came from the S-3 section at GEN MacArthur's Headquarters, especially his Operations Chief LTG Stephen Chamberlain. Neither Swing nor Eichelberger supported Chamberlain's plan and thankfully that awful concept was dropped at Swing's insistence.

On January 21 the 11th Airborne held a division review at Tarragona for GEN Eichelberger who flew in. Swing's troopers, recovered as they could be from their ordeals, stood ramrod straight in polished boots and khaki uniforms and carried personal sidearms.

RHQ-511's 2LT William Abernathy wrote, "It was really classy,

## 16. On to Tokyo... via Luzon

*BG Albert Pierson presents the Angels to GEN Eichelberger*

despite cramped space on the beach. It was for the awarding of Silver Star medals to those that got them during the campaign. Naturally this regiment (the 511th PIR) looked the snappiest and got the lion's share of the medals. There were more stars floating around than there are stars in Hollywood. I mean the stars worn on collars. I saw a three-star general for the first time." (this was GEN Eichelberger).

A stick of 511th Paratroopers worked hard to land on the beach's narrow strip and some dropped from Piper Cubs much to GEN Eichelberger's pleasure (he had never seen static line jumping from a liaison plane before). A few of the jumpers drifted out into the surf, but managed to make it to shore without problems. Shortly thereafter BG Albert Pierson presented the Angels to Eichelberger who distributed the Silver Stars and other awards.

Eichelberger then climbed atop a small tower for a speech in which he recalled that when the Angels had unloaded the ships at New Guinea's Oro Bay that Summer, they had been called "General Swing's eight thousand thieves." Eichelberger then smiled and said that the Angels also managed to slip past the "defenses" and MPs guarding the Women's Army Auxiliary Corps (WAAC) compound near Dobodura, adding that "anyone who can do that is good enough for me." The Angels cheered and Eichelberger left to lunch with MG Swing. GEN Eichelberger later wrote in his journal, "I like Joe's outfit. They look like they'll fight plenty." They would and they did.

Eichelberger wrote decades later, "There is one thing one must realize, however, and that is that the 11th ABD paratrooper was magnificent fighting soldier. They were also veterans and had fought much better on Leyte than most of the other troops. They were on the south of our line in Leyte and had gone clear across the island while the infantry division on the right managed to advance only a few hundred yards. So, here you have not only disciplined, selected troops but also have brave leadership in General Swing, the (commanding general) of the 11th ABD."

General Eichelberger, the former West Point superintendent knew what was waiting on Luzon and he believed that even after their brutal month in Leyte's mountains, GEN Swing's men could be counted on to get the job done. As Swing himself noted proudly, "My men fought harder than any of them - the high command knows it..."

Their new "job" had come from GEN MacArthur himself who wanted Eichelberger to "undertake a daring expedition against Manila with a small mobile force using tactics that would have delighted Jeb Stuart." With the right transportation and planning, the Angels' nimble airborne forces excelled at such operations.

But outside of GEN Swing and his staff, plus some regimental commanders, the Angels had no idea where they would be fighting next. They all knew that Sixth Army under GEN Walter Krueger had landed at Lingayan Gulf on Luzon's northwest coast, but where would that leave the 11th Airborne Division?

The answer came on on January 22, the day after the division's review for GEN Eichelberger who issued Field Order No. 17:

*11th A/B will land one regimental combat team on X-day at H-hour in the Nasugbu area, seize and defend a beachhead; 511th Parachute Regimental Combat team will be prepared to move by air from Leyte and Mindoro bases, land by parachute on Tagaytay Ridge, effect a junction with the force of the 11th A/B Div moving inland from Nasugbu; the 11th A/B Div, reinforced, after assembling on Tagaytay Ridge will be prepared for further action to the north and east as directed by Commanding General, Eighth Army.*

Eichelberger wanted Swing's division to land on southern Luzon on January 31, which only left the Angels six days to prepare. GEN Swing decided that his Regimental Combat Team (the amphibious landing force) would consist of the 187th and 188th Glider Infantries

## 16. On to Tokyo... via Luzon

*Down From Heaven Comes Eleven and There Will be Hell to Pay Below...on Luzon*

supported by elements from the 127th Airborne Engineers and the 674th and 675th Glider Artilleries.

The RCT would set sail for Luzon on January 27, so after GEN Eichelberger pinned the Legion of Merit on GEN Swing on January 25, Swing departed to oversee his division's preparations. Numerous lectures were held around sand tables which represented the areas between Nasugbu, Batangas and Manila, many of which were given by Angels who had served in the area before the war.

The division's 408th Quartermaster Company had one of the toughest jobs at the time since nearly 90% of the division's supplies of personal equipment and equipment had been destroyed by the Japanese during their surprise attacks on airstrips around Burauen (not to mention all the equipment damaged by Leyte's environment).

And many hands were called to the deck to help clean two months'-worth of mud out of the division's vehicles and repair them for use in time for the landings on Luzon.

Troopers across the Division discussed with their squads, platoons and companies what Leyte had taught them and the Angels made small, yet significant changes which included reducing the fuses on their grenades to three seconds to deny the enemy time to throw them back. Given the weight of their .30 Browning machine guns, resourceful machine gunners from the parachute units "acquired" lighter Browning Automatic Rifles (BARs) from the glider regiments to increase their firepower (crates of new BARs were also liberated from a nearby supply dump).

The Angels also discussed the effectiveness of turning the enemy's propensity to attack at all hours against him, something the Angels had had great success with as displayed by D-511's Rat's Ass Charge on December 22, 1944. The 11th's troopers also talked about the effectiveness of using their artillery support to both destroy enemy defenses and to stun the defenders. Aggressive actions taken during the few minutes after such a barrage allowed for higher rates of success along with lower rates of casualties, a fact that would come into play during the Angels' operations on Luzon.

Leyte's terrain had also been a nightmare for GEN Swing's troopers, but they recognized that such a difficult environment could, if utilized properly, allow them to gain the upper hand over the enemy in most, if not all, cases. Nor could one overemphasize perimeter discipline and fire sectors in defensive situations, more lessons that the 11th Airborne Division would apply in the months to come.

And so the discussions went as the Angels continued to pack supplies, clean their weapons and write final letters home. Many troopers included sparse details about their Leyte ordeals, and more thoughts of the future, as indicated in a letter written by RHQ-511's 2LT William Abernathy. Bill told his fiancee Naomi, "First there is a job to do. Until we can be with each other once more, I'll continue to love you more each day."

Bill noted, "As to the length of my stay over here, I must confess that I haven't given the matter enough thought to arrive at any conclusion. The optimistic ones say 'Christmas of '45' and others say 'Golden Gate in '48', so you can draw you own conclusions. Don't let anyone fool you on this '6 months after Germany falls' stuff."

The Angels now knew the enemy and every one of GEN Swing's troopers believed that Imperial Japan was going to fight to defend every one of their strongholds to the last man, especially Japan itself.

For now, the war for Luzon was raging and the Angels of the 11th Airborne Division were going to fight it, down from heaven into hell.

# Conclusion:

Thank you for reading *Down From Heaven: The 11th Airborne Division in World War II, Volume 1 - Camp Toccoa to Leyte Campaign*. I truly hope you enjoyed it and gained a greater appreciation for the men of the mighty 11th Airborne Division.

The words of HQ1-511's SGT Kenneth Fuller, who became a pastor after the war, come to mind when he prayed, "Our gracious heavenly father, we come before thee on this memorable occasion to offer thanks for all those who have so nobly served in the defense of our liberty, our homes and our sacred way of life."

*H-511 on the move*

All I can say to Pastor Fuller's words is: amen!

You'll find the Angels' battle for Luzon and their time in Japan covered in the second book of this series: *Down From Heaven: The 11th Airborne Division in World War II, Volume 2 - Luzon and the Occupation of Japan*.

You can also learn more about the Angels through our two online historical websites, **www.511pir.com** for the 511th Parachute Infantry Regiment and **www.11thAirborne.com** for the 11th Airborne Division and its veterans association.

If I can help you research an Angel or answer any questions for you regarding the history of the 11th Airborne Division, please don't hesitate to reach out to me.

**Jeremy C. Holm**
Salt Lake City, UT

**Author - Bobsled Athlete - Historian**
**11th Airborne Division Association, Secretary**

www.JeremyCHolm.com
jeremy@jeremycholm.com

## Selected Bibliography:

11th Airborne Division Parachute Maintenence Company After Action Report, 1945

511th Parachute Infantry Regiment S-1, S-2, S-3, S-4 Journals and casualty lists, author's collection

Becker, Carl M., unpublished manuscript, "Eyebrow Easy, Eyebrow Easy: A Draftee's Story"Devlin, Gerard M., *Paratrooper!*, St. Martin's Press, New York (1979)

Carrico, Andrew, Oral Interviews, 2005-2016

Cavanaugh, Stephen, Oral Interviews, 2015-2018

Ellis, John T., THE AIRBORNE COMMAND CENTER STUDY 25, 1946

Flanagan, Edward M. Jr., *The Angels: A History of the 11$^{th}$ Airborne Division 1943-1946*, Infantry Journal Press, Washington, DC (1948)

FM-130 TACTICS AND TECHNIQUES OF AIR-BORNE TROOPS, 1942

Fullilove, Cecil and Mary Ann, *Dear General: World War II Letters, 1944-1945*; Palo Alto, CA, 1987

Giordano, Joseph, "The Operations of Company G 187th Glider Infantry Regiment (11th Airborne Division) In The Breakthrough to the Ormoc Corridor, 22-23 December 1944", 1947

Haugen, Orin D., Memorandum 1943, author's collection

Kitchen, William C., *Angels At War*

Muller, Henry, Oral Interviews, 2018-2020

Rottman, Gordon L., *US Army Paratrooper in the Pacific Theater 1943-1945*, Osprey Publishing, 2012

Sams, Margaret, *Forbidden Family: Wartime Memoir of the Philippines, 1941-1945*, University of Wisconsin Press, 1997

Swing, Joseph, Oral Interview, 1971

Wilson, James, Oral Interview, 2020

Young, Stanley, Oral Interviews, 2019-2022

Made in United States
Orlando, FL
16 June 2023